Real-Resumes For U.S. Postal Service Jobs

...including real resumes used to change careers
and transfer skills to other industries

Anne McKinney, Editor

PREP PUBLISHING

FAYETTEVILLE, NC

PREP Publishing
1110 ½ Hay Street
Fayetteville, NC 28305
(910) 483-6611

Library of Congress Cataloging-in-Publication Data

McKinney, Anne, 1948-
Real-resumes for U.S. Postal service jobs : --including real resumes used to change careers and transfer skills to other industries / Anne McKinney.
      p. cm. -- (Government jobs series)
 ISBN 1-885288-43-3 (trade paper)
  1. Postal service--Vocational guidance--United States. 2. Resumes (Employment)--United States.
3. Applications for positions. I. Title. II. Series.

  HE6499.M26 2004
  650.14'2--dc22   2004053407

Printed in the United States of America

PREP Publishing

Business and Career Series:

RESUMES AND COVER LETTERS THAT HAVE WORKED, Revised Edition

RESUMES AND COVER LETTERS THAT HAVE WORKED FOR MILITARY PROFESSIONALS

GOVERNMENT JOB APPLICATIONS AND FEDERAL RESUMES

COVER LETTERS THAT BLOW DOORS OPEN

LETTERS FOR SPECIAL SITUATIONS

RESUMES AND COVER LETTERS FOR MANAGERS

REAL-RESUMES FOR COMPUTER JOBS

REAL-RESUMES FOR MEDICAL JOBS

REAL-RESUMES FOR FINANCIAL JOBS

REAL-RESUMES FOR TEACHERS

REAL-RESUMES FOR STUDENTS

REAL-RESUMES FOR CAREER CHANGERS

REAL-RESUMES FOR SALES

REAL ESSAYS FOR COLLEGE & GRADUATE SCHOOL

REAL-RESUMES FOR AVIATION & TRAVEL JOBS

REAL-RESUMES FOR POLICE, LAW ENFORCEMENT & SECURITY JOBS

REAL-RESUMES FOR SOCIAL WORK & COUNSELING JOBS

REAL-RESUMES FOR CONSTRUCTION JOBS

REAL-RESUMES FOR MANUFACTURING JOBS

REAL-RESUMES FOR RESTAURANT, FOOD SERVICE & HOTEL JOBS

REAL-RESUMES FOR MEDIA, NEWSPAPER, BROADCASTING & PUBLIC AFFAIRS JOBS

REAL-RESUMES FOR RETAILING, MODELING, FASHION & BEAUTY JOBS

REAL-RESUMES FOR HUMAN RESOURCES & PERSONNEL JOBS

REAL-RESUMES FOR NURSING JOBS

REAL-RESUMES FOR AUTO INDUSTRY JOBS

REAL RESUMIX & OTHER RESUMES FOR FEDERAL GOVERNMENT JOBS

REAL KSAS--KNOWLEDGE, SKILLS & ABILITIES--FOR GOVERNMENT JOBS

REAL BUSINESS PLANS & MARKETING TOOLS

REAL-RESUMES FOR ADMINISTRATIVE SUPPORT, OFFICE & SECRETARIAL JOBS

REAL-RESUMES FOR FIREFIGHTING JOBS

REAL-RESUMES FOR JOBS IN NONPROFIT ORGANIZATIONS

REAL-RESUMES FOR SPORTS INDUSTRY JOBS

REAL-RESUMES FOR LEGAL & PARALEGAL JOBS

REAL-RESUMES FOR ENGINEERING JOBS

REAL-RESUMES FOR U.S. POSTAL SERVICE JOBS

Judeo-Christian Ethics Series:

SECOND TIME AROUND

BACK IN TIME

WHAT THE BIBLE SAYS ABOUT...Words that can lead to success and happiness

A GENTLE BREEZE FROM GOSSAMER WINGS

BIBLE STORIES FROM THE OLD TESTAMENT

Contents

A WORD FROM THE EDITOR:
ABOUT THE GOVERNMENT JOBS SERIES

Welcome to the Government Jobs Series. The Government Jobs Series is a series of books which have been developed based on the experiences of real job hunters and which target specialized fields or types of employment. As the editor of the series, I have carefully selected applications, documents, resumes, and cover letters (with names and other key data disguised, of course) which have been used successfully in real job hunts. What you see in this book are *real* resumes and applications which helped real people get ahead in their careers.

The Government Jobs Series is based on the work of the country's oldest resume-preparation company known as PREP Resumes. If you would like a free information packet describing the company's resume preparation services, call 910-483-6611 or write to PREP at 1110½ Hay Street, Fayetteville, NC 28305. If you have a job hunting experience you would like to share with our staff at the Government Jobs Series, please contact us at preppub@aol.com or visit our website at www.prep-pub.com.

The resumes, applications, and cover letters in this book are designed to be of most value to people already in a job hunt or contemplating a career change. If we could give you one word of advice about your career, here's what we would say: Manage your career and don't stumble from job to job in an incoherent pattern. Try to find work that interests you, and then identify prosperous industries which need work performed of the type you want to do. Learn early in your working life that a great resume and job application can blow doors open for you and help you maximize your salary.

We hope the superior samples will help you manage your career and job campaign and your career so that you will find work aligned to your career interests.

FACTS ABOUT USPS© EMPLOYMENT!

In this section, we want you to see how the U.S. Postal System describes itself on its own website. According to the USPS, ever since Benjamin Franklin was named the first Postmaster General in 1775, the US postal system has been keeping America connected. USPS says that it realizes that "it's our people who provide customer satisfaction, drive innovation, and ensure our continued success."

Mail delivery is big business!

According to the USPS, as of 2004, the Postal Service is at the heart of the $900 billion mailing industry—which employs nine million people—and three of the Postal Service's six product lines would qualify as Fortune 500 companies:

Correspondence & transactions	$37 billion business
Business advertising	$17.2 billion business
Expedited delivery	$5.4 billion business
Publications delivery	$2.2 billion business
Standard package delivery	$2.2 billion business
International mail	$1.5 billion business

According to statements on its website, the USPS estimates 2004 annual operating revenue of $68.5 billion. USPS claims 700,000 career employees and pays $2 billion in salaries and benefits every two weeks.

According to the USPS website, the organization delivers 202 billion pieces of mail a year, or five pieces per address per day to over 141 million homes, businesses, and post office boxes. Each of its 300,000 carriers delivers an estimated 2,300 pieces of mail a day to about 500 addresses, and more than 1.8 million new addresses are added each year. More than 3 billion pieces of First-Class Mail are redirected to new addresses for the 17% of the nation's population that moves annually, generating over 44 million address changes. The USPS claims that it delivers more than 46% of the world's mail volume while serving 7 million customers daily at 37,579 postal retail outlets. Stamps are now available on the Internet, by mail, by phone, through 32,000 vending machines and 40,000 commercial retail outlets and Automatic Teller Machines (ATMS).

According to the U.S. Postal Service, it is a first-class organization that is appreciated by its residential and business customers. The USPS claims that performance for on-time local delivery of First-Class Mail for 2003 was 95%, and 94% of households surveyed in 2003 had a positive perception of the Postal Service. To do its job, the USPS operates a transport and delivery fleet of 213,585 vehicles driving approximately 1.15 billion miles a year. It leases 25,987 facilities at a rental cost of $869.7 million, and it operates 30,000 alternative-fuel vehicles (AFVs), the nation's largest fleet of AFVs, using ethanol, compressed natural gas and electricity. The USPS purchases $200 million worth of products with recycled content, including pallets and trays, stamp products and mailing envelopes. The USPS believes it is a leader in innovation, and it strives to utilize the latest technology to improve service, increase productivity, and reduce costs. The USPS has been a leader in developing and using optical character recognition, and USPS claims that installation of its upgraded flat-sorting equipment that deciphers hard-to-read addresses saved $292.5 million.

Mail Processing Jobs

Many mail processing jobs in the USPS have exam requirements. By visiting the USPS website, you can learn more about specific job requirements and how to apply for the exam in the areas of Maintenance, Operations, and Transportation.

Corporate Jobs

The USPS offers supervisory, administrative, professional, and technical staff positions in the following categories, and you can learn more about the precise job requirements in these categories by visiting the USPS website.

- Administrative/Clerical
- Customer Service
- Diversity Development
- Economics
- Engineering/Architecture
- Facilities/Real Estate
- Finance/Accounting
- Government Relations
- Human Resources
- Information Technology
- Law Enforcement/Investigation
- Labor Relations
- Legal
- Marketing/Sales
- Operations-Research & Analysis
- Processing Operations
- Statistician
- Strategic Planning
- Supply Management/Purchasing
- Transportation/Network Operations

MAIL IS BIG BUSINESS

In this section you see how the U.S. Postal Service describes itself and its career opportunities.

EMPLOYMENT REQUIREMENTS

Eligibility requirements for USPS employment are as follows:

Age Requirement: 18 years at the time of appointment or 16 years with a high school diploma.

Citizenship: Employees must be a U.S. citizen or permanent resident alien.

Basic competency in English: This is a requirement.

Selective Service: Males born after 12/31/59 must be registered with the Selective Service System.

Employment History: Applicants must provide the names of their current employer and all previous employers for the 10-year period immediately preceding the date of application or to their 16th birthday, whichever is most recent.

Military Service: Military service is treated as prior employment. Veterans must indicate service and submit Copy 4 of the DD Form 214, Certificate of Release or Discharge from Active Duty.

Criminal Conviction History: A local criminal check is required prior to employment. A more extensive criminal history check is completed at employment.

Drug Screen: A qualification for postal employment is to be drug free, and is determined through a urinalysis drug screen.

Medical Assessment: A medical assessment is conducted to provide information about an applicant's ability to physically or mentally perform in a specific position.

Safe Driving Record: A safe driving record is required for employees who drive at work (i.e., city carriers, motor vehicle operators, etc.).

COMPENSATION AND BENEFITS

USPS believes that it offers highly competitive compensation and benefits packages. Most Postal Service employees receive regular salary increases, overtime pay, night shift differential, and Sunday premium pay. Overtime is paid at one and one-half times the applicable hourly rate for work in excess of 8 hours per day, or 40 hours within a workweek. Night shift differential is paid at a specified dollar rate for all hours worked between 6 pm and 6 am. Sunday premium is paid at 25 percent for work scheduled on Sunday.

POSTAL FACTS
In this section you see how the U.S. Postal Service describes itself and its career opportunities.

Health Insurance: According to its website, the Postal Service participates in the Federal Employees Health Benefits (FEHB) Program, which provides excellent coverage and flexibility with most of the cost paid by the Postal Service. There are many plans available, including both traditional insurance coverage and Health Maintenance Organizations (HMOs). Employee premium contributions are not subject to most taxes, making health insurance even more affordable.

Retirement: The Postal Service participates in the federal retirement program, which provides a defined benefit annuity at normal retirement age as well as disability coverage.

Thrift Savings Plan: Career postal employees may contribute to the Thrift Savings Plan (TSP), which is similar to 401(k) retirement savings plans offered by private sector employers. Employees contribute to TSP on a tax-deferred basis, and may receive automatic and matching contributions (up to 5 percent of pay), after a waiting period, from the Postal Service.

Social Security and Medicare: Newly hired postal employees are covered under Social Security and Medicare.

Life Insurance: The Postal Service offers coverage through the Federal Employees' Group Life Insurance (FEGLI) Program. The cost of basic coverage is fully paid by the Postal Service, with the option to purchase additional coverage through payroll deduction.

Flexible Spending Accounts: Career employees may participate in the Flexible Spending Accounts (FSA) Program after one year of service. Tax-free FSA contributions can be used to cover most out-of-pocket health care and dependent care (day care) expenses.

Leave: The Postal Service offers a generous leave program to career employees that includes annual (vacation) leave and sick leave. For the first 3 years of service, full-time employees earn 13 days of annual leave per year, increasing to 20 days per year after 3 years of service, and to 26 days per year after 15 years of service. In addition, full-time employees earn 13 days of sick leave per year as insurance against loss of income due to illness or accident.

Holidays: The Postal Service observes 10 holidays each year. They are Martin Luther King Jr's Birthday, Washington's Birthday (President's Day), Memorial Day, Independence Day, Labor Day, Columbus Day, Veteran's Day, Thanksgiving Day, Christmas Day, and New Year's Day.

CAREER DEVELOPMENT OPPORTUNITIES

National Center for Employee Development

According to the USPS's website, the National Center for Employee Development (NCED) is the U.S. Postal Service's national center for employee training. NCED oversees and conducts hands-on training for postal employees who manage and maintain major high-technology postal systems, vehicles, and mail processing equipment. Training offered at NCED supports postal automation efforts and national job skills training. NCED is a nationally recognized leader in the use of distance learning technology. NCED expands on its resident classrooms by using national networks for live satellite broadcasts, audio teletraining, and computer-driven audiographics courses as well as computer, video, and internet technology to deliver critical job skill training to postal employees.

Associate Supervisor Program

According to the USPS, the Associate Supervisor Program (ASP) is designed to attract, select, and train the best possible candidates for first-line supervisory positions. ASP will develop technical, operational, administrative, and leadership skills through its comprehensive classroom training and on-the-job assignments. Applicants who meet the requirements will learn the critical knowledge and skills necessary to become highly effective leaders of the U.S. Postal Service. ASP is a 16-week training program, combining classroom training and on-the-job assignments, to provide a practical hands-on experience. Coaching is an important aspect of the program. ASP trainees are assigned a coach who provides leadership and guidance throughout the program. If you like working with people, want to make a difference, and be associated with a winning team, supervisory positions with the USPS may be right for you.

Career Management Program

The USPS believes that its Career Management Program (CMP) prepares supervisors, managers, and postmasters for the future by providing them the skills and knowledge they need to guide employees and operations toward greater efficiency, continued improvement, and outstanding customer service. CMP is a training program that provides supervisory employees with a roadmap for continuous learning within the Postal Service. Course curricula cover skills and knowledge identified by the field as critical for effective supervision and management. The core components of the training are leadership/management, functional/administrative, and supporting curricula. Employees enter CMP by completing the managerial and functional enrollment guides with their manager to determine the skill areas they want to strengthen and initial course they should attend.

Advanced Leadership Program

According to the USPS, the Advanced Leadership Program (ALP) was developed to assist the U.S. Postal Service in ensuring that a base of qualified and capable leaders is available for the next several years. ALP is aimed at experienced managers who exhibit high potential for increased levels of responsibility. Thus, a particular type of learner was anticipated for ALP and the program was designed consistent with those expectations. ALP provides the knowledge, skills, and experience necessary for participants to positively impact and support future postal management decisions and direction. The program seeks to develop a highly competent managerial base from which future organizational leadership will emerge.

USPS© INTERNSHIPS

USPS offers management intern programs. These include the Management Intern Program and the Summer Intern Program. According to the USPS, its internships are highly selective programs through which interns are assigned to a hands-on management position in processing, delivery, or retail operations in one of the Postal Service's nine geographic areas. According to the USPS, interns enter the program as a manager on the Executive Administrative Schedule (EAS-19), overseeing front-line supervisors who supervise personnel performing mail processing, delivery, and retail operations. Assuming satisfactory performance in the intern program, the first post-internship position would be at least at a mid-level management level. Examples of mid-level management operational responsibilities include managing a large post office or branch facility with numerous routes, a shift operation in a processing plant, a substantial fleet operation, or a large financial operation.

The USPS believes that its intern programs offer structured developmental assignments in different aspects of postal operations within the area where the intern is assigned. Responsibilities include problem analysis, staffing, resource management, scheduling, labor relations, interpersonal relations, training, transportation, and working with customers, both internal and external. A select senior manager serves as the intern's mentor throughout the two-year program, and the mentor functions as a personal coach to guide the intern in the corporate culture, help the intern establish a personal network among managers, and help the intern learn the practical techniques of postal management. Developmental work assignments include stints in processing and delivery operations, customer service and sales, and finance. Interns participate in formal quarterly training activities. According to the USPS, the starting annual salary for management interns would be approximately $44,000, and upon completion of the two-year program, the salary would advance to $50,000 or more, depending upon performance. The career development gained as a Management Intern is designed to accelerate advancement up the organizational career ladder.

Eligibility requirements for Management Interns.
The program is open to all who possess the required qualifications.
Citizenship: Be a native-born or naturalized U.S. Citizen or a fully documented Permanent Resident Alien (possess a "Green Card").

Education: Hold a Master's Degree in Business Administration; or an M.S. or equivalent degree in Management, Finance, Logistics, Supply-Chain Management, or Operations; or a Masters in Engineering (specifically Industrial Operations, Operations Research, Manufacturing or Engineering Management) from an accredited graduate school.

Leadership: In addition to these qualifications, successful applicants must demonstrate capacity for leadership, potential for future professional growth as a manager or executive, and commitment to a career in management.

The purpose of the Management Intern Program is to prepare persons capable of assuming operational positions critical to the future of the Postal Service. The program seeks individuals with an ability to manage diverse people and technologies in a high-speed plant-processing, retail, or delivery operations environment; solve problems creatively; take initiative; work in teams; and help direct the high-tech future of the Postal Service.

SELECTION PROCESS
Selection process for the Management Intern Program.
Applicants will be required to complete a two-step application process as described in the "Apply for Internship" section in the USPS website. Applicants selected on the basis of this two-step process will be invited to participate in a one-day Assessment Center process.

Those applicants who best meet the Management Intern Program requirements as identified by the Assessment Center will be invited to interview with Postal Service managers to whom they may be assigned. Those applicants who best meet the Program needs of these management officials may be offered a position in the Program.

Employment will be contingent upon successful completion of a Background Investigation and a drug test.

MANAGEMENT INTERN Frequently Asked Questions (FAQs)
Q. May I apply for the Management Intern Program if I do not yet have a Master's Degree?
A. To be eligible, you must hold a Master's Degree in Business Administration; or an M.S. Degree in Management, Finance, Logistics, Supply-Chain Management, or Operations; or a Masters in Engineering (specifically Industrial Operations, Operations Research, Manufacturing or Engineering Management) from an accredited graduate school in the United States.

Q. May I apply if I am not a United States Citizen?
A. Yes, you may apply but only if you are a documented Permanent Resident Alien (possess a "Green Card"). The program is open to U.S. Citizens and Resident Aliens.

Q. Will I always be working a normal 9 to 5 workday?
A. No, the intern position entails shift work operations and hands-on management in mail processing, retail services, and delivery services. In most cases you will be working some evening and night tours.

Q. When will my internship start, and how long will it last?
A. The intern class typically begins in June and lasts for two years.

Q. What subjects will be covered in the one-day assessment?
A. The assessment center will evaluate your problem-solving, oral and written communication, interpersonal, and leadership and teambuilding skills. The assessment center will include an individual presentation, a group discussion, and a writing exercise.

Q. If I qualify, where and when will my one-day assessment be held?
A. The assessment centers will be held in several locations throughout the United States. Visit the USPS website for specific details.

Q. Can I claim Veterans Preference for this program?
A. Yes, Veterans Preference claims can be made in the application.

For information regarding requirements and how to apply, including paper applications, send an email to uspsintern@opm.gov or call 202-268-4259.

Real-Resumes For U.S. Postal Service Jobs

Anne McKinney, Editor

PART ONE:
The 171, The 612, The Form 2591, and Federal Resumes Used in Applying for Federal Government Jobs

You may already realize that applying for a federal government position requires some patience and persistence in order to complete rather tedious forms and get them in on time. Depending on what type of federal job you are seeking, you may need to prepare an application such as the SF 171 or OF 612, or you may need to use a federal resume, sometimes called a "Resumix," to apply for a federal job. But that may not be the only paperwork you need.

In this section you see samples of applications used to apply for USPS employment.

Many people feel that their "dream job" would be a job working for the U.S. Postal Service. If you wish to apply for employment with the U.S. Postal Service, the forms 171 or 612 or the federal resume are, as of this date, the basic application with which you would apply for work. Getting a full-time job in the postal service right "off the bat" can be very difficult. Part-Time Flex (PTF) and Rural Carrier positions are the majority of the jobs available. The Veterans Administration and the local Employment Security Commission handle the "casual" or part-time positions, so they are your best points of initial contact. On rare occasions, where a job is hard to fill, a full-time postal service job will be posted in the newspaper.

If you are trying to get your foot in the door at the Post Office, you would be well advised to consider applying for any type of part-time or casual position, even if they are not what you are ideally looking for. As in most organizations, it is easier to move around and transfer into a better job once you are "in the system." Although there are few full-time jobs available to outsiders, once you get inside the postal service, there are many openings that become available.

In this section you will see examples of the Standard Form (SF) 171 and the Optional Form (OF) 612 as well as the USPS 2591 and federal resumes. Also included are the forms you may encounter in the pre-employment screening process as well as applications for non-career employment eligibility and the Assessment Worksheet for motor vehicle operators and tractor-trailer operators.

Applicants for career mail handling positions are required to take the Postal Exam Battery 470 (or Battery 460 for Rural Carrier Associate, identical to test 470). Applicants that pass with a score of 70% or higher are then listed on the "Register" based on their exam scores. They are then interviewed accordingly, highest exam scores first, as positions become available. Each job classification has a separate register, and the USPS recommends that you test for as many positions as you can qualify for. There are various ways you can prepare for the examination. Exam scheduling is done at the discretion of the Regional Postmaster as they see a need to update their Register. The exam is free. When you take the exam, you can apply for full-time, part-time regular, part-time flexible, and/or casual positions. Examples of the types of work you might be asked to do are Clerk, Carrier, Machine Distribution Clerk, Mail Handler, Mail Processor, and Mark-Up Clerk.

This section is intended to illustrate the documents and paperwork used when you apply for employment in the USPS.

Application for Federal Employment - SF 171

Read the instructions before you complete this application. *Type or print clearly in dark ink.*

Electronic Approved 08/31/1999
Form Approved:
OMB No. 3206-0012

GENERAL INFORMATION

1 What kind of job are you applying for? *Give title/announcement no. (If any)*

2 Social Security Number

999-99-9999

3 Sex

☒ Male ☐ Female

4 Birth date *(MM, DD, YY)*

01/01/1961

5 Birthplace *(City, State, Country)*

Plainview, TX

6 Name *(Last, First, Middle)*

COX, Christopher Landon

Mailing address *(Include apartment number, if any)*

1110 1/2 Hay Street

City	State	ZIP Code
Fayetteville,	NC	28305

7 Other names ever used *(e.g., maiden name, nickname, etc.)*

N/A

8 Home Phone

Area Code	Number
910	483-6611

9 Work Phone

Area Code	Number	Ext.
910	483-6611	

10 Were you ever employed as a civilian by the Federal Government? If "NO", go to item 11. If "YES", mark each type of job you held with an "X".

☐ Temporary ☐ Career-Conditional ☐ Career ☐ Excepted

What is your highest grade, classification series and job title?

Dates at highest grade: FROM ___ TO ___

DO NOT WRITE IN THIS AREA

FOR USE OF EXAMINING OFFICE ONLY

Date entered register

Form reviewed:
Form approved:

Option	Grade	Earned Rating	Veteran Preference	Augmented Rating
			No Preference	
			☐ Claimed	
			5 Points *(Tentative)*	
			10 Pt.*(30%) Or More* Comp. Dis.)	
			10 Pt. *(Less Than 30% Comp. Dis.)*	
			Other ☐ 10 Pt.	
Initials and Date			☐ Dis-allowed	☐ Being Investigated

FOR USE OF APPOINTING OFFICE ONLY

Preference has been verified through proof that the separation was under honorable conditions, and other proof as required.

☐ 5-Point ☐ 10-Pt.-30% or More Comp. Disability ☐ 10-Pt.-Less Than 30% Comp. Disability ☐ 10-Point-Other

Signature and Title

Agency ___ Date ___

AVAILABILITY

11 When can you start work? *(MM, YY)* *(4-Digits)*

12/2004

12 What is the lowest pay you will accept? *(You will not be considered for jobs which pay less than you indicate.)*

Pay $ ___ per ___ OR Grade GS-3

13 In what geographic area(s) are you willing to work?

Fort Jackson/Columbia, SC

14 Are you willing to work:

	YES	NO
A. 40 hours per week *(full-time)*?	X	
B. 25-32 hours per week *(part-time)*?	X	
C. 17-24 hours per week *(part-time)*?	X	
D. 16 or fewer hours per week *(part-time)*?		X
E. An intermittent job *(on-call/seasonal)*?		X
F. Weekends, shifts, or rotating shifts?	X	

15 Are you willing to take a temporary job lasting:

	YES	NO
A. 5 to 12 months *(sometimes longer)*?	X	
B. 1 to 4 months?	X	
C. Less than 1 month?		X

16 Are you willing to travel away from home for:

	YES	NO
A. 1 to 5 nights each month?	X	
B. 6 to 10 nights each month?	X	
C. 11 or more nights each month?	X	

MILITARY SERVICE AND VETERAN PREFERENCE

17 Have you served in the United States Military Service? *If your only active duty was training in the Reserves or National Guard, answer "NO". If "NO" go to item 22.*

YES	NO
X	

18 Did you or will you retire at or above the rank of major or lieutenant commander?

YES	NO
	X

MILITARY SERVICE AND VETERAN PREFERENCE (Cont.)

19 Were you discharged from the military service under honorable conditions? *(If your discharge was changed to "honorable" or "general" by a Discharge Review Board, answer "YES". If you received a clemency discharge, answer "NO".)* If "NO", provide below the date and type of discharge you received.

YES	NO
	X

Discharge Date (MM/DD/YY)	Type of Discharge
02/28/2004	Honorable

20 List the dates *(MM/DD/YY)*, and branch for all active duty military service.

From	To	Branch of Service
01/15/1983	02/28/2004	U.S. Army

21 If all your active military duty was after 10/14/76, list the full names/dates of all campaign badges/expeditionary medals you received/were entitled to receive.

22 Read the instructions that came with this form before completing this item. When you have determined your eligibility for veteran preference from the instructions, place an "X" in the box next to your veteran preference claim.

☐ NO PREFERENCE

☒ 5-POINT PREFERENCE – You must show proof when you are hired.

☐ 10-POINT PREFERENCE – If you claim 10-point preference, place an "X" in the box below next to the basis for your claim. To receive 10-point preference, you must also complete a Standard Form 15, Application for 10-Point Veteran Preference, which is available from any Federal Job Information Center. Attach The Completed SF 15 And Requested Proof To This Application.

☐ Non-compensably disabled or Purple Heart recipient.

☐ Compensably disabled, less than 30 percent.

☐ Spouse, widow(er), or mother of a deceased or disabled veteran.

☐ Compensably disabled, 30 percent or more.

THE FEDERAL GOVERNMENT IS AN EQUAL OPPORTUNITY EMPLOYER
PREVIOUS EDITION USABLE UNTIL 12-31-90

NSN 7540-00-935-7150 171-110 Standard Form 171 (Rev. 6-88)
U.S. Office of Personnel Management, FPM Chapter 295

WORK EXPERIENCE *If you have no work experience, write "NONE" in A below and go to 25 on page 3.*

23	May we ask your present employer about your character, qualifications, and work record? A "NO" will not affect our review of your qualifications. If you answer "NO" and we need to contact your present employer before we can offer you a job, we will contact you first.	YES	NO
		X	

24 READ **WORK EXPERIENCE** IN THE INSTRUCTIONS BEFORE YOU BEGIN.

- ? Describe your current or most recent job in Block A and work backwards, describing each job you held during the **past 10 years.** If you were unemployed for longer **than 3 months** within the past 10 years, list the dates and your address(es) in an experience block.
- ? You may sum up in one block work that you did **more than 10 years ago.** But if that work **is related** to the type of job you are applying for, describe each related job in a separate block.
- ? INCLUDE VOLUNTEER WORK *(non-paid work)*--If the work *(or a part of the work)* is like the job you are applying for, complete all parts of the experience block, just as you would for a paying job. You may receive credit for work experience with religious, community, welfare, service, and other organizations.

- ? INCLUDE MILITARY SERVICE-You should complete all parts of the experience block just as you would for a non-military job, including all supervisory experience. Describe each major change of duties or responsibilities in a separate experience block.
- ? IF YOU NEED MORE SPACE TO DESCRIBE A JOB–Use sheets of paper the same size as this page (be sure to include all information we ask for in A and B below). On **each** sheet show your name, Social Security Number, and the announcement number or job title.
- ? IF YOU NEED MORE EXPERIENCE BLOCKS, use the SF 171-A or a sheet of paper.
- ? IF YOU NEED TO UPDATE (ADD MORE RECENT JOBS), use the SF 172 or a sheet of paper as described above.

A Name/address of employer's organization *(include ZIP Code, if known)*	Dates employed *(give MM/DD/YY)* From: To:	Average number of hr. per week	No. of employees you supervise
	Salary or earnings Starting$ per Ending $ per	Your reason for wanting to leave	
Your immediate supervisor Name Area Code Telephone No.	Exact title of your job	If Federal employment *(civilian or military)* list series, grade or rank, and, if promoted in this job, the date of your last promotion	

Description of work: Describe your specific duties, responsibilities and accomplishments in this job, including the job title(s) of any employees you supervise. *If you describe more than one type of work (for example, carpentry, painting, or personnel and budget), write the approximate percentage of time you spent doing each.*

See attached CONTINUATION SHEET FOR ITEM 24.A.

For Agency Use (skill codes, etc.)

B Name/address of employer's organization *(include ZIP Code, if known)*	Dates employed *(give MM/DD/YY)* From: To:	Average number of hours per week	Number of employees you supervise
	Salary or earnings Starting$ per Ending $ per	Your reason for wanting to leave	
Your immediate supervisor Name Area Code Telephone No.	Exact title of your job	If Federal employment *(civilian or military)* list series, grade or rank, and, if promoted in this job, the date of your last promotion	

Description of work: Describe your specific duties, responsibilities and accomplishments in this job, including the job title(s) of any employees you supervise. *If you describe more than one type of work (for example, carpentry and painting, or personnel and budget), write the approximate percentage of time you spent doing each.*

See attached CONTINUATION SHEET FOR ITEM 24.B.

For Agency Use (skill codes, etc.)

Page   IF YOU NEED MORE EXPERIENCE BLOCKS, USE SF 171-A *(SEE BACK OF INSTRUCTION PAGE).*

Standard Form 171-A— *Continuation Sheet for SF 171 (Back)*
• Attach all SF 171-A's to your application at the top of page 3.

Form Approved:
OMB No. 3206-0012

1. Name *(Last, First, Middle Initial)*	2. Social Security Number
COX, Christopher L.	999-99-9999

3. Job Title or Announcement Number You Are Applying For	4. Date Completed

ADDITIONAL WORK EXPERIENCE BLOCKS

A

Name and address of employer's organization *(include ZIP Code, if known)*	Dates employed *(give month, day and year)*	Average number of hours per week	Number of employees you supervise
U.S. Army AG 483rd Postal Company Fort Jackson, SC 27000	From: 07/02 To: 10/04	45	15

Salary or earnings	Your reason for wanting to leave
Starting $ E-7 per year Ending $ E-7 per year	Retired

Your immediate supervisor Name	Telephone No.	Exact title of your job	If Federal employment *(civilian or military)* list series, grade or rank, and, if promoted in this job, the date of your last promotion
LTC Jones	(910) 483-6611	Postal Supervisor	E-7

Description of work: Describe your specific duties, responsibilities and accomplishments in this job, **including the job title(s) of any employees you supervise.** *If you describe more than one type of work (for example, carpentry and painting, or personnel and budget), write the approximate percentage of time you spent doing each.*

Served as Postal Finance Officer and Custodian of Postal effects in the only contingency and TOE Postal Company; responsible for maintaining stockage levels of over $23,000.00 in stamps and money orders for the unit's soldier-operated post offices; issued stocks to clerks for operational missions; assumed position of First Sergeant. Supervised performance of administrative functions of the Battalion administrative section. Reviewed and edited correspondence prior to release submission for signature or other disposition. Conducted periodic review of files to ensure proper filing of correspondence. Planned and organized office operations, wrote office Standard Operating Procedures (SOPs), job descriptions, and directives. Determined requirements for office equipment (to include automation), supplies, and space.

During the War on Terror in Iraq, I deployed to a combat zone and established "from scratch" a postal operation which supported military professionals. From January 2003 until August 2003, I established standard operating procedures while managing more than 20 individuals who included clerks, carriers, mail handlers, mail processors, and mark-up clerks. I received two prestigious medals in recognition of my exceptional results in providing highly efficient postal services to deployed soldiers.

For Agency Use (skill codes, etc.)

Standard Form 171-A (BACK) (Rev. 6-88)
U.S. Office of Personnel Management
FPM Chapter 295

Standard Form 171-A— *Continuation Sheet for SF 171 (Back)*

• Attach all SF 171-A's to your application at the top of page 3.

Form Approved:
OMB No. 3206-0012

1. Name *(Last, First, Middle Initial)*	2. Social Security Number
COX, Christopher L.	999-99-9999

3. Job Title or Announcement Number You Are Applying For	4. Date Completed

ADDITIONAL WORK EXPERIENCE BLOCKS

B

Name and address of employer's organization *(include ZIP Code, if known)*	Dates employed *(give month, day and year)*	Average number of hours per week	Number of employees you supervise
U.S. Army	From: 05/01 To: 06/02	48	17
Training Group (ABN)	**Salary or earnings**	**Your reason for wanting to leave**	
Fort Jackson, SC 27000	Starting $ E-7 per year	PCS	
	Ending $ E-7 per year		

Your immediate supervisor Name	Telephone No.	Exact title of your job	If Federal employment *(civilian or military)* list series, grade or rank, and, if promoted in this job, the date of your last promotion
SGM Kent Taylor	(910) 483-6611	Battalion Adjutant (CPT Pos.)	E-7

Description of work: Describe your specific duties, responsibilities and accomplishments in this job, **including** the job title(s) of any employees you supervise. *If you describe more than one type of work (for example, carpentry and painting, or personnel and budget), write the approximate percentage of time you spent doing each.*

Provided administrative and personnel support to a Special Forces Battalion with 268 soldiers and 60 civilians assigned; managed the processing of critical documents, including efficiency reports, awards, personnel transfers, and finance documents; advised the Battalion and Company Commanders on administrative matters; coordinated Sponsorship Program; supervised two NCOs and two civilians.

For Agency Use (skill codes, etc.)

Standard Form 171-A (BACK) (Rev. 6-88)
U.S. Office of Personnel Management
FPM Chapter 295

Standard Form 171-A– *Continuation Sheet for SF 171 (Back)*
• Attach all SF 171-A's to your application at the top of page 3.

Form Approved:
OMB No. 3206-0012

1. Name *(Last, First, Middle Initial)*	2. Social Security Number
COX, Christopher L.	999-99-9999

3. Job Title or Announcement Number You Are Applying For	4. Date Completed

ADDITIONAL WORK EXPERIENCE BLOCKS

C	Name and address of employer's organization *(include ZIP Code, if known)*	Dates employed *(give month, day and year)*	Average number of hours per week	Number of employees you supervise
	U.S. Army	From: 01/00 To: 04/01	40	14

Salary or earnings	Your reason for wanting to leave
Starting $ E-7 per year	PCS
Ending $ E-7 per year	

Fort Jackson, SC 27000

Your immediate supervisor Name	Telephone No.	Exact title of your job	If Federal employment *(civilian or military)* list series, grade or rank, and, if promoted in this job, the date of your last promotion
SGM Kent Taylor	(910) 483-6611	Administrative Supervisor	E-7

Description of work: Describe your specific duties, responsibilities and accomplishments in this job, **including** the job title(s) of any employees you supervise. *If you describe more than one type of work (for example, carpentry and painting, or personnel and budget), write the approximate percentage of time you spent doing each.*

As the principal staff NCO of a Special Forces Training Battalion consisting of five training companies housing 268 soldiers and 60 civilians, was responsible for the administrative preparedness of the battalion. Managed the processing of critical documents to include efficiency reports, awards, personnel transfers, and finance documents. Exercised staff supervision over the PAC, legal, reenlistment, and safety programs. Established policies and procedures for the administration of awards, staff duty, and recreation programs. Managed OER and NCOER system. Advised the Executive Officer on civilian personnel and administrative matters. Coordinated Sponsorship Program and supervised two NCOs and two civilians.

Served as Adjutant in 2d Battalion Staff. Performed assigned duties and tasks in the accomplishment of the unit's mission.

Was appointed as Publications Officer and Battalion Unit Fund Custodian.

For Agency Use (skill codes, etc.)

Standard Form 171-A (BACK) (Rev. 6-88)
U.S. Office of Personnel Management
FPM Chapter 295

Standard Form 171-A– *Continuation Sheet for SF 171 (Back)*
• Attach all SF 171-A's to your application at the top of page 3.

Form Approved:
OMB No. 3206-0012

1. Name *(Last, First, Middle Initial)*	2. Social Security Number
COX, Christopher L.	999-99-9999

3. Job Title or Announcement Number You Are Applying For	4. Date Completed

ADDITIONAL WORK EXPERIENCE BLOCKS

D

Name and address of employer's organization *(include ZIP Code, if known)*	Dates employed *(give month, day and year)*	Average number of hours per week	Number of employees you supervise
U.S. Army	From: 09/99 To: 03/00	45	240
Fort Jackson, SC 27000	Salary or earnings	Your reason for wanting to leave	
	Starting $ E-7 per year	PCS	
	Ending $ E-7 per year		

Your immediate supervisor Name	Telephone No.	Exact title of your job	If Federal employment *(civilian or military)* list series, grade or rank, and, if promoted in this job, the date of your last promotion
1SG Turner	(910) 483-6611	Operation Training Sup.	E-7

Description of work: Describe your specific duties, responsibilities and accomplishments in this job, **including** the job title(s) of any employees you supervise. *If you describe more than one type of work (for example, carpentry and painting, or personnel and budget), write the approximate percentage of time you spent doing each.*

Supervised personnel performing typing, general clerical, and administrative duties. Cross-trained personnel in job duties which resulted in reduced supervision requirements and a saving in overtime hours. Trained personnel in the maintenance of records and preparation of work orders.

Served as a Training Noncommissioned Officer for a Basic Combat Training company consisting of 17 cadre organized into a headquarters and four platoons. Responsible for the in- and out-processing of approximately 240 soldiers every eight-week cycle. Initiated and maintained training records for all assigned cadre and soldiers. Scheduled, coordinated, and inspected unit training. Procured and maintained training aids and lesson plans. Assisted the Commander and 1SG with all administrative matters.

Was very proficient in preparing and managing the training records of both Initial Entry soldiers and permanent party soldiers. On a formal audit, received a perfect evaluation of our recordkeeping.

Willingly accepted the responsibility of the company administration in the absence of the First Sergeant. Became respected for my top-notch organizational skills which resulted in top scores on internal inspections.

Was formally recognized as "primarily responsible for the unit's smooth transition into the 'Train your own trainer' concept." Continually monitored training, ensuring that all training was scheduled and conducted in accordance with the prescribed Program of Instruction and Post Policy Letters. Was evaluated in writing as being "superb in the processing and separation of soldiers in a timely manner."

For Agency Use (skill codes, etc.)

Standard Form 171-A— *Continuation Sheet for SF 171 (Back)*
• Attach all SF 171-A's to your application at the top of page 3.

Form Approved:
OMB No. 3206-0012

1. Name *(Last, First, Middle Initial)*	2. Social Security Number
COX, Christopher L.	999-99-9999

3. Job Title or Announcement Number You Are Applying For	4. Date Completed

ADDITIONAL WORK EXPERIENCE BLOCKS

E	Name and address of employer's organization *(include ZIP Code, if known)*	Dates employed *(give month, day and year)*	Average number of hours per week	Number of employees you supervise
	U.S. Army Fort Jackson, SC and Italy	From: 12/95 To: 12/99	40	0

Salary or earnings	Your reason for wanting to leave
Starting $ E-7 per year	PCS
Ending $ E-7 per year	

Your immediate supervisor Name	Telephone No.	Exact title of your job	If Federal employment *(civilian or military)* list series, grade or rank, and, if promoted in this job, the date of your last promotion
CSM Pearle	(910) 483-6611	Training Supervisor	E-7

Description of work: Describe your specific duties, responsibilities and accomplishments in this job, **including** the job title(s) of any employees you supervise. *If you describe more than one type of work (for example, carpentry and painting, or personnel and budget), write the approximate percentage of time you spent doing each.*

Served as a Training Noncommissioned Officer for a Basic Combat Training company consisting of 17 cadre organized into a headquarters and four platoons. Managed the in- and out-processing of approximately 240 soldiers every eight-week cycle. Initiated and maintained training records for all assigned cadre and soldiers. Scheduled, coordinated, and inspected unit training. Procured and maintained training aids and lesson plans. Assisted the Commander and 1SG with all administrative matters.

Consistently received excellent ratings from the Directorate of Plans and Training during the end of cycle training records inspections. Have been recognized for saving time and greatly enhancing the quality of training through my "uncanny ability in gathering and managing training materials and resources."

Served as Headquarters Detachment First Sergeant of a remote installation in Italy which supports 14 tenant units. Served as Headquarters First Sergeant responsible for supervision of the Installation Transportation Office, Transportation Motor Pool, Property Book Office, Dining Facility, and Personnel Administration Center (PAC).

Was appointed to Club Council, Dining Facility Council, Unit Fund Custodian, Test Site Manager, Key Control Custodian, and Member of Area II Morale Support Fund Council.

For Agency Use (skill codes, etc.)

Standard Form 171-A (BACK) (Rev. 6-88)
U.S. Office of Personnel Management
FPM Chapter 295

Standard Form 171-A— *Continuation Sheet for SF 171 (Back)*
• Attach all SF 171-A's to your application at the top of page 3.

Form Approved:
OMB No. 3206-0012

1. Name *(Last, First, Middle Initial)*	2. Social Security Number
COX, Christopher L.	999-99-9999

3. Job Title or Announcement Number You Are Applying For	4. Date Completed

ADDITIONAL WORK EXPERIENCE BLOCKS

F Name and address of employer's organization *(Include ZIP Code, if known)*

U.S. Army

Italy

Dates employed *(give month, day and year)*	Average number of hours per week: 40 / Number of employees you supervise: 0
From: 01/92 To: 10/95	
Salary or earnings	Your reason for wanting to leave
Starting $ E-6 per year	PCS
Ending $ E-6 per year	

Your immediate supervisor Name	Telephone No.	Exact title of your job	If Federal employment *(civilian or military)* list series, grade or rank, and, if promoted in this job, the date of your last promotion
LTC Wilkins	(910) 483-6611	Education Coordinator	E-6 (11 November 1993)

Description of work: Describe your specific duties, responsibilities and accomplishments in this job, including the job title(s) of any employees you supervise. *If you describe more than one type of work (for example, carpentry and painting, or personnel and budget), write the approximate percentage of time you spent doing each.*

Managed and coordinated the function of the Operations Division, Security Plans, and Operations Directorate. Planned, coordinated, and oversaw participation in major exercises to include REFORGER, WINTEX, CRESTED EAGLE, and ABLE ARCHER. Developed and maintained contingency plans for wartime operations and peacetime community operations. Served as NCOIC, Operations Center. Was responsible for Emergency Actions (EA) operations.

During NATO Exercise CRESTED EAGLE was not only responsible for exercise participation, but was also charged with the reception and logistical support of three Reserve component units that were located in five different areas.

Personally planned and supervised 6th Area Support Group participation in exercise FIRST RESPONSE '94, an exercise conducted in Louisiana and sponsored by the Louisiana Army National Guard.

Received two prestigious medals recognizing my outstanding leadership ability and personnel management skills. During this time, organized and directed more than a dozen successful training projects, each of which included up to 2,000 people.

For Agency Use (skill codes, etc.)

Standard Form 171-A (BACK) (Rev. 6-88)
U.S. Office of Personnel Management
FPM Chapter 295

COX, Christopher Landon   999-99-9999

CONTINUATION SHEET FOR ITEM 31 (1)

NAME AND LOCATION OF SCHOOL	MONTH AND YEAR ATTENDED	CLASSROOM HOURS	SUBJECTS STUDIED	TRAINING COMPLETED
Postal Supervisor Training Course Fort Jackson, SC	09/99–07/00	40	Postal Supervision	Yes
Supervisor Principles and Techniques Fort Jackson, SC	01/99	40	Supervisor Principles and Techniques	Yes
Postal Supervisor Course Fort Campbell, KY	07/98–09/98	320	Postal Supervision	Yes
Senior Commander and First Sergeant Course Fort Leonard Wood, MO	01/96–02/96	80	Senior Commander and First Sergeant Training	Yes
(ANCOC) Advance Noncommission Officer Course Fort Campbell, KY	09/93–11/93	320	Advance Noncommission Officer Training	Yes
Commander/First Sergeant Course Italy	07/94	80	Commander/First Sergeant Training	Yes
Security Management Course Italy	05/94–06/94	80	Security Management	Yes

COX, Christopher Landon   999-99-9999

CONTINUATION SHEET FOR ITEM 31 (2)

NAME AND LOCATION OF SCHOOL	MONTH AND YEAR ATTENDED	CLASSROOM HOURS	SUBJECTS STUDIED	TRAINING COMPLETED
Law for Legal Clerk Course Columbia, SC	06/91	80	Law for Legal Clerks	Yes
(1SG) First Sergeant Administrative Course Fort Jackson, SC	03/91-04/91	80	First Sergeant Administration	Yes
Human Relations Course Fort Jackson, SC	03/89-04/89	120	Human Relations	Yes
NCO Academy Italy	02/86-03/86	160	Noncommissioned Officer Academy	Yes
Advance Leadership Training Course Fort Benning, GA	11/85-12/85	120	Advance Leadership Training	Yes
Race Relation Leadership Course Fort Benning, GA	09/85-09/85	40	Race Relation Leadership	Yes
Airborne School Fort Benning, GA	01/84-02/84	120	Airborne School	Yes
Clerk Typist School Fort Campbell, KY	03/83-04/83	320	Clerk Typist	Yes

EDUCATION

25 Did you graduate from high school? *If you have a GED high school equivalency or will graduate within the next nine months, answer "YES".*

If "YES", give month and year graduated

		or received GED equivalency:................	05/1980
YES	X		
NO		If "NO", give the highest grade you completed:.	

26 Write the name and location *(city and state)* of the last high school you attended or where you obtained your GED high school equivalency.

Sparkling High School, Columbia, SC

27 Have you ever attended college or graduate school?

YES	X	If "YES", continue with 28.
NO		If "NO", go to 31.

28 NAME/LOCATION *(City, state, ZIP Code)* OF COLLEGE OR UNIVERSITY. *If you expect to graduate within 9 months, give the month/year you expect to receive your degree:*

	Name	City	ST.	ZIP Code	MONTH AND YEAR ATTENDED From	To	NO. OF CR. HRS. COMPLETED Sem.	Quarter	TYPE OF DEGREE *(e.g. BA, MA)*	MONTH AND YEAR OF DEGREE
1)	Benedict College	Columbia	SC		09/80	05/82	60		A.A.	05/82
2)	University of South Carolina, Columbia		SC		03/04	05/04	12			
3)										

29 CHIEF UNDERGRADUATE SUBJECTS *Show major on the first line*

		NO. CR. HRS. COMPLETED Sem.	Quarter
1)	Business Administration	60	
2)	Sexual Harassment	5	
3)	Organization & Management	3	

30 CHIEF GRADUATE SUBJECTS *Show major on the first line*

		NO. CR. HRS. COMPLETED Sem.	Quarter
1)			
2)			
3)			

31 If you have completed any other courses or training related to the kind of jobs you are applying for *(trade, vocational, Armed Forces, business)* give information below.

NAME AND LOCATION *(City, State and ZIP Code)* OF SCHOOL	MO./YR. ATTENDED From	To	CLASS-ROOM HOURS	SUBJECT(S)	TRAINING COMPLETE? YES	NO
School Name 1) City / State / ZIP Code				See attached CONTINUATION SHEET FOR ITEM 31		
School Name 2) City / State / ZIP Code						

SPECIAL SKILLS, ACCOMPLISHMENTS AND AWARDS

32 Give the title /year of honors, awards or fellowships you have received. List special qualifications, skills or accomplishments that may help you get a job. *Some examples are: skills with computers; most important publications (do not submit copies); public speaking/writing experience; membership in societies; patents or inventions; etc.*

Guest Speaker, VFW Post #1110; Instructor; Member of Columbia Lodge #48 Columbia, SC; SWA: 283055-283056//Humanitarian Service Medal//Armed Forces Expeditionary Medal// Parachutist Badge//Joint Service Commendation Medal//Meritorious Medal-10LC

33 How many words per minute can you: Type? Take Dictation?

65 wpm

Agencies may test your skills before hiring you.

34 List job-related licenses or certificates that you have, such as: *registered nurse; lawyer; radio operator, driver's; pilot's; etc.*

	LICENSE OR CERTIFICATE	DATE OF LATEST LICENSE OR CERTIFICATE	STATE OR OTHER LICENSING AGENCY
1)	Driver's License	01/2003	SC DMV
2)			

35 Do you speak or read a language other than English *(Include sign language)? Applicants for jobs that require a language other than English may be given an interview conducted solely in that language.*

YES		If "YES", list each language and place an "X" in each column that applies to you.
NO	X	If "NO", go to 36.

LANGUAGE(S)	CAN PREPARE AND GIVE LECTURES Fluently	With Difficulty	CAN SPEAK AND UNDERSTAND Fluently	Passably	CAN TRANSLATE ARTICLES Into English	From English	CAN READ ARTICLES FOR OWN USE Easily	With Difficulty
1)								
2)								

REFERENCES

36 List three people who are not related to you and are not supervisors you listed under 24 who know your qualifications and fitness for the kind of job for which you are applying. At least one should know you well on a personal basis.

	FULL NAME OF REFERENCE	TELEPHONE NUMBER(S) *(Include Area Code)*	PRESENT BUSINESS OR HOME ADDRESS *(Number, street and city)*	STATE	ZIP CODE
1)	David Cantu, (SGM RET)	(910) 483-6611	Fort Jackson	SC	27000
2)	Kent Taylor, (SGM RET)	(910) 483-6611	Fort Jackson	SC	27000
3)	Suzanne Lillard, (BN CDR)	(910) 483-6611	Fort Jackson	SC	27000

Page

BACKGROUND INFORMATION-- *You must answer each question in this section before we can process your application.*

		YES	NO
37	Are you a citizen of the United States? *(In most cases you must be a U.S. Citizen to be hired. You will be required to submit proof of identity and citizenship at the time you are hired.)* If "NO", give the country or countries you are a citizen of:		
		X	

NOTE: It is important that you give complete and truthful answers to questions 38 through 44. If you answer "YES" to any of them, provide your explanation(s) in **Item 45. Include** convictions resulting from a plea of nolo contendere *(no contest).* **Omit:** 1) traffic fines of $100.00 or less; 2) any violation of law committed before your 16th birthday; 3) any violation of law committed before your 18th birthday, if finally decided in juvenile court or under a Youth Offender law; 4) any conviction set aside under the Federal Youth Corrections Act or similar State law; 5) any conviction whose record was expunged under Federal or State law. We will consider the date, facts, and circumstances of each event you list. In most cases you can still be considered for Federal jobs. However, **if you fail to tell the truth or fail to list all relevant** events or circumstances, this may be grounds for not hiring you, for firing you after you begin work, or for criminal prosecution (18 USC 1001).

		YES	NO
38	During the last **10 years**, were you **fired from any job** for any reason, did you **quit after being told that you would be fired**, or did you leave by mutual agreement because of specific problems?...............		X
39	Have you **ever** been convicted of, or forfeited collateral for **any felony violation?** *(Generally, a felony is defined as any violation of law punishable by imprisonment of longer than one year, except for violations called misdemeanors under State law which are punishable by imprisonment of two years or less.)*		X
40	Have you **ever** been convicted of, or forfeited collateral for **any firearms or explosives violation?**..........		X
41	Are you **now** under charges for **any** violation of law?		X
42	During the **last 10 years** have you forfeited collateral, been convicted, been imprisoned, been on probation, or been on parole? Do **not** include violations reported in 39, 40, or 41, above.		X
43	Have you **ever** been convicted by a military **court-martial?** If no military service, answer "NO".............		X
44	Are you **delinquent** on any Federal debt? *(Include delinquencies arising from Federal taxes, loans, overpayment of benefits, and other debts to the US Government **plus** defaults on Federally guaranteed or insured loans such as student or home mortgage loans.)*		X

45   If "YES" in: **38** - Explain for each job the problem(s) and your reason(s) for leaving. Give the employer's name and address.
39 through 43 - Explain each violation. Give place of occurrence and name/address of police or court involved.
44 - Explain the type, length and amount of the delinquency or default, and steps you are taking to correct errors or repay the debt. Give any identification number associated with the debt and the address of the Federal agency involved.
NOTE: If you need more space, use a sheet of paper, and include the item number.

Item No.	Date (Mo./Yr.)	Explanation	Mailing Address
			Name of Employer, Police, Court, or Federal Agency
			City State ZIP Code
			Name of Employer, Police, Court, or Federal Agency
			City State ZIP Code
			Name of Employer, Police, Court, or Federal Agency
			City State ZIP Code

		YES	NO
46	Do you receive, or have you ever applied for retirement pay, pension, or other pay based on military, Federal civilian, or District of Columbia Government service?	X	
47	Do any of your relatives work for the US Government or the United States Armed Forces? Include: *father; mother; husband; wife; son; daughter; brother; sister; uncle; aunt; first cousin; nephew; niece; father-in-law; mother-in-law; son-in-law; daughter-in-law; brother-in-law; sister-in-law; stepfather; stepmother; stepson; stepdaughter; stepbrother; stepsister; half brother; and half sister*............	X	

If "YES", provide details below. If you need more space, use a sheet of paper.

Name	Relationship	Dept., Agency or Branch of Armed Forces
Peter Cox	Son	U.S. Army
Jason Cox	Son	U.S. Army

SIGNATURE, CERTIFICATION, AND RELEASE OF INFORMATION

YOU MUST SIGN THIS APPLICATION. Read the following carefully before you sign.

? A false statement on any part of your application may be grounds for not hiring you, or for firing you after you begin work. Also, you may be punished by fine or imprisonment (U.S. Code, title 18, section 1001).
? If you are a male born after December 31, 1959, you must be registered with the Selective Service System or have a valid exemption in order to be eligible for Federal employment. You will be required to certify as to your status at the time of appointment.
? **I understand** that any information I give may be investigated as allowed by law or Presidential order.
? **I consent** to the release of information about my ability and fitness for Federal employment by *employers, schools, law enforcement agencies and other individuals and organizations, to investigators, personnel staffing specialists, and other authorized employees of the Federal Government.*
? **I certify** that, to the best of my knowledge and belief, **all** of my statements are true, correct, complete, and made in good faith.

48 SIGNATURE *(Sign each application in dark ink)*	49 DATE SIGNED *(Month, day, year)*

Page

Form Approved
OMB No. 3206-0219

OPTIONAL APPLICATION FOR FEDERAL EMPLOYMENT - OF 612

You may apply for most jobs with a resume, this form, or other written format. If your resume or application does not provide all the information requested on this form and in the job vacancy announcement, you may lose consideration for a job.

1 Job title in announcement	**2** Grade(s) applying for	**3** Announcement number

4 Last name Cox,	First and middle names Christopher Landon	**5** Social Security Number 999-99-9999

6 Mailing Address 1110 1/2 Hay Street		**7** Phone Numbers (incl area code) Day 910-483-6611
City Fayetteville,	State NC — Zip Code 28305	Eve 910-483-6611

WORK EXPERIENCE

8 Describe your paid and nonpaid work experience related to the job for which you are applying. Do not attach job descriptions.

1) Job Title (if Federal, include series and grade)
Postal Supervisor

From (MM/YY) July 2002	To (MM/YY) October 2004	Salary per $ E-7	Hours per week 45

Employer's name and address U.S. Army, AG 483rd Postal Company, Fort Jackson, SC 27000	Supervisor's name and phone number LTC Jones (910) 483-6611

Describe your duties and accomplishments

Served as Postal Finance Officer and Custodian of Postal effects in a Postal Company. Maintained stock levels of $23,000.00 in stamps and money orders for soldier-operated post offices; issued stocks to clerks for operations; assumed position of First Sergeant. Supervised administrative functions of the Battalion. Reviewed and edited correspondence prior to release for signature. Conducted review of files to ensure proper filing. Planned and organized office operations, wrote office Standard Operating Procedures (SOPs), job descriptions, and directives. Determined requirements for office equipment (to include automation), supplies, and space.

2) Job Title (if Federal, include series and grade)
Battation Adjutant (CPT)

From (MM/YY) May 2001	To (MM/YY) June 2002	Salary per $ E-7	Hours per week 48

Employer's name and address U. S. Army, Training Group (ABN), Fort Jackson, SC 27000	Supervisor's name and phone number SGM Kent Taylor ( )

Describe your duties and accomplishments

Provided administrative and personnel support to a Special Forces Battalion with 268 soldiers and 60 civilians assigned; managed the processing of critical documents, including efficiency reports, awards, personnel transfers, and finance documents; advised the Battalion and Company Commanders on administrative matters; coordinated Sponsorship Program; supervised two NCOs and two civilians.

9 May we contact your current supervisor?

     YES [X]   NO [ ] if we need to contact your current supervisor before making an offer, we will contact you first.

EDUCATION

10 Mark highest level completed. **Some HS [ ] HS/GED [X] Associate [ ] Bachelor [ ] Master [ ] Doctoral [ ]**

11 Last high school (HS) or GED school. Give the school's name, city, State, ZIP Code (if known), and year diploma or GED received. Sparkling High School, Columbia, SC 22222

12 Colleges and universities attended. Do **not** attach a copy of your transcript unless requested.

1) Name				Total Credits Earned		Major(s)	Degree - Year
				Semester	Quarter		(if any) Received
City		State	Zip Code				
2)							
3)							

OTHER QUALIFICATIONS

13 **Job-related** training courses (give title and year). **Job-related** skills (other languages, computer software/hardware, tools, machinery, typing speed, etc.). **Job-related** certificates and licenses (current only). **Job-related** honors, awards, and special accomplishments (publications, memberships in professional/honor societies, leadership activities, public speaking, an d performance awards). Give dates, but do **not** send documents unless requested.

Guest Speaker, VFW Post #1110; Instructor; Member of Columbia Lodge #48 Columbia, SC; SWA: Humanitarian Service Medal//Armed Forces Expeditionary Medal//Parachutist Badge//Joint Service Commendation Medal//Meritorious Medal-10LC.

Strong working knowledge of Word, Excel, Access, and PowerPoint. Experienced in utilizing spreadsheets for management analysis and decision making.

Held Top Secret security clearance. Firearms expertise includes skills with rifles and pistols.

GENERAL

14 Are you a U.S. citizen?   YES [X]   NO [ ]▶ Give the country of your citizenship. _____

15 Do you claim veterans' preference?   NO [ ] YES [X]▶ Mark your claim of 5 or 10 points below.
    5 points [X]▶ Attach your DD 214 or other proof. **10 points [   ]▶** Attach an *Application for 10-Point Veterans' Preference* (SF 15) and proof required.

16 Were you ever a federal civilian employee?
     NO [X] YES [ ]▶ For highest civilian grade give: Series   Grade   From   To

17 Are you eligible for reinstatement based on career or career-conditional Federal status?
     NO [ ] YES [❱ if requested, attach SF 50 proof.

APPLICANT CERTIFICATION

18 I **certify** that, to the best of my knowledge and belief, all of the information on and attached to this application is true, correct, complete and made in good faith. **I understand** that false or fraudulent information on or attached to this application may be grounds for not hiring me or for firing me after I begin work, and may be punishable by fine or imprisonment. **I understand** that any information I give may be investigated.

SIGNATURE   **DATE SIGNED**

UNITED STATES POSTAL SERVICE®

Application for Employment
The US Postal Service is an Equal Opportunity Employer
(Shaded Areas for Postal Service Use Only)

Rated Application			Veteran preference has been verified through proof that the separation was under honorable conditions, and other proof as required. *(See Section D below.)*	Check One:
Rated For	**Rating**	**Date Rcvd.**		☐ 10 pts. CPS
		Time Rcvd.	**Type of Proof Submitted & Date Issued**	☐ 10 pts. CP
				☐ 10 pts. XP
Signature & Date			**Verifier's Signature, Title & Date**	☐ 5 pts. TP

A. General Information

1. Name *(First, MI, Last)* Robert L. Charles	2. Social Security No. (SSN) 123-45-6789	3. Home Telephone (910) 483-6611
4. Mailing Address *(No., Street, City, State, ZIP Code)* 1110 1/2 Hay Street Fayetteville, NC 28305	5. Date of Birth January 1, 1960	6. Work Telephone (910) 483-6611
	7. Place of Birth *(City & State or City & Country)* Chicago, IL	

8. Kind of Job Applied for and Postal Facility Name & Location *(City & State)*	9. Will You Accept: Temporary/Casual (Noncareer) Work? ☒ Yes ☐ No	10. When Will You Be Available? Immediately	11. Are You Willing to Travel? *(Complete only if you are applying for an executive or professional position.)* ☒ Yes ☐ No

B. Educational History

1. Name and Location *(City & State)* of Last High School Attended Windy City High School Chicago, IL	2. Are You a High School Graduate? Answer "Yes" if you expect to graduate within the next 9 months, or you have an official equivalency certificate of graduation. ☒ Yes - Month & Year: June 1998 ☐ No - Highest Grade Completed:

3a. Name and Location of College or University *(City, State, and ZIP Code if known. If you expect to graduate within 9 months, give month and year you expect degree.)*	Dates Attended		No. of Credits Completed		Type Degree (BA, etc.)	Year of Degree
	From	To	Semester Hrs.	Quarter Hrs.		
See Continuation Sheet						

3b. Chief Undergraduate College Subjects	Semester Hrs. Completed	Quarter Hrs. Completed	3c. Chief Graduate College Subjects	Semester Hrs. Completed	Quarter Hrs. Completed

4. Major Field of Study at Highest Level of College Work

5. Other Schools or Training *(For example, trade, vocational, armed forces, or business. Give for each: Name, City, State, and ZIP Code, if known, of school; dates attended; subjects studied; number of classroom hours of instruction per week; certificates; and any other pertinent information.)*

See Continuation Sheet for College and Other Schools and Training.

6. Honors, Awards, and Fellowships Received

See Continuation Sheet for Honors and Awards.

7. Special Qualifications and Skills *(Licenses; skills with machines, patents or inventions; publications - do not submit copies unless requested; public speaking; memberships in professional or scientific societies; typing or shorthand speed, etc.)*

See Continuation Sheet for Special Qualifications.

PS Form **2591**, March 1999 *(Page 1 of 4)*

Name *(First, MI, Last)* Robert L. Charles	Social Security No. 123-45-6789	Date

C. Work History

(Start with your present position and go back for 10 years or to your 16th birthday, whichever is later. You may include volunteer work. Account for periods of unemployment in separate blocks in order. Include military service. Use blank sheets if you need more space. Include your name, SSN, and date on each sheet.)

May the US Postal Service ask your present employer about your character, qualifications, and employment record? A "No" will not affect your consideration for employment opportunities. ☒ Yes ☐ No

1.

Dates of Employment *(Month & Year)*	Grade If Postal, Federal Service or Military	Starting Salary/Earnings
From May 2004 To **Present**	N/A	$ 9.50 per hour

Exact Position Title	Average Hours per Week	Number and Kind of Employees Supervised	Present Salary/Earnings
Service Coordinator	30	3 cooks	$ 10.00 per hour

Name of Employer and Complete Mailing Address	Kind of Business *(Manufacturing, etc.)*	Place of Employment *(City & State)*
Burger King	Fast Food	Chicago, IL
987 West 1st Street	Name of Supervisor	Telephone No. *(If known)*
Chicago, IL 00000	Thomas Evans	(910) 483-6611

Reason for Wanting to Leave
To improve my skills.

Description of Duties, Responsibilities, and Accomplishments

Quickly promoted from cook to service coordinator within three months. Supervise three cooks in their jobs of cooking regular hamburgers, specialty sandwiches, and salads. Responsible for the cleanliness of the grill, oven, and stock room. Ensure food waste is at a minimum. Accountable for assets valued at $75,000.

2.

Dates of Employment *(Month & Year)*	Grade If Postal, Federal Service or Military	Starting Salary/Earnings
From April 2003 To April 2004	N/A	$ 8.00 per hour

Exact Position Title	Average Hours per Week	Number and Kind of Employees Supervised	Present Salary/Earnings
Sales Associate	20	-0-	$ 9.00 per hour

Name of Employer and Complete Mailing Address	Kind of Business *(Manufacturing, etc.)*	Place of Employment *(City & State)*
Best Buy	Retail Store	Chicago, IL
123 Old Main Street	Name of Supervisor	Telephone No. *(If known)*
Chicago, IL 60600	Rita Moore	(910) 483-6611

Reason for Leaving
Desire to improve job skills.

Description of Duties, Responsibilities, and Accomplishments

Sold computers, video camera equipment, software, games, and digital cameras. Accountable for assets valued at $250,000. Received the "top sales professional" award in three separate months.

3.

Dates of Employment *(Month & Year)*	Grade If Postal, Federal Service or Military	Starting Salary/Earnings
From April 2001 To April 2003	E-6, SSG	$ per

Exact Position Title	Average Hours per Week	Number and Kind of Employees Supervised	Present Salary/Earnings
Company Physical Security	40+	-0-	$ per

Name of Employer and Complete Mailing Address	Kind of Business *(Manufacturing, etc.)*	Place of Employment *(City & State)*
U.S. Army	Military	Fort Bragg, NC
Fort Bragg, NC 22233	Name of Supervisor	Telephone No. *(If known)*
	1SG Sweeney	( )

Reason for Leaving

Description of Duties, Responsibilities, and Accomplishments

Responsible for the security of the company's arms room, vehicles, motor pool in a field and garrison environment.

Responsible for updating the SOPs and to make sure they were followed.

PS Form **2591**, March 1999 *(Page 2 of 4)*

Name (First, MI, Last) Robert L. Charles	Social Security No. 123-45-6789	Date

4.	Dates of Employment (Month & Year) From May 2000 To April 2001	Grade If Postal, Federal Service or Military E-6, SSG	Starting Salary/Earnings $ per
	Exact Position Title Average Hours per Week Platoon Sergeant 40+	Number and Kind of Employees Supervised 10	Present Salary/Earnings $ per

Name of Employer and Complete Mailing Address U.S. Army Fort Dix, NJ 33445	Kind of Business (Manufacturing, etc.) Military	Place of Employment (City & State) Fort Dix, NJ
	Name of Supervisor CPT Lincoln	Telephone No. (If known) ( )

Reason for Leaving

Description of Duties, Responsibilities, and Accomplishments

Supervised the training of ten soldiers in MP duties. Oversaw the upkeep of the squad's vehicles and equipment valued at $50,000. Patrol supervisor responsible for law enforcement of the military community. Received two prestigious medals recognizing my leadership ability, attention to detail, and willingness to train and mentor other employees.

D. Veteran Preference (Answer all parts. If a part does not apply, answer "No".)

	Yes	No
1. Have you ever served on active duty in the US military service? (Exclude tours of active duty for training as a reservist or guardsman.)	X	
2. Have you ever been discharged from the armed service under other than honorable conditions? You may omit any such discharge changed to honorable by a Discharge Review Board or similar authority. (If "Yes," give details in Section F.)		X
3. Do you claim 5-point preference based on active duty in the armed forces? (If "Yes," you will be required to furnish records to support your claim.)	X	
4. Do you claim a 10-point preference? If "Yes," check type of preference claimed and attach Standard Form 15, Claim for 10-Point Veteran Preference, together with proof called for in that form.		X

☐ Compensable Disability (Less than 30%)   ☐ Compensable Disability (30% or more)   ☐ Non-Compensable Disability (includes Receipt of the Purple Heart)   ☐ Wife/Husband

☐ Widow/Widower   ☐ Mother   ☐ Other:

5. List for All Military Service: (Enter N/A if not applicable)

Date (From - To)	Serial/Service Number	Branch of Service	Type of Discharge
April 1983-April 2003	123-45-6789	U.S. Army	Honorable

THE LAW (39 U.S. CODE 1002) PROHIBITS POLITICAL AND CERTAIN OTHER RECOMMENDATIONS FOR APPOINTMENTS, PROMOTIONS, ASSIGNMENTS, TRANSFERS, OR DESIGNATIONS OF PERSONS IN THE POSTAL SERVICE. Statements relating solely to character and residence are permitted, but every other kind of statement or recommendation is prohibited unless it either is requested by the Postal Service and consists solely of an evaluation of the work performance, ability, aptitude, and general qualifications of an individual or is requested by a government representative investigating the individual's loyalty, suitability, and character. Anyone who requests or solicits a prohibited statement or recommendation is subject to disqualification from the Postal Service and anyone in the Postal Service who accepts such a statement may be suspended or removed from office.

PS Form 2591, March 1999 (Page 3 of 4)

Name (First, MI, Last) Robert L. Charles	Social Security No. 123-45-6789	Date

E. Other Information

	Yes	No
1. Are you one of the following: a United States citizen, a permanent resident alien, a citizen of American Samoa or any other territory owing allegiance to the United States?	X	
2. RESERVED FOR OFFICIAL USE		
3. RESERVED FOR OFFICIAL USE		

If you answer "Yes" to question 4 and/or 5, give details in Section F below. Give the name, address (including ZIP Code) of employer, approximate date, and reasons in each case. ▶	4. Have you ever been fired from any job for any reason?		X
	5. Have you ever quit a job after being notified that you would be fired?		X

	Yes	No
6. Do you receive or have you applied for retirement pay, pension, or other compensation based upon military, postal, or federal civilian service? *(If you answer "Yes," give details in Section F.)*		X
7a. Have you ever been convicted of a crime or are you now under charges for any offense against the Law? You may omit: (1) any charges that were dismissed or resulted in acquittal; (2) any conviction that has been set aside, vacated, annulled, expunged, or sealed; (3) any offense that was finally adjudicated in a juvenile court or juvenile delinquency proceeding; and (4) any charges that resulted only in a conviction of a non-criminal offense. **All felony and misdemeanor convictions and all convictions in state and federal courts are criminal convictions and must be disclosed. Disclosure of such convictions is required even if you did not spend any time in jail and/or were not required to pay a fine.**		X
7b. While in the military service were you ever convicted by special or general court martial? **If you answer "Yes" to question 7a and/or 7b, give details in Section F. Show for each offense: (1) Date of conviction; (2) Charge convicted of; (3) Court and location; (4) Action taken. Note: A conviction does not automatically mean that you cannot be appointed. What you were convicted of, and how long ago, are important. Give all of the facts so that a decision can be made.**		X
8. Are you a former Postal Service or Federal Employee not now employed by the US Government? If you answer "Yes," give in Section F, name of employing agency(ies), position title(s), and date(s) employed.		X
9. Does the US Postal Service employ any relative of yours by blood or marriage? Postal officials may not appoint any of their relatives or recommend them for appointment in the Postal Service. Any relative who is appointed in violation of this restriction can not be paid. Thus it is necessary to have information about your relatives who are working for the USPS. These include: mother, father, daughter, son, sister, brother, aunt, uncle, first cousin, niece, nephew, wife, husband, mother-in-law, father-in-law, daughter-in-law, son-in-law, sister-in-law, brother-in-law, stepfather, stepmother, stepdaughter, stepson, stepsister, stepbrother, half sister, and half brother. If you answer "Yes" to question 9, give in section F for such relatives: (1) Full name; (2) Present address and ZIP Code; (3) Relationship; (4) Position title; (5) Name and location of postal installation where employed.		X
10. Are you now dependent on or a user of ANY addictive or hallucinogenic drug, including amphetamines, barbiturates, heroin, morphine, cocaine, mescaline, LSD, STP, hashish, marijuana, or methadone, other than for medical treatment under the supervision of a doctor?		X

F. Use This Space for Detailed Answers *(Use blank sheets if you need more space. Include your name, SSN, and date on each sheet.)*

G. Certification

Enter number of additional sheets you have attached as part of this application:

I certify that all of the statements made in this application are true, complete, and correct to the best of my knowledge and belief and are in good faith.	Signature of Applicant	Date Signed

Disclosure by you of your Social Security Number (SSN) is mandatory to obtain the services, benefits, or processes that you are seeking. Solicitation of the SSN by the USPS is authorized under provisions of Executive Order 9397, dated November 22, 1943. The information gathered through the use of the number will be used only as necessary in authorized personnel administration processes.

A false or dishonest answer to any question in this application may be grounds for not employing you or for dismissing you after you begin work, and may be punishable by fine or imprisonment. (US Code, Title 18, Sec. 1001). All information you give will be considered in reviewing your application and is subject to investigation.

PS Form **2591**, March 1999 *(Page 4 of 4)*

CONTINUATION SHEET FOR ITEM B5

EDUCATION & TRAINING

- Battalion training management system, platoon trainers (40 hours), Central Texas College, Fort Drum, NY, December 1997
- M-60 machine gun leaders course (80 hours), Central Texas College, Fort Drum, NY, September 1997
- Spanish (40 hours), Language School, Fort Drum, NY, June 1997
- Battalion training management system (40 hours), Central Texas College, Fort Drum, NY, August 1994
- Human Relations (120 hours), Human Relations School, Fort Drum, NY, June 1991
- Physical Security (120 hours), Physical Security School, Fort Rucker, AL, March 1990
- Primary NCO course (200 hours), Noncommissioned Officer's Academy, Fort Drum, NY, June 1987
- Training in military police procedures (320 hours), Advance Individual Training, Fort Jackson, SC, December 1985
- How to be a Team and Squad Leader (40 hours), Leadership Prep Course, Fort Jackson, SC, August 1985
- Basic Military Training (560) hours, Basic Training, Fort Benning, GA, July 1985
- Basic Training for Corrections Officer (40 hours), Corrections School Central Prison, Chicago, IL, January 1983
- Riot Control Training (80 hours), Corrections School Central Prison, Chicago, IL, August 1982

CONTINUATION SHEET FOR ITEM B7

HONORS/MEDALS

- Overseas Ribbon, three awards, 2003
- Army Good Conduct Medal, five awards, 2000
- Humanitarian Service Medal, 2000
- Army Service Medal, 1999
- NCO Development, 1994
- Armed Forced Expedition Medal, 1987
- Nation Defense Medal, 1985

EQUIPMENT EXPERTISE

Can operate and maintain the following:

Truck Carry all ½ ton	Truck 6x6 M35A2 2 ½ ton
Truck Scout	Truck CJ5 4x4 ½ ton
Truck J5F 4x2 Hyd. ½ ton	Truck Panel 4x2 ¾ ton
Truck pickup 4x2 ½ ton	Truck utility 4x4 ¼ ton

PUBLIC SPEAKING   Have taught to groups of up to 100 people on several occasions.

SECURITY CLEARANCE   Secret

Charles, Robert L.   123-45-6789

CONTINUATION SHEET FOR ITEM C

5. **Dates:** April 1998-April 2000
   Grade: E-6, SSG
   Exact Position Title: Platoon Sergeant
   Number and Kind of Employees Supervised: 40
   Name of Employer and Complete Mailing Address: U.S. Army, Fort Bragg, NC
   Kind of Business: Military
   Place of Employment: Fort Bragg, NC
   Name of Supervisor: CPT Forbes
   Reason for Wanting to Leave: Transferred
   Duties: Responsible for the training and welfare of 40 soldiers in military police duties
       and combat tactics.
         Oversaw the maintenance of the platoon's equipment.

6. **Dates:** April 1993-April 1998
   Grade: E-6, SSG
   Number and Kind of Employees Supervised: 10
   Name of Employer and Complete Mailing Address: U.S. Army, Fort Drum, NY
   Kind of Business: Military
   Place of Employment: Fort Drum, NY
   Name of Supervisor: CPT Ray
   Reason for Wanting to Leave: Transferred
   Duties: Responsible for training of ten soldiers and their welfare. Oversaw the upkeep of
       the squad's equipment.
       Patrol supervisor for law enforcement of Fort Drum, NY.

FEDERAL RESUME or RESUMIX

JAMES D. CAMERON
1110 1/2 Hay Street
Fayetteville, NC 28305
910-483-6611
E-mail: PREPub@aol.com

SSN: 000-00-0000
Country of Citizenship: United States
Veteran's Preference: _____ preference
Vacancy Announcement Number:
Position Title:

POSTAL FINANCE CLERK

MILITARY EXPERIENCE

2003-present: POSTAL FINANCE CLERK. United States Air Force, 315th Communication Squadron, Postal Division (USAF), Charleston Air Force Base, South Carolina 29418. Salary: $38,500 Hours per week: 40+. Supervisor: Dillon McPherson, Phone: 222-222-2222. Perform postal financial services using the UNISYS III Integrated Retail Terminal, and sell postage stamps, postal validation imprinter labels, and money orders. Maintain a minimum $2,750 flexible-credit account and adequate postage stock to service postal patrons. Remit funds derived daily from selling postage stock and money orders to the Custodian of Postal Effects. Accept items for mailing and advise patrons of applicable postal and customs requirements. Compute charges for postage and special-service fees and affix appropriate endorsements for category mail and special services. Prepare receipts on items accepted as Express, Insured, and Certified mail. Safeguard all mail items. Worked overtime hours to complete all daily assignments.

Accomplishments:

- Qualified as a Postal Finance Clerk within 4 weeks instead of the usual 6 weeks.
- Processed over $42,500 in financial transactions monthly with flawless accuracy.
- During an operational surge, worked extra hours to reduce mail delivery time by 45%.
- Was nominated as the "Finance Clerk of the Year" because of my "knowledge of the finance section and continued drive to understand new operations and train new finance clerks."
- Provided exceptional customer service while working the finance window; produced an 89% customer service satisfaction rating.

2001-03: POSTAL CLERK. United States Air Force, 315th Communication Squadron, Postal Division (USAF), Charleston Air Force Base, South Carolina 29418. Salary: $36,350. Hours per week: 40+. Supervisor: Thomas Guillard, Phone: 333-333-3333. Processed more than 2,750 pieces of incoming mail weekly. Unloaded incoming mail trucks and break down personal and official correspondence to include express, first, second, third, and fourth class mail. Processed express mail in a timely manner. Opened pouches and broke down letter trays and flats using sorting equipment. Distributed personal mail to individual U.S. Postal Service lock boxes. Wrote up accountable mail and large items using delivery notices of receipt and provided customer service at the parcel pick-up window. Off-loaded and processed mail from Moore Drums containers. Assisted patrons in completion of mail disposition forms and standing delivery forms.

Accomplishments:

- Ensured the efficient processing of 98,000 pounds of mail to 4,325 patrons and their families monthly.
- Was commended for my initiative in aggressively researching and reviewing postal guidelines, which led to 95% compliance with all U.S. government and host country rules and regulations.
- Was evaluated as an outstanding supervisor; was praised in writing for strong communication skills, and was commended for my skill in briefing the entire postal branch on current initiatives, programs, and quality of life improvements.

1999-01: PASSENGER SERVICE SPECIALIST. United States Air Force, 52nd Transportation Squadron, Travel Division (USAF), Tyndall Air Force Base, Florida 33948. Salary: $34,000. Hours per week: 40+. Supervisor: Carl Stephenson, Phone: 444-444-4444. Obtained passenger travel reservations for military personnel, DoD civilians, and temporary duty personnel. Issued transportation requests, travel authorizations, and related documents. Maintained files and registers. Prepared military travel warrants via air, rail, and ferry. Made reservations for military professionals and civilians. Audited commercial reservations provided by the Scheduled Airline Travel Office (SATO). Operated the Global Air Transportation Execution System (GATES).

Accomplishments:

- Was evaluated as "an extremely skilled and reliable transporter with a high level of knowledge and expertise."
- Played a key role in the expedient processing of over 1,125 passengers monthly involved in transactions valued at over $965,000.
- Aggressively collected over $27,500 in excess costs from travelers exceeding their authorized travel entitlement and returned those monies to the government.
- Continuously utilized my strong communications and public relations skills: provided briefings to military and federal employees on travel entitlements.
- Was credited with making a significant contribution toward achieving a 90% customer satisfaction rate; noted for my commitment to teamwork and completing tasks above expectations.

1996-99: QUALITY CONTROL PERSONAL PROPERTY SPECIALIST. United States Air Force, Defense Courier Service (USAF), Vance Air Force Base, Oklahoma 77485. Salary: $32,700. Hours per week: 40+. Supervisor: Suzanne Ramsey, Phone: 555-555-5555. Maintained surveillance over transportation policies and procedures pertinent to the movement of personal property from the largest U.S. military community overseas. Maintained the courier performance files of over 125 stateside couriers. Evaluated and monitored courier performance scores, performed witness reweighs, and inspected agents' facilities and equipment. Prepared semiannual carrier performance reports and identified negative trends in the movement of personal property. Resolved disputes between agents' personnel and customers, and negotiated and managed contracts with local firms. Monitored the performance of 95 personal property couriers.

Accomplishments:

- Was cited as "instrumental in maintaining a 89 percent inspection rate, which minimized loss and damages while also reducing overall claims filed against the government." Ensured all shipments received top quality service.
- During routine quality control inspections over a nine-month period, accurately identified 185 out of 750 shipments as being out of tolerance, which permitted early resolution of the problem and saved over $34,500 in government funds. On another occasion, saved $13,500 in excess weight costs.

- As a Quality Assurance Evaluator, ensured the error-free expenditure and processing of over $96,500 of contractual services for the local Direct Procurement Method Packing and Crating Contract.
- Monitored 14,333 inspection documents and identified the substandard performance of 12 carriers while making recommendations for appropriate actions.
- Was commended in writing for "possessing the ability to handle many and varied problems associated with the movement of personal property" and for effectively resolving problems "with laudatory comments from customers."
- Updated the Transportation Operational Personal Property Standard System (TOPS) computer system, which enabled end users to access up-to-date information when performing inquiries in the TOPS system.

1992-96: OUTBOUND PERSONAL PROPERTY SPECIALIST. United States Air Force, Defense Courier Service (USAF) Vance Air Force Base, Oklahoma 77485. Salary: $30,350. Hours per week: 40+. Supervisor: Eric S. Linwood, Phone: 666-666-6666. Prepared and reviewed International Through Government Bills of Lading for commercial carriers for accuracy and completeness. Advised Personal Property Processing Offices in writing of carrier/agent selection and confirmation pick-up dates. Prepared Government Bills of Lading and other shipping documents for International, Direct Procurement Method, Door-to-Door, and Local Moves. Maintained documents and files. Acted as a liaison between Personal Property Shipping Offices and carriers' local agents. Maintained surveillance over transportation policies and procedures pertinent to the performance files of over 135 stateside carriers. Evaluated and monitored carrier performance scores.

Accomplishments:

- Was described in writing as "an excellent performer who provided outstanding service to over 6,250 government personnel members relocating from other communities."
- Expertly prepared 1,950 Government Bills of Lading for household goods shipments worldwide.
- Was instrumental in collecting $10,500 on personal property shipments; ensured strict compliance with guidelines related to waste, fraud, and abuse.
- Earned a reputation as an outstanding communicator: A formal performance evaluation praised my "ability to articulate personal property issues during briefings for 2,750 inbound personnel." Also earned praise for my written communication skills: prepared and submitted articles on constantly changing personal property entitlements.
- On my own initiative, prepared a guide for administrative policies and procedures for the Outbound Section which eliminated redundancy, increased productivity, and resulted in a 95% customer satisfaction rate.
- On one occasion, streamlined the processing of over 450 Government Bill of Lading correction notices, which saved more than $4,500 in supplies and labor yearly.

EDUCATION	**Master of Public Administration degree**, Charleston Southern University, Charleston, SC, 2003. Excelled academically with a 4.0 GPA. **Bachelor of Arts degree in Management**, University of Oklahoma, Enid, OK, 1998.
AFFILIATIONS	Member of General Administration Society Affiliate of the Honorary Society of Public Administrators in South Carolina
CLEARANCE	Secret security clearance
COMPUTERS	Gained working knowledge of Microsoft Word, Excel, Access, and PowerPoint
HONORS & AWARDS	Recipient of Meritorious Service Medal and Air Force Commendation Medals Air Force Good Conduct Award 2001 and 2000 Air Force Achievement Award 1999 and 1997

FEDERAL RESUME or RESUMIX

MICHAEL A. WHITE
1110½ Hay Street
Fayetteville, NC 28305 USA
Home Phone: 910-483-6611
www.prep-pub.com
E-mail: preppub@aol.com

SSN: 000-11-2222
Date of birth: January 01, 1959
Country of Citizenship: United States
Veteran's Preference: 10 point compensable

PROGRAM ANALYST

EXPERIENCE

01/01/2004-present: **PROGRAM ANALYST.** U.S. Army, S-3, 5th Special Forces Group, Fort Hood, TX 48361. 40 hours per week. Rank: SFC. Supervisor: MSG Woodrow, 910-483-6611. In the intensive environment of special operations during wartime, worked with the S-3/Program Manager (a Major) as I performed complex financial analysis and statistical accounting in support of the 5th Special Forces Group's training program. While acting as a consultant, obtained input from managers in three battalions and three companies in order to develop—and annually revise—a five-year plan which forecast training and personnel needs. Conducted detailed analyses of cost effectiveness, identified potential problems, and predicted future efficiency of programs. Data and predictions I developed were used to create the five-year plan that became the "master plan" and "training bible" to ensure that 1,000 Special Forces team members received on-time training in areas such as SCUBA, electronics, communications, and airborne operations. Performed cost-benefit analyses and trend analyses. Developed cost data and performed cost analyses of expenditures.

- Developed Excel spreadsheets, Access databases, and reports that monitored spending monthly and quarterly. Utilized the Army Training, Readiness, and Resource System (ATRRS). Developed a new Access database that forecast future training deficiencies and other problems. Created and delivered PowerPoint presentations praised for clarity.

- When training needs exceeded resources, procured funding for specialty training. Established strong working relationships with the Marines, Air Force, and Navy. Became the "go-to" professional when program managers from other services sought guidance about coordinating specialty training. Helped the Schools program become the best within USASOC.

- In my spare time, attended college in the evenings and earned my B.S. in Accounting with a 3.67 GPA as I completed courses including cost accounting, managerial accounting, and statistics. In my senior year, served as a company's Chief Financial Officer on a two-month project. Prepared balance sheets, profit and loss statements, cash flow statements, and other documents.

- Received Tax Preparer's ID issued by the IRS in 2004 (have prepared tax documents since 1984).

01/01/2002-12/31/2003: **RESOURCES MANAGER.** U.S. Army, S-3, 5th Special Forces Group, Fort Hood, TX 48361. 40 hours per week. Rank: SFC. Supervisor: SGM Heinz, 910-483-6611. When I took this job, inherited a situation in which key Special Forces individuals were unaware of their specific training requirements, which jeopardized their ability to remain ready to deploy on highly specialized teams.

- Because of my analytical skills and ability to use software programs as a management tool, I was handpicked to assume responsibility for PERSTEMPO projections. Developed a new software program that monitored PERSTEMPO projections so that unit deployments could occur on time and in compliance with regulatory and legal requirements. Developed a PERSTEMPO tracking database system that accommodated the new Global Forces Management Database System (GFMDS). Instructed personnel in the use of the new GFMDS Report.
- Expertly utilized Excel spreadsheets, Access databases, PowerPoint software, and the ATRRS system while analyzing resources and forecasting training needs. Utilized a classified software program to perform accounting and control functions. Processed over 303 school allocations with a 98.4% utilization rating. Performed research, statistical analysis, and cost analyses while making adjustments based on recommendations from staff and commanders. Established and maintained an automated school database that controlled expenditures by unit. Analyzed and evaluated personnel and equipment authorizations using Tables of Organization and Equipment (TOES) and Modified Tables of Organization and Equipment (MTOES).
- Developed and delivered outstanding PowerPoint presentations. Prepared written justifications of resource requirements.
- Maintained accountability of NBC equipment and supplied valued at $1 million, and directed the storage and monitoring of radioactive materials.

01/01/2000-12/31/2001: **OPERATIONS MANAGER.** U.S. Army, 75th MSB, 3rd Infantry Division, Fort Benning, GA 28305. 40 hours per week. Rank: SFC. MSG Mitchell, phone unknown. For a 655-person battalion, coordinated battalion operations while also supervising intelligence gathering and analysis. Was continuously involved in budgetary analysis and cost analysis as I ensured that funds were properly allocated to meet training needs. On a formal performance evaluation, was praised for "unparalleled technical expertise; always provides sound recommendations."

- On my own initiative, developed and implemented standard operating procedures (SOPs) for the schools program and for the Standard Army System program.
- Developed training plans using the software program known as the Standard Army Training (SATS) program. Initiated the SATS program in the battalion and trained Training NCOs on the SATS program, which became a model within the 3rd Infantry Division.
- On my own initiative, developed a tracking system to track all on-post and off-post schools.
- Prepared PowerPoint presentations and conducted briefings.
- Analyzed personnel and equipment authorizations using Tables of Organization and Equipment (TOES) and Modified Tables of Organization and Equipment (MTOES) for each company.

09/15/1998-12/31/1999: **FIRST-LINE SUPERVISOR.** U.S. Army, 3rd Chemical Company, 3rd Infantry Division, Fort Benning, GA 28305. 40 hours per week. Rank: SFC. 1LT Patrick, phone unknown. As Platoon Sergeant for the only forward deployed dual-purpose chemical company in the Pacific Basin, trained and supervised 27 people. With 100% accuracy, accounted for $2 million in equipment. Performed detailed research and cost analyses in order to ensure that training was complete within the projected budget.

- Assessed proficiency of platoon during NBC operations. Routinely anticipated and resolved a wide range of problems using my strong analytical and problem-solving abilities.
- Mentored three soldiers who were selected as Soldiers of the Month and Battalion Operator of the Quarter. Trained the platoon to achieve outstanding results on the Physical Fitness Test and on numerous decon and smoke missions. Was commended for my ability to establish strong working relationships with people at all levels.

PROGRAM ANALYST

- Became skilled in utilizing Excel spreadsheets as a management tool in conducting research and in developing recommendations for future courses of action.

01/01/1997-09/14/1998: **OPERATIONS MANAGER & COST ANALYST.** U.S. Army, 3rd Infantry Division, Fort Benning, GA 28305. 40 hours per week. Rank: SFC. CPT Sweeney, phone unknown. As Force Integration NCO, determined requirements and established priorities while providing guidance to various activities in the formulation, planning, and execution of the Command operating budget. Tracked funds distribution while also reconciling commitments/ obligations and reallocating organizational funds as directed. Monitored costs and prepared reports projecting use of available resources. Used advanced office automation skills to support budget operations such as updating, revising, sorting, calculating, manipulating, and converting spreadsheet data into various formats, programs, and reports. Prepared written justification of resource requirements, and prepared data in support of requirements. Analyzed and evaluated the documentation of personnel and equipment authorizations and requirements in Tables of Organization and Equipment (TOES) and Modified Tables of Organization and Equipment (MTOES) for a five-year window. Analyzed and reviewed trends in battlefield capability and determined cost factors related to the brigade's long-range plan.
- Acted as the Brigade Chemical NCO for a 2,400-person Brigade Combat Team. Developed standard operating procedures related to nuclear, biological, and chemical (NBC) matters and integrated all NBC equipment. Developed standard operating procedures (SOPs) related to contaminated casualty treatment, and trained personnel in proper contaminated casualty handling procedures. Improved the brigade's readiness and safety postures through my development of garrison SOPs and radiation safety SOPs.
- Was praised for my ability to prepare and deliver effective PowerPoint presentations on a wide variety of subjects. Conducted conferences and presentation and briefs pertaining to USR, NBC, Force Modernization, and the Quarterly Training Brief.

01/01/1995-12/31/1996: **OPERATIONS MANAGER.** U.S. Army, 483rd Maintenance Battalion, 3rd Infantry Division, Fort Benning, GA 28305. 40 hours per week. Rank: SFC. Supervisor: CPT Gibbs, Phone unknown. Established reporting methods to monitor costs involved in operating the training program for six separate companies with more than 800 personnel. Automated manual procedures to improve the timeliness of information provided to management. Served as the central point of authoritative information on administrative policies, NBC training, and chemical defense supplies and equipment. Developed and implemented plans for fielding new equipment. Planned and supervised the issuing and training related to the M40A1 protective mask. Compiled a variety of statistical data and information requiring research into reports, guidance memorandums, and data charts for incorporation into briefings, presentations, talking papers, information summaries, and impact statements. Reviewed budget data and recommended movement of funds based on analysis of historical execution rates, planning programmatic decisions, program manager input, and justification by key managers. Frequently performed duties of a Budget Analyst as I examined all phases of program, planning, and analysis necessary to formulate and support the budgetary needs of activities related to battalion operations and NBC Schools. Analyzed, maintained, gathered, compiled, and verified all data required to produce reports, charts, graphs, information papers, and briefings. Checked accuracy of budget justification data. Advised program managers of cost effectiveness, problems found, and future operational efficiency of programs.

EDUCATION

B.S. degree in Accounting, Central Texas College, Killeen, TX, awarded Dec 2004. Excelled academically with a 3.67 GPA. Total credit hours earned: 157.
Graduated from Ladybug Senior High School, Houston, TX, 1977.
Extensive on-the-job training in tax preparation since 1987.

TRAINING

NBC training: (1) Technical Escort, Killeen, TX, 15 Jan-10 Feb 2004: Became skilled in performing Tech Escort duties involving field sampling, detection, identification, limited decontamination, and mitigation/remediation of hazards associated with chemical, biological, and radiological materials. (2) Chemical Advanced Noncommissioned Officer Course (54B40), Fort Bragg, NC, 02 Jan-02 Mar 1997. (3) Chemical Basic Noncommissioned Officer Course (54B30), Fort Benning, GA, 10 Aug-12 Sep 1988. (4) Chemical Recon Course, Fort Benning, GA, June 1992.
Computer training: Army Training, Readiness, and Resource System (ATRRS), 2001. Extensive training since 1993 related to Word, Excel, PowerPoint, Access, and other software programs.
Battlefield operations: Battle Staff Noncommissioned Officer Course, Fort Bragg, NC, 10 May-20 Jun 1998. Training focused on the BN and BDE level, and task performance standards are from ARTEP Mission Training Plans for light and maneuver forces and all battlefield operating systems.
Other: Master Fitness Trainer Course, Germany, July 1996. Equal Opportunity Course, Jan 2001. Administrative Specialist Course, Fort Riley, KS, 20 Oct-15 Nov 1986.

AWARDS

Academic: Inducted into Alpha Beta Business Honor Society, Nov 2004. Inducted into Beta Kappa Evening College Honor Society, Nov 2003.
Military: Meritorious Service Medal; Army Commendation Medal (8); Army Achievement Medal (4); Good conduct Medal (7); Korean Defense Service Medal; Kuwait Liberation Medal; Southwest Asia Medal; National Defense Medal; Overseas Ribbon (4).

OTHER INFORMATION

Computer expertise: Highly proficient with Word, Excel, Access, and PowerPoint. Skilled in utilizing specialized databases including the Global Forces Management Database System (GFMDS) and the Army Training, Readiness, and Resource System (ATRRS). Have utilized computer programs daily for 15 years.
Accounting expertise: Highly experienced tax preparer since 1987. Hold an official Tax Preparer's ID issued by the IRS. Skilled at preparing balance sheets, profit and loss statements, cash flow statements, and other financial documentation. Skilled at analyzing financial documentation to determine problems and flaws.
Volunteer experience: Volunteer Income Tax Assistance (VITA) Volunteer for 2003 and 2004, Central Texas College.
Security clearance: Secret security clearance

FEDERAL RESUME or RESUMIX

HEIDI TALLSTONE
1110 1/2 Hay Street
Fayetteville, NC 28305
910-483-6611
E-mail: PREPub@aol.com

SSN: 000-00-0000
Country of Citizenship: United States
Veteran's Preference: _____ preference

SUPERINTENDENT, POSTAL OPERATIONS

Vacancy Announcement Number:
Position Title:

EMPLOYMENT

SUPERINTENDENT, POSTAL OPERATIONS. U.S. Postal Service, Chapel Hill, NC 27514 (2004 present). Salary: $75,000. Hours per week: 40+. Supervisor: Grace Black, Phone: 222-222-2222. Directly supervised clerks/carriers in the distribution, dispatch, collection and delivery of mail and window service activities. Established work schedules and allocated manpower to meet service requirements. Rescheduled assignments based on changes in mail volume and manpower availability. Approved vacation schedules, leave and overtime. Trained employees for safe working environment habits and practices. Issued government driver's licenses and ensured carriers possessed state licenses. Performed street observation to ensure compliance with safety and delivery rules and regulations. Held weekly safety meetings and prepared quarterly job safety analysis. Performed audits such as miscase, undeliverable bulk business mail, and quality control. Counseled employees in relation to work performance and habits. Investigated customer complaints, which involved dealing with customers in a tactful manner. Met with large volume mailers in an attempt to resolve mail problems. Inspected and participated in adjustment of city and rural routes, and in establishment, discontinuance and relocation of collection boxes. Ensured compliance with vehicle maintenance schedules and inspected vehicles weekly. Monitored vehicle service contracts. Supervised and participated in recordkeeping and report preparation in areas such as man hours, mail volume, carrier transportation costs (gas reports and payment thereof and vehicle usage hours and mileage, etc.), injuries and accidents, growth management, and time and attendance. Prepared quarterly collection on delivery and numbered insured report and performed collection tests. Investigated, documented, and acted on industrial and vehicle accidents. Prepared database for zip +four for automation purposes. Input information into hand-held Hewlett-Packard computer to determine if carrier needed additional time and/or assistance. Underwent conversion to Integrated Retail Terminal computers at window counters. Planned operating budget for fiscal year based on funds allocated, previous year expenditures, estimates on projected growth affecting possible deliveries, workload (mail volume increases), peak times and holidays, etc. Broke down planned budget by separate cost accounts. After receiving approved budget, set daily expenditure goals for work hours (office, street, parcels, branch delivery, special delivery, collection, etc.), mail volume and possible deliveries. Gained knowledge of National Agreement and EEO policies. Communicated orally and in writing on a daily basis with customers, employees, and associate offices, etc. While in this position, implemented the Incentive Awards Program which lowered office hours and decreased no record percentages in computerized forwarding system.

CITY CARRIER. U.S. Postal Service, Charlotte, NC 28834 (1999-2003). Salary: $38,500 Hours per week: 40+. Supervisor: Edith Brown, Phone: 222-222-2222. Immediately upon clocking in, inspected vehicle to ensure it was operational. Received all classes of mail at carrier case and sequenced for efficient delivery. Entered "change of address" cards, forwarded mail under computerized forwarding system, recorded "hold" orders, and held mail. Received and signed for accountable mail items such as certified, registered, Express mail, collection on delivery, customs, postage due, etc. Endorsed all undeliverable mail for return to sender. Delivered all mail (all classes-letters, flats, circulars, parcels, etc.) along prescribed route and collected mail from mailboxes, customers and collection boxes. Obtained receipts for registered, certified, and insured mail. Collected charges on customs, postage due and collect-on-delivery mail. Recorded usage information on vehicle cards such as mileage and time. Cleared accountable items. Maintained "special order" records. Protected mail, money and equipment. Conducted work in a safe manner. This office had 36 city routes and as part-time flexible carries was required to deliver mail on any one of these routes at any given time.

CITY CARRIER. U.S. Postal Service, Caldwell, ID 88334 (1993-98). Salary: $38,500 Hours per week: 40+. Supervisor: Desiree Forbes, Phone: 222-222-2222. This office had eleven city routes, and as a part-time flexible carrier, I was required to deliver mail on any one of these routes at any given time. During this period, I later became a "regular" (40 hours per week) employee with a permanently assigned route.

CLERICAL ASSISTANT. Department of the Army, Fort Sill, OK 33355 (1991-93). Salary: $28,000. Hours per week: 40+. Supervisor: Martha Wooten, Phone: 222-222-2222. Assisted the USAR Facility Manager in all clerical and procedural phases of engineer support for 33 USAR centers and ten AMSA shops in Oklahoma and Kansas. Reviewed work requests from USAR centers and higher headquarters for funding requirements, establishing priority with available funds. Received inquiries and reviewed requests pertaining to provisions covered in leases, deeds, permits, etc. Prepared requests along with specifications for service type contracts (grounds, custodial, refuse, and entomology) for contract award to Contracting Division. Obtained necessary documents from USAR Center to certify payment for these services. Monitored all budget actions assuring availability of funds, provided data and recommendations on which to base decisions to support requests for additional funds, services, priorities, and other adjustments. Maintained records in support of cost accounts for expenditure payments, contract modification, and adjusted account balances. Compiled cost for commitments and expenditures and maintained a running balance of available funds and cost account. Based on known variables, such as percentage increase in costs, changed requirements, prior FY costs, compiled budget and planning data and provided information to the Budget Branch. Made cost projections for annual reviews with trends noted in under and over expenditures, amounts required to complete projects, priority of projects, and status of funds within USAR Centers by cost account. In this position, I received three different awards: two Exceptional Performance Ratings and one Sustained Superior Performance with cash award of $1,000.00.

ACCOUNTING TECHNICIAN. Department of the Army, Commissary, Fort Sill, OK 29418 (1990-91). Salary: $25,000. Hours per week: 40+. Supervisor: Dixon Platter, Phone: 222-222-2222. Validated transaction documents, taking action to reflect or correct price changes and extensions. Researched to discover extent to which discrepancies had been carried into account, initiating any necessary correction. Noted daily price changes.

Ensured price changes reached store manager within 24 hours. Maintained Block Control Register and Document Number Log. Prepared and distributed transmittal documents to headquarters in Fort Lee, VA. Updated price book and price list card deck. Compiled revised issue and resale price books. Assisted in maintenance and inventory account for meat and produce. Computed weekly gains and losses, monitoring and reporting excess in authorized dollar amounts. Computed quarterly and annual inventories. Assisted in inventory reconciliation. Coded as necessary for processing the various transactions into the account identification of department, to whom charged, issued, etc.

VOUCHER EXAMINER. Finance and Accounting, Fort Sill, OK 88990 (1988-90). Salary: $20,000. Hours per week: 40+. Supervisor: Len Black, Phone: 222-222-2222. Performed complete examinations of difficult vouchers and transactions. Complicating factors included progress payments, reservation of funds, numerous modifications to contracts, requiring close study and summary sheet preparation, maintenance of fiscal and contract control records, recurring requirement for reconstruction of transactions which had occurred after contract and control sheets were established, and was responsible for performing and balancing contract closeout computation. Performed examination of vouchers and related supporting documents (invoices, certificates of shipment, contracts, receiving reports, and other records) to determine accuracy and adequacy of all facts and the presence of necessary supporting documents. This included complete verification of facts in the invoice and identification of any errors, omissions, duplications or other irregularities. Determined necessary corrections, adjustments, modifications or additional data needed to support request for payment. Initiated action, either oral or in writing, to obtain data documentation information. Used contracts and guidelines to assure accuracy and allowability of facts, figures and charges, identification numbers, shipping instructions, quantities ordered and shipped, purchase authorization, allowability of transportation charges, prices, costs, etc. Summarized from contracts/modifications the terms and clauses pertinent to payment of invoices. Prepared running balance sheets and records. Performed retroactive and partial payments. Control sheets contained information such as funds expended, time left under contract, and any increases or decreases in time, funds expended, discount allowances, required withholdings and final payment reports. Reviewed contract files monthly to ensure pending vouchers or irregularities. Computed prices, extensions, costs, and discounts to ensure proper application, calculation, and consideration of factors such as terms, price variations, cost increase/decrease, FOB origin-destination charges and modification of orders or contract affecting amount payable. Posted payment information, after payment, to the office records and filed vouchers. Received Certificate of Achievement Award while in this position and numerous letters of appreciation/commendation for outstanding accomplishment of duties.

CLERK (TYPING). Department of the Army, Administrative Office, Fort Sill, OK 29418 (1985-88). Salary: $18,000. Hours per week: 40+. Supervisor: Lee Penn, Phone: 222-222-2222. Skillfully processed accounts for USAR centers and AMSA shops located in Oklahoma and Kansas. Received and reviewed utility bills, expenditure documents and small purchase requests. Checked monthly utility bills against rate schedules for verification of charges. Certified payment and prepared voucher for Finance and Accounting. Compiled budget information and maintained balances. Reviewed contract certificates for service type contracts and verified and forwarded to Finance for payment. Prepared correspondence. Assisted in maintenance of employee record cards for approximately 600 personnel. Also was responsible for distribution of incoming and outgoing mail. In this position, I received an Outstanding Performance Rating with cash award of $150, Sustained Superior Performance and Special Act of Service Award with cash award of $150 along with letters of appreciation.

CLERK TYPIST. Department of the Army, Real Estate Office, Fort Sill, OK 29418 (1983-85). Salary: $15,500. Hours per week: 40+. Supervisor: D.K. Smith, Phone: 222-222-2222. Recorded information for input into Integrated Facilities System. Updated Real Property Inventory and Building Information Schedule. Maintained information on leases, permits, licenses and outgrants for Fort Sill, HAAF and USAR Centers. Made changes to building and facility utilization by units/activities. Typed correspondence and reports, etc.

EDUCATION	**Bachelor of Arts degree in Public Administration**, University of North Carolina at Chapel Hill, NC, 2002.
AFFILIATIONS	Society of Public Administrators in North Carolina
CLEARANCE	Secret security clearance
COMPUTERS	Proficient with Microsoft Word, Excel, Access, and PowerPoint
HONORS	Recipient of more than 23 medals, awards, and certificates of achievement

 **UNITED STATES POSTAL SERVICE** ®

Application for Former Casual (Non-Career) Employment Eligibility
The U.S. Postal Service is an Equal Opportunity Employer

Please review the statements on the reverse of this form before completing this application. Your answers to the questions below will be considered together with other information in your record in determining your *present* fitness for postal employment and are subject to investigation. A false statement or dishonest answer to any question in this application may be grounds for not employing you or for dismissing you after you begin work, and may be punishable by fine or imprisonment (US Code, Title 18, Sec. 1001). ***PLEASE PRINT ALL INFORMATION ENTERED BELOW.***

A. General Information

1. Name *(Last, First, MI)* Charles, Robert L.	2. Social Security No. 123-45-6789

3. Date of Birth January 1, 1960	4. Place of Birth *(City/State OR City/Country)* Chicago, IL	5. Home Telephone No. (910) 483-6611	6. Work Telephone No. (910) 483-6611

7. Mailing Address *(No., Street, City, State, ZIP + 4)*
1110 1/2 Hay Street, Fayetteville, NC 28305

B. Casual (Non-Career) Job Information

8. Casual Position Applied For:

☐ Clerk   ☐ Mail Handler   ☐ Carrier   ☐ Other *(Position Title)*: _____

9. Postal Facility Name and Location *(City/State)* Chicago, IL	10. Earliest Date You Are Available Immediately

C. Prior Casual Work History

11. Dates of Last Casual Employment From _____ To _____	12. Salary $ _____ per hour	13. Title of Former Casual Position ☐ Clerk ☐ Mail Handler ☐ Carrier ☐	Other *(Position Title)*: _____

14. Postal Facility Name and Location *(City/State)*	15. Name of Supervisor	16. Telephone No. *(If known)*

17. Reason Assignment Ended:

☐ Expiration of Appointment   ☐ Resignation *(Give Reason)*: _____   ☐ Termination *(Give Reason)*: _____

D. Updated Non-Postal Work History

List all employment since the postal employment shown in Section C, above. Start with your present position and go back to the dates in Item C. Account for periods of unemployment on a separate line. If needed, continue on reverse.

18. Dates of Employment or Unemployment	Exact Position Title	Name of Employer and Complete Mailing Address	Supervisor's Name and Telephone No.	Reason for Leaving (or Unemployment)	Hours Worked Per Week	Hourly Salary Begin End
1. ____ to ____	_____	_____	_____	_____	____	$ ___ $ ___
2. ____ to ____	_____	_____	_____	_____	____	$ ___ $ ___
3. ____ to ____	_____	_____	_____	_____	____	$ ___ $ ___

E. Military Service *(Attach a copy of your military discharge records covering all periods of active duty service.)*

19. Since Your Last Postal Employment, Have You Performed Active Duty in the Armed Forces?

☐ No ☐ Yes If "Yes," indicate: (A) Branch of Service: U.S. Army (B) Period of Service: 04/83 to 04/03 (C) Type of Discharge: Honorable

20. If You Claim Veteran Preference, Indicate Type of Preference Claimed:

☐ 5-Point   ☐ 10-Point Non-Compensable Disability   ☐ 10-Point Compensable Disability *(30% or more)*

☐ 10-Point Compensable Disability *(at least 10% but less than 30%)*   ☐ 10-Point Other *(Wife/Husband, Widow/Widower, Mother)* *(Attach required proof to support your claim.)*

F. Other Information

The following questions should be answered so that an assessment can be made of your continued qualification and suitability for postal employment. If you answer "Yes" to any questions, give a detailed explanation on the reverse or attach a separate statement, including the date, explanation of the violation or offense, place of occurence, name and address of the police department or court involved; name and address of employer, explanation of the problem or reason for leaving employment.

	No	Yes
21. Have you been fired, quit after being notified that you would be fired, or resigned by mutual agreement because of specific problems from any employment listed in Section D.	☒	☐
22. Have you been convicted of a crime or are you now under charges for any offense against the Law? You may omit: (1) any charges that were dismissed or resulted in acquittal; (2) any conviction that has been set aside, vacated, annulled, expunged, or sealed; (3) any offense that was finally adjudicated in a juvenile court or juvenile delinquency proceeding; and (4) any charges that resulted only in a conviction of a non-criminal offense. **All felony and misdemeanor convictions and all convictions in state and federal courts are criminal convictions and must be disclosed. Disclosure of such convictions are required even if you did not spend any time in jail and/or were not required to pay a fine.**	☒	☐
23. Are you now dependent on or a user of ANY addictive or hallucinogenic drug, including amphetamines, barbiturates, heroin, morphine, cocaine, mescaline, LSD, STP, hashish, marijuana, or methadone, other than for medical treatment under the supervision of a doctor?	☒	☐
24. Have you been convicted by a military court-martial? *(If yes, give details on reverse.)* *(If no military service, answer "No".)*	☒	☐
25. Does the U.S. Postal Service employ any relative of yours by blood or marriage? *(Give name, present address, relationship, position title, and name and location of postal installation where employed on reverse.)*	☒	☐

PS Form **2591-C**, August 1998 *(Page 1 of 2)*

The law (939 U.S. Code 1002) prohibits political and certain other recommendations for appointments, promotions, assignments, transfers, or designations of persons in the Postal Service. Statements relating solely to character and residence are permitted, but every other kind of statement or recommendation is prohibited unless it either is requested by the Postal Service and consists solely of an evaluation of the work performance, ability, aptitude. and general qualifications of an individual or is requested by a Government representative investigating the individual's loyalty, suitability, and character. Anyone who requests or solicits a prohibited statement or recommendation is subject to disqualification from the Postal Service and anyone in the Postal Service who accepts such a statement may be suspended or removed from office.

PRIVACY ACT: Collection of this information is authorized by 39 U.S.C. 401; 1001; and 1005; 42 U.S.C. 2000e-16; and Executive Orders 11478 and 11590. This information will be used to determine qualifications and suitability of applicants for USPS employment. It may be disclosed to an appropriate government agency, domestic or foreign, for law enforcement purposes; where pertinent, in a legal proceeding to which the USPS is a party or has an interest; to a government agency in order to obtain information relevant to a USPS decision concerning employment, security clearances, contracts, licenses, grants, permits or other benefits; to a government agency upon its request when relevant to its decision concerning employment, security clearances, security or suitability investigations, contracts, licenses, grants or other benefits; to a congressional office at your request; to an expert, consultant, or other person under contract with the USPS to fulfill an agency function; to the Federal Records Center for storage; to the Office of Management and Budget for review of private relief legislation; to an independent certified public accountant during an official audit of USPS finances; to an investigator, adminstrative judge or complaints examiner appointed by the Equal Employment Opportunity Commission for investigation of a formal EEO complaint under 29 CFR 1614; to the Merit Systems Protection Board or Office of Special Counsel for proceedings or investigations involving personnel practices and other matters within their jurisdiction; to a labor organization as required by the National Labor Relations Act; to a prospective employer for consideration of employment; to management for compilation of a local seniority list for posting; to the EEOC for enforcement of federal EEO regulations; to the appropriate finance center as required under the provisions of the Dual Compensation Act; to the Office of Personnel Management (OPM) for processing retirement benefits; to OPM and private carriers for the provision of health, life insurance and retirement benefits; to state employment security agencies for unemployment compensation claim processing; and to a federal or state agency or other authorized person providing parent locator services pursuant to Pub. L. 93-647. In addition, limited information may be disclosed to a federal, state, or local government admistering benefits or other programs pursuant to statute for the purpose of conducting computer matching programs under the Act. These programs include, but are not limited to, matches performed to verify an individual's initial or continuing eligibility for, indebtedness to, or compliance with requirements of a benefit program.

Disclosure by you of your Social Security Number (SSN) is mandatory to obtain the services, benefits, or processes that you are seeking. Solicitation of the SSN by the USPS is authorized under the provisions of Executive Order 9397, dated November 22, 1943. The information gathered through the use of the number will be used only as necessary in authorized personnel administration processes.

G. Applicant Statements

(Use the space below to give detailed explanations and indicate item number to which answers apply. Use blank sheets if you need more space. Include your name, social security number, and date on each sheet.)

H. Certification

I certify that all of the statements made in this application are true, complete, and correct to the best of my knowledge and belief and are in good faith.

_____   _____
Signature of Applicant   Date Signed

PS Form **2591-C**, August 1998 *(Page 2 of 2)*

Government Jobs Series edited by Anne McKinney **51**

This worksheet for the Motor Vehicle Operator (MVO) and Tractor Trailer Operator (TTO) positions in the United States Postal Service® is provided to assist you in completing the assessment part of your employment application. It is recommended that you fill out this worksheet and use it as a guide when completing your assessment. **You can only complete your assessment on the Internet at www.usps.com/employment or on a Touch Tone Phone by calling 1-866-999-8777 (TTY 1-800-800-8776) and following the prompts.** You will need the Announcement Number for the MVO/TTO opening for which you wish to apply when completing your assessment. You can only apply once per Announcement Number. Duplicate applications will not be accepted.

Section A: Biographical Information *(* Required Information)*

We will need your Social Security Number to maintain your records. The information requested will be kept confidential and handled in accordance with the Privacy Act. Information regarding the Privacy Act is provided at the end of this worksheet and will also be available when you complete your assessment on the Internet or by Touch Tone Phone.

Announcement Number *	Social Security Number *
PRPXYX123	555-55-5555

First Name *	Middle Initial *	Last Name *
Douglas	X.	Johnston

Street Address (No., street, ste./apt. no.) *	ZIP Code™
1110 1/2 Hay Street	28305

Telephone Number *(Include area code)*	Email Address
(910) 483-6611	preppub@aol.com

Section B. Driving Experience

Please enter your responses in whole numbers only *(For example: 0, 1, 2, 3, etc.).*

1. How many drug, alcohol or other controlled substance driving offenses have you been convicted of in the past 5 years?	0
2. How many hit and run convictions have you had in the last 5 years?	0
3. How many convictions for reckless or careless driving have you had in the past 5 years?	0
4. How many fatal accidents have you been involved in that were judged to be your fault?	0
5. How many times in the last 3 years has your driver's license of any kind been suspended?	0
6. How many times in the last 5 years has your driver's license of any kind been revoked?	0
7. Within the last 5 years, how many accidents are on your driving record that were judged to be your fault?	0
8. How many traffic/driving offenses (moving violations) have you had in the past 3 years?	0
9. How many traffic/driving offenses (moving violations) have you had in the last year?	0
10. How many years of driving experience have you had with passenger cars or larger vehicles?	3
11. How many months of full-time experience do you have driving a 7 or more ton truck, tractor trailer, or 16 or more passenger bus?	11
12. Within the past 7 years, how many months of full-time experience do you have driving a 7 or more ton truck, tractor trailer, or a 16 or more passenger bus?	40
13. How many months of full-time experience do you have driving a tractor trailer?	6
14. Within the past 7 years, how many months of full-time experience do you have driving a tractor trailer?	35

PS Form **5999**, July 2004 *(Page 1 of 2)*

Section C. Veterans' Preference Status

The United States Postal Service® is a federal agency and complies with the Veterans' Preference Act which permits 5 or 10 points to be added to a qualifying score of 70 or better. Not all military veterans are entitled to veterans' preference. **If you claim veterans' preference for this purpose, your claim will have to be supported by submitting a Form(s) DD 214**, *Certificate of Release or Discharge From Active Duty*, **and other required documentation during the hiring process.**

1. Are you claiming veterans' preference points? --------------------------- ☐ Yes ☒ No *(If No, proceed to Section D)*

2. Are you claiming 5 points veterans' preference? ---------------------- ☐ Yes ☐ No

3. Are you claiming 10 points for a compensable service-connected disability rated at least
   10% but less than 30%? --- ☐ Yes ☐ No

4. Are you claiming 10 points for a compensable service-connected disability rated
   30% or more? -- ☐ Yes ☐ No

5. Are you claiming 10 points veterans' preference for other reasons? --------------- ☐ Yes ☐ No

Section D. Voluntary Data Request *(See Privacy Act Statement Below)*

The U.S. Postal Service wants to make sure that its part in the recruitment and hiring of Postal employees is fair to everyone. To do this we need your answers to two questions. These responses are entirely voluntary and have no bearing on your selection for a job. The first question asks you to identify your sex. The second question asks you to identify your race and national origin. If you are of mixed race and/or national origin, indicate the category with which you most closely identify yourself. Again, your responses are voluntary and have no bearing on your selection. We appreciate your cooperation.

The information requested will be kept confidential and handled in accordance with the Privacy Act. Information regarding the Privacy Act is provided at the end of this worksheet and will also be available when you complete your assessment on the Internet or by Touch Tone Phone.

1. Gender

☒ Male ☐ Female ☐ None Selected

2. Race/National Origin *(The definition of each race/national origin category is provided below)*

☐ **American Indian or Alaska Native:** A person having origins in any of the original peoples of North America, and who maintains cultural identification through community recognition or tribal affiliation.

☐ **Asian or Pacific Islander:** A person having origins in any of the original peoples of the Far East, Southeast Asia, the Indian subcontinent, or the Pacific Islands. This area includes, for example, China, India, Japan, Korea, the Philippine Islands, Samoa, and Vietnam.

☒ **Black, not of Hispanic Origin:** A person having origins in any of the black racial groups of Africa. Does not include persons of Mexican, Puerto Rican, Cuban, Central or South American, or other Spanish cultures or origins.

☐ **Hispanic:** A person of Mexican, Puerto Rican, Cuban, Central or South American, or other Spanish cultures or origins. Does not include persons of Portuguese culture or origin.

☐ **White, not of Hispanic Origin:** A person having origins in any of the original peoples of Europe, North Africa, or the Middle East. Does not include persons of Mexican, Puerto Rican, Cuban, Central or South American, or other Spanish cultures or origins. Also includes persons not included in other categories.

☐ **None Selected**

Privacy Act Statement: The collection of this information is authorized by 39 U.S.C. 401, 1001 and 5 U.S.C. 7201. This information will be used to determine your qualifications for an appointment. As a routine use, the information may be disclosed to an appropriate government agency, domestic or foreign, for law enforcement purposes; where pertinent, in a legal proceeding to which the USPS® is a party or has an interest; to a government agency in order to obtain information relevant to a USPS decision concerning employment, security clearances, contracts, licenses, grants, permits or other benefits; to a government agency upon its request when relevant to its decision concerning employment, security clearances, security or suitability investigations, contracts, licenses, grants or other benefits; to a congressional office at your request; to an expert, consultant, or other person under contract with the USPS to fulfill an agency function; to the Federal Records Center for storage; to the Office of Management and Budget for review of private relief legislation; to an independent certified public accountant during an official audit of USPS finances; to an investigator, administrative judge, or complaints examiner appointed by the Equal Employment Opportunity Commission for investigation of a formal EEO complaint under 29 CFR 1614; for determining the adverse effects in the total selection process, and for assessing the status of compliance with federal law; to the Merit Systems Protection Board or Office of Special Counsel for proceedings or investigations involving personnel practices and other matters within their jurisdiction; and to a labor organization as required by the National Labor Relations Act. Completion of this form is voluntary; however, if this information is not provided, you may not receive full consideration for a position. Completion of race, sex, national original and disability status has no bearing on personal selections. It will be used for research purposes only and equal opportunity recruitment programs to help ensure compliance with federal Law. Such information will not be disclosed outside the Postal Service except to a federal representative auditing program compliance or as part of a statistical aggregate in which case your name and Social Security Number will not be involved.

COMPUTER MATCHING: Limited information may be disclosed to a federal, state, or local government administering benefits or other programs pursuant to statute for purpose of conducting computer matching programs under the Act. These programs, include but are not limited to, matches performed to verify an individual's initial or continuing eligibility for, indebtedness to, or compliance with requirements of a benefit program.

UNITED STATES POSTAL SERVICE®

Pre-Employment Screening — Authorization and Release

Applicant: Carefully read the following information before you complete and sign this form.

Privacy Act Statement: The collection of this information is authorized by 39 USC 410(b) and 1001; it may be used to obtain information from organizations and individuals pertaining to your character and current or prior employment as may be relevant and necessary to determine your fitness and suitability for employment in the United States Postal Service. As a routine use, the information may be disclosed to an appropriate government agency, domestic or foreign, for law enforcement purposes; where pertinent, in a legal proceeding in which the USPS is a party or has an interest; to a government agency in order to obtain information relevant to a USPS decision concerning employment, security clearances, contracts, licenses, grants, permits or other benefits; to a government agency upon its request when relevant to its decision concerning employment, security clearances, security or suitability investigations, contracts, licenses, grants or other benefits; to a congressional office at your request; to an expert, consultant, or other person under contract with the USPS to fulfill an agency function; to the Federal Records Center for storage; to the Office of Management and Budget for review of private relief legislation; to an independent certified public accountant during an official audit of USPS finances; to an investigator, administrative judge or complaints examiner appointed by the Equal Employment Opportunity Commission for investigation of a formal EEO complaint under 29 CFR 1614; to the Merit Systems Protection Board or Office of Special Counsel for proceedings or investigations involving personnel practices and other matters within their jurisdiction; and to a labor organization as required by the National Labor Relations Act.

Completion of this form is voluntary; however, if consent to obtain this information is not given, it may have an adverse effect on your employment opportunities with the USPS.

Applicant's Name *(Last, First, Middle)*		Mailing Address
Charles, Robert L.		1110 1/2 Hay Street
Date of Birth *(Month, Day, Year)*	Home Phone Number	Fayetteville, NC 28305
January 1, 1960	(910) 483-6611	

This constitutes my consent and authorization to the disclosure or furnishing of any relevant and necessary information or records to any duly authorized employment official of the USPS by any person, corporation, agency, or association concerning my character, employment, or military service as may be relevant and necessary for a determination of my suitability for employment with the USPS.

This authorization is executed with full knowledge and understanding that the USPS will take measures to protect the aforementioned information against unauthorized disclosure to any parties not having a legitimate need for it in the discharge of official business of the United States, or its agencies and instrumentalities.

I hereby RELEASE the aforementioned persons, corporators, agencies, associations and their employees, agents and representatives from any and all liability for damages resulting from a decision by the USPS not to employ me on account of compliance, or any attempts at compliance with this authorization, except for any damages resulting from knowingly providing false or misleading information or records about me.

A copy of this authorization shall be as effective and valid as the original. This authorization shall be valid for 12 months from the date it is signed.

Date Signed	Signature of Applicant

PS Form **2181-A,** March 1996

You might be interested to learn what happens once you submit your 171 or 612 in hopes of being tapped for a postal service position. Human Resources at a central location will screen all the applications, and up to five people will be chosen to interview for the position. A three-person board of local postal personnel will actually do the interviewing; one of the interviewers will be from Human Resources and the other two will be people who are knowledgeable of the position being filled. Bear in mind that there can be very long lead times throughout this whole process. But let's assume that you are one of those selected for the interview. After the interview, the board will make a decision on whom to hire, and you may receive a phone call if you are selected. If you are not selected, you will learn by mail. Background checks and physical exams requested will be paid for by the USPS.

Once you are inside the system, you apply for positions with the Form 991, and your 991 will go through the same evaluation process as described above.

If you are lucky enough to get an interview, you need to understand that a post office interview is like any other interview. You are trying to sell yourself! Since it may have been a long time (months probably) between submitting your paperwork and interviewing for the job, it's wise to prepare for the interview by reading the documents you submitted. As you will see on the next page, applicants for initial-level supervisor positions are required to submit written narrative statements addressing specific "requirements" in order to demonstrate their knowledge, skills, or abilities ("KSAs") in specific areas such as these: oral communications, leadership, human relations, problem analysis, decision making, written communication, mathematical computations, safety, and job knowledge. Sample KSAs used by real people to apply for postal positions are shown in this section.

The U.S. Postal Service prefers that you demonstrate your knowledge, skills, or abilities by presenting your information within a precise framework referred to as "STAR." STAR stands for Situation, Task, Action, and Result, and you are asked to describe a situation or event in which you did, said, produced, or accomplished something which illustrated your level of proficiency related to that requirement or KSA. Postal Service KSAs based on the STAR format can be shorter than KSAs for other federal service jobs. Often a single incident will reveal your competence in a certain area. Remember here to be very detailed, and try to make sure that you clearly show the result you were able to achieve by your involvement in the situation or event you are describing. In KSAs for non-postal-service jobs, you often need to "translate" jargon into language that can be understood by others. For example, military professionals need to make sure that their experience is "translated" into terminology that civilians can understand. In the case of postal service KSAs, however, you are often writing about technical matters for an audience that is very familiar with the "language" of the postal service, so you can feel comfortable using technical terminology and acronyms.

You may find this section to be the most helpful part of this book, because you will see several examples of 991s and Statements of Qualifications used by real people to advance within the USPS.

This application provides the review committee and selecting official a summary of your education, work experience, and capabilities in specific areas pertinent to the vacant position. List your education or training and work experience in the spaces provided. Number your entries consecutively in the Reference No. columns, e.g., education or training 1-6, postal positions 7-10, etc.

The vacancy announcement to which you are responding lists a number of job requirements. In this application you are to provide your qualifications in reference to those requirements. Your statement of qualification should include a demonstration of the required knowledge, skill, or ability (KSA). All of the requirements should be addressed. Failure to address each requirement results in an incomplete application which may lead to your being found unqualified.

Read each of the requirements listed on the vacancy announcement. Consider carefully achievements which demonstrate the KSA specified for that requirement. Achievements may be either a specific instance or sustained high performance over a period of time. These achievements may have occurred in all kinds of settings, e.g., paid work in the Postal Service or any other organization, volunteer work, or education or training activities. For each requirement try to give several examples of achievements that demonstrate that you possess the KSA. Achievements may be best described by telling of a situation or task which needed to be done; stating what action you took; and finally, describing the result of that action. Be sure it is clear to the reader that:

1. What you are describing actually demonstrates the KSA.

2. The situation, action, and result are fully described.

3. You yourself were in some way responsible for the result.

4. If you displayed initiative or innovation, it is explained.

If your achievement was the acquisition of education or training, then your achievement description should indicate the following:

1. What you learned and how that learning relates to the KSA specified in the requirement.

2. Details or nature of the course - topics covered, level of complexity.

3. Evidence of the quality of your performance in the course, if available. Simply mentioning that you took a course may not indicate you gained much knowledge from it.

4. Any application of what you learned.

The content of the description you write is much more important than writing style. You must communicate to the reader how you have demonstrated the KSA. Be specific about what you personally did. Merely saying that you possess a KSA is not adequate.

Write your achievement descriptions as though none of the review committee members or the selecting official knows anything about you (it's very likely the truth). After each achievement description, indicate the reference person(s) who could verify your achievements. Your supervisor may also be contacted to verify any work-related statements you write. Also indicate for each achievement the reference number of your education or training, or work experience connected to your achievements.

If you are applying for a managerial or supervisory position, read the following:

When the ability to manage or supervise is listed as a requirement, applicants should present achievements (examples) that demonstrate their current ability to undertake the full range of responsibility for the position being sought. If the position involves the supervision of lower-level supervisors and managers, applicants are generally expected to indicate sustained high performance in a supervisory or managerial position previously held.

Following are the three components of managerial ability that should guide the applicant's demonstration of achievement. Not all considerations listed here need be addressed. The objective is for the applicant to demonstrate managerial ability as it applies to the position being sought.

1. **Structuring/Organizing.** Identifying problems and their causes and securing relevant information; developing solutions to problems and making logical decisions that make effective use of resources and accomplish organizational goals; making innovations, investing effort, and keeping high standards to ensure a product of high quality; and following up on activities to see that they were on target, on time, and within budget.

2. **Establishing Effective Work Relationships.** Encouraging employees to participate in decisions that affect their work and the quality of their life at work; supporting management's mission and representing the unit at the next higher management level; engaging in teamwork with other managers; maintaining effective relationships with clients and customers; acting on EEO, Affirmative Action, EI/QWL, Management by Participation policies and programs; maintaining cooperative labor-management relations; providing honest and constructive feedback and positive recognition; training and developing subordinates; and handling interpersonal conflicts.

3. **Communicating.** Communicating information and instructions in writing and orally to achieve desired results; presenting technical information at a level appropriate to the audience; and facilitating information flow within the organizational unit.

NOTES TO APPLICANT AND PRIVACY ACT STATEMENT ARE ON REVERSE

Detached from PS Form **991,** October 1993

Requirements for Intitial-Level Supervisor Positions
When applying for Initial-Level Supervisor Positions, use the requirements listed below. *(Copy the bolded heading to page 3.)*

1. **Oral Communications.** Ability to communicate information, instructions, or ideas orally in a clear and concise manner in individual and group situations.

2. **Leadership.** Ability to direct or coordinate individual or group action in order to accomplish a task or goal.

3. **Human Relations.** Ability to interact tactfully and relate well with others.

4. **Problem Analysis.** Ability to analyze problems, work performance, suggestions, and complaints by listening, observing, gathering, organizing, and interpreting information.

5. **Decision Making.** Ability to develop plans, evaluate their anticipated effectiveness, make decisions, and take appropriate action.

6. **Written Communication.** Ability to write letters, simple reports, and employee evaluations clearly and effectively and to complete standardized reporting forms accurately.

7. **Mathematical Computations.** Ability to perform addition, subtraction, multiplication, and division with whole numbers, fractions, and decimals.

8. **Safety.** Knowledge of safety procedures needed to ensure that safe working conditions are maintained, including knowledge of the procedures and techniques established to avoid injuries, and of normal accident prevention measures and emergency procedures.

9. **Job Knowledge.** Knowledge of the operating procedures and the goal of the function to be supervised.

Factors for Postmaster Positions
When applying for Postmaster Positions, use the factors listed below. *(Copy the bolded heading to page 3.)*

1. **Decision Making/Problem Solving.** Ability to carry out operational plans and procedures within the framework of policy. Ability to obtain and interpret relevant facts; analyze problems, complaints, and suggestions; devise effective plans and procedures; and take appropriate action. Ability to analyze problems and to devise improvements.

2. **Budget Operations.** Ability to prepare a budget and maintain financial records. Ability to carry out operations economically and efficiently. Ability to maintain operating cost and expenditures in proper relationship to the authorized budget.

3. **Planning and Scheduling of Work.** Ability to plan operations over appropriate time periods, taking into account variations in workload and available resources. Ability to adjust work activities and schedules to meet emergency operations.

4. **Safety and Health.** Knowledge of safety procedures needed to ensure that safe working conditions are maintained. Knowledge of procedures and techniques established to avoid injuries to self, employees, and customers. Knowledge of normal accident prevention measures and emergency procedures. Knowledge of a postmaster's safety and health responsibilities. Knowledge of the relationships of safety and health considerations to efficient operations, including absenteeism and operating costs.

5. **Customer and Community Relations.** Ability to conduct operations in an attitude of responsive service to customers. Ability to present a favorable Postal Service image to the community. Ability to be active in community life. Ability to comprehend and communicate information, both orally and in writing. Knowledge of operating procedures and standards, postal rates and classes, and commonly encountered customer needs. Ability to sell ideas, positions, and recommendations to others. Ability to interact tactfully and relate well with others.

NOTE: **Factors 6-9 need to be addressed only when the postmaster position under consideration has subordinate career employees.**

6. **Labor Relations.** Knowledge of labor relations policies, including management's rights, the rights of employees and their representatives, national and local labor agreements, and applicable laws and regulations. Ability to negotiate effectively with employee groups.

7. **Equal Employment Opportunity.** Knowledge of policy pertaining to equal employment opportunity and affirmative action. Ability to deal sensitively with minority groups. Ability to deal fairly with all employees, customers, and business contacts.

8. **Employee Development.** Ability to train and develop employees. Ability to delegate work to subordinates according to their current ability and capacity for growth.

9. **Supervision.** Ability to define assignments or projects clearly. Ability to delegate authority, and to work with and through others effectively. Ability to direct or coordinate individual or group action in order to accomplish a task or goal. Ability to motivate and lead employees of varied backgrounds and skill levels. Ability to deal fairly and objectively with subordinates.

PS Form **991,** October 1993 *(Page 5 of 5)*

Date

Exact Name of Person
Title or Position
Name of Company
Address
City, State, Zip

991 and Statements of Qualifications

In this section you see the 991 of a Distribution Clerk who seeks to advance to a position as a Delivery Service Analyst.

Dear Exact Name of Person (or Dear Sir or Madam if answering a blind ad.):

With the enclosed 991 and Statements of Qualifications, I am expressing my interest in further contributing to the U.S. Postal Service as a Delivery Service Analyst.

As you will see from my enclosed application, I offer a "track record" of accomplishments in jobs with the U.S. Postal Service and the U.S. Army. I am sure that my leadership and management skills, along with my attention to detail, will enable me to excel in this position.

I look forward to taking the next step toward advancing into a position as Delivery Service Analyst, and I thank you in advance for your time.

Yours sincerely,

Jason M. Schultz

Applicant Information

Name (Last, First, MI)	Title of Present Position
Schultz, Jason M.	Distribution Clerk

Mailing Address	Name and Location of Employing Office
1110 1/2 Hay Street Fayetteville, NC 28305	Lexington Sectional Center 123 Bulk Mail Drive Lexington, KY

Home Phone (Area Code)	Work Phone (Area Code/PEN)	Social Security Number	Grade	Years of Service
(910) 483-6611	(910) 483-6611	999-88-7777	P05-B	1 year

Information About Vacant Position

Vacancy Announcement Number	Closing Date	Position Applied For	Grade
Not Listed	10/04/2004	Delivery Service Analyst	EAS-15

Name of Vacancy Office	Location of Vacancy Office
Lexington Sectional Center	123 Bulk Mail Drive, Lexington, KY

Education/Training

Ref. No.	Date (Mo./Yr.) From	Date (Mo./Yr.) To	Name of Educational Institution (Address Not Required)	Major Fields of Study	No. of Credits (Hours) Semester	No. of Credits (Hours) Quarter	Type of Degree	Date
	08/02	02/04	Lexington Community College	Postal Service Tech.	71			
	05/98	08/98	Central Texas College	Industrial Management	13			
	03/96	05/96	Central Texas College	Industrial Management	3			
	02/95	07/95	Central Texas College	Industrial Management	6		A.A.	08/98
	02/88	01/91	University of Kentucky	Law Enforcement	27			
	09/68	05/72	High School Lexington High School					

Ref. No.	From	To	Name of Postal or Other Training Facility	Course Name
	01/03	01/03	Lexington PED	Newly Appointed Window Clerks
	01/03	01/03	Lexington PECC	Scheme Training for Fort Campbell

Postal Positions

List permanent positions first, then temporary/detail assignments of 30 or more consecutive days. List in reverse chronological order. Use additional space on page 2.

Ref. No.	Date (Mo./Yr.) From	Date (Mo./Yr.) To	Position Title	Name & Location of Organization	Grade
	01/03	Present	Distribution Clerk	Fort Campbell Post Office Fort Campbell, KY	P05-B

PS Form **991**, October 1993 (Page 1 of 5)

Nonpostal Positions

List permanent positions first, then temporary/detail assignments of 30 or more consecutive days.
List in reverse chronological order. Use additional space below.

Ref. No.	Date (Mo./Yr.) From	To	Position Title	Grade or Salary	Name & Location of Organization
	07/02	01/03	Mill Operator	$17.00/hr	Firestone Tires, Lexington, KY
	02/02	06/02	Trucker	$17.00 hr	Mayflower Trucker, Lexington, KY
	07/01	02/02	Supervisor/Leadman	$17,000	Mideastern Lumber Co., Lexington, KY
	02/00	07/01	Command Sergeant Major	E-9	U.S. Army, Italy
	06/98	02/00	Command Sergeant Major	E-9	U.S. Army, Fort Bragg, NC
	10/97	06/98	Command Sergeant Major	E-9	U.S. Army, Fort Drum, NY
	07/95	10/97	Chief Intelligence Sergeant	E-9	U.S. Army, Fort Drum, NY
	01/92	07/95	First Sergeant (Continued below)	E-8	U.S. Army, Germany

Additional space for use in completing preceding information and listing any special assignments, projects, civic and professional organizations, awards, honors, special skills, etc.

	01/91	01/92	Intelligence Sergeant	E-8	U.S. Army, Germany
	01/88	01/91	Intelligence Analyst	E-7	U.S. Army, Fort Carson, CO
	12/87	01/88	Intelligence Evaluation Advisor	E-7	U.S. Army, Fort Carson, CO
	11/85	12/87	Supply Supervisor	E-7	U.S. Army, Korea
	05/84	11/85	Truck Master	E-7	U.S. Army, Korea
	01/82	05/84	Ordnance Supply Sergeant	E-6	U.S. Army, Fort Lewis, WA
	01/73	01/82	Supply Specialist	E-6	U.S. Army, Fort Bragg, NC

AWARDS

Meritorious Service Medal
Bronze Star with Oak Leaf Cluster
Korea Honor Medal, 2nd Class
Army Commendation Medal

PROFESSIONAL ORGANIZATIONS

Metro Golf Association
AUSA (Association of U.S. Army)
VFW (Veterans of Foreign War)

Application must be received at vacancy office by closing date.

I hereby certify that the foregoing information is true, complete, and accurate, to the best of my knowledge and belief.

Signature of Employee	Date

☐ If you are applying for a specific position, complete pages 1-4 of this form and submit the completed form to your supervisor, who will complete the evaluation for each requirement. If you want a copy of the evaluation, check the box at left. If you are completing this form for another reason, disregard pages 3 and 4, unless otherwise instructed.

PS Form **991,** October 1993 *(Page 2 of 5)*

Statement of Qualifications	Name
	Schultz, Jason M.

Announcement Number	Position Applied For
Not Listed	Delivery Service Analyst

Applicant position requirements are enumerated on the vacancy announcement. Enter the requirement in the space provided and explain your qualifications in reference to the requirement. A situation/task-action-result format for describing qualifications is recommended.

APPLICANT - COPY THIS PAGE. USE ONE PAGE PER REQUIREMENT/FACTOR.

Requirement/Factor   Educational Accomplishment

With an Associate's degree in General Studies, emphasis in Management, I am completing a second Associate's degree in Postal Service Technology while maintaining a GPA of 3.5 or higher. I have excelled in a variety of course work related to math, communications, and postal service operations including:

     Postal Delivery and Collection
     Industrial Engineering
     Business Math
     Speech
     Supervision
     Human Relations

I have continuously demonstrated my strong personal initiative in seeking out educational programs that would allow me to contribute to the USPS in even greater ways. For example, I obtained my Associate's degree in General Studies at night while excelling in full-employment which allowed me to finance 100% of my education.

On three occasions during 2003 and 2004, I volunteered for training opportunities sponsored by the USPS in order to enhance my knowledge and technical skills. In February 2003, I gained insight into Customer Relations by completing a three-hour seminar taught by Dr. Jack Bradley, well-known author of the book "Seven Steps for Enhancing Customer Satisfaction." In August 2003, I volunteered for a course taught at night related to Bulk Mail Handling Procedures. I completed that 40-hour course and gained specialized knowledge of bulk mailing procedures. In March 2004, I volunteered for a USPS course which trained me in computerized mail screening procedures.

Reference Number	Reference Name & Phone Number (For use of review committee & selector)

PS Form **991**, October 1993 (Page 3 of 5)

Requirements Page __1__ of _3_

Government Jobs Series edited by Anne McKinney **61**

Statement of Qualifications	Name
	Schultz, Jason M.

Announcement Number	Position Applied For
Not Listed	Delivery Service Analyst

Applicant position requirements are enumerated on the vacancy announcement. Enter the requirement in the space provided and explain your qualifications in reference to the requirement. A situation/task-action-result format for describing qualifications is recommended.

APPLICANT - COPY THIS PAGE. USE ONE PAGE PER REQUIREMENT/FACTOR.

Requirement/Factor   Training and Experience

Through 28 years of military and civilian work experience and training, I have acquired outstanding management, planning, analytical, and communication skills. While in the U.S. Army, I was rapidly promoted over my peers and achieved the highest enlisted rank of Command Sergeant Major.

I earned a reputation as a superior manager and motivator while managing organizations of all sizes. I have expertly managed up to 8,500 personnel while coordinating operations, training, and administrative functions for maximum operating effectiveness. As a supervisor at Mideastern Lumber, Co., I supervised 15 employees to achieve the highest levels of productivity and quality. A graduate of two U.S. leadership schools and the Sergeant Major Academy, I learned excellent supervisory and leadership techniques.

In an earlier job as an Intelligence Analyst, I developed exceptional skills in the assembly and analysis of information and the production of detailed reports. I wrote extensive correspondence/reports in numerous administrative positions.

Known as a highly effective communicator, I have spoken before up to 600 people and been chosen to brief executives and VIP's because of my ability to communicate complex ideas in a clear, concise manner.

While working in the supply/logistics field, I gained outstanding skills related to customer service and arithmetic computations. As a Supply/Inventory Manager, I accurately computed the food and supply needs for a 12,000-person organization.

As a Transportation Manager (a job very similar to Delivery Service Analyst), I acquired expertise in routing, dispatching, and compiling time/mileage/load data.

As a Distribution Clerk, I learned to interpret postal regulations.

Reference Number	Reference Name & Phone Number (For use of review committee & selector)

PS Form **991**, October 1993 (Page 3 of 5)   Requirements Page 2 of 3

Applicant position requirements are enumerated on the vacancy announcement. Enter the requirement in the space provided and explain your qualifications in reference to the requirement. A situation/task-action-result format for describing qualifications is recommended.

APPLICANT - COPY THIS PAGE. USE ONE PAGE PER REQUIREMENT/FACTOR.

Requirement/Factor Other Pertinent Information

In both my civilian and military careers, I have distinguished myself as a person who will "go the extra mile" to get the job done. I have consistently been chosen for difficult jobs requiring superior planning, problem-solving, and decision-making skills and have always produced outstanding results.

I have been recognized for my exceptional job performance, leadership, and dedication by numerous U.S. Army and civic awards and honors including:
> Bronze Star (2)
> Meritorious Service Medal (2)
> Nominee, Outstanding Citizen of Kentucky Award
> Army Commendation Medal (2)
> Numerous Letters of Commendation and Appreciation

In my personal life, I have become known for my willingness to help others and provide my leadership to the less fortunate. As a lifelong church member, I volunteered for 15 years (from 1985-2000) as a Boy Scout Troop Leader, and I take pride in the fact that I have shaped the attitudes of many youth who are today productive and contributing citizens. My financial abilities also have been recognized by my church, and I served in a volunteer role from 1999-2004 as Treasurer of my 1500-person church. During my tenure, the church raised more than $2 million in order to build and finance a new youth facility, and I directed the fundraising as well as the construction management associated with that new 4,000 square ft. structure.

Reference Number	Reference Name & Phone Number *(For use of review committee & selector)*

Date

Exact Name of Person
Title or Position
Name of Company
Address
City, State, Zip

991 and Statements of Qualifications

In this section you see the 991 of an individual who was selected for the Management Associate Program.

Dear Exact Name of Person (or Dear Sir or Madam if answering a blind ad.):

I would appreciate an opportunity to talk with you soon about how I could contribute to your organization through my outstanding skills in computer operation, data entry, and computer programming.

As you will see from my enclosed application, I can offer you a "track record" of accomplishments in previous jobs.

- With graduate and undergraduate degrees in Business Administration, I have studied Java and Pearl programming languages and know how to write, document, debug, and input computer programs.

- With more than seven years of experience in computer operation and data entry, I have been detailed to computer operator jobs, including Flow Control Operator and Supervisor of Flat Sorter Machines, by the U.S. Postal Service.

- A U. S. Postal Service employee for seven years, I have won several awards and was selected as a Candidate for the Management Associate Program because of my leadership, dedication, and performance. I refined my supervisory and management abilities while managing personnel and assets in the U.S. Postal Service jobs as Officer-in-Charge, Supervisor-of-Mails, and Supervisor of Flat Sorter Machines. I was selected as Officer-in-Charge (temporary Postmaster) for the Miami Main Post Office in 2004 until a new Postmaster was appointed. I supervised and scheduled five employees and managed all daily operations. In the Supervisor-of-Mails position, I supervised 25 personnel in a large technical operation, staffing each keying station based on the projected volume of mail for that shift. While the Supervisor of Flat Sorter Machines, I effectively supervised 15 data entry and mail processing personnel.

I hope you will contact me soon to suggest a time convenient for us to meet and discuss your current and future needs and how I might serve them. Thank you in advance for your time.

Yours sincerely,

Drake V. Hanson

Applicant Information

Name (Last, First, MI)	Title of Present Position
Hanson, Drake V.	Postal Clerk

Mailing Address	Name and Location of Employing Office
1110 1/2 Hay Street Fayetteville, NC 28305	6611 Postal Lane Orlando, FL

Home Phone (Area Code) (910) 483-6611	Work Phone (Area Code/PEN) (910) 483-6611	Social Security Number 999-88-7777	Grade PS-5	Years of Service 8 years

Information About Vacant Position

Vacancy Announcement Number Not Listed	Closing Date Until Filled	Position Applied For Detail	Grade

Name of Vacancy Office National Information Systems Development Center, USPS	Location of Vacancy Office 1 USPS Court, Orlando, FL

Education/Training

Ref. No.	Date (Mo./Yr.) From	To	Name of Educational Institution (Address Not Required)	Major Fields of Study	No. of Credits (Hours) Semester	Quarter	Type of Degree	Date
	01/00	05/03	University of Central Florida	Business Administration	60		MBA	05/03
	09/90	05/94	University of Central Florida	Business Administration	125		BS	05/94
	06/88	05/90	High School B.J. Moore High School					

Ref. No.	From	To	Name of Postal or Other Training Facility	Course Name
	11/03	11/03	USPS, Miami, FL	Florida State Awareness Conference
	08/03	09/03	USPS, Orlando, FL	Florida State Awareness Conference
	08/02	08/02	Orlando Main Post Office	Affirmative Action
	07/00	08/00	Postal Employee Development Center	Origin-Destination Information Systems
	01/96	02/96	Postal Employee Development Center	Introduction to Postal Management

Postal Positions

List permanent positions first, then temporary/detail assignments of 30 or more consecutive days.
List in reverse chronological order. Use additional space on page 2.

Ref. No.	Date (Mo./Yr.) From	To	Position Title	Name & Location of Organization	Grade
	12/04	Present	Postal Clerk	Orlando Main Post Office	PS-5
	02/03	11/04	MPFSM Operator	Orlando Main Post Office	PS-6
	07/00	02/03	Window/Distribution Clerk	Crestwood Post Office, Orlando, FL	PS-5
	07/94	08/97	Parcel Postal Clerk	Bulk Mail Center, Orlando, FL	PS-5
	04/94	08/97	Mail Handler	Bulk Mail Center, Orlando, FL	PS-4
			DETAILED ASSIGNMENTS		
	08/04	11/04	Officer-in-Charge	Miami Main Post Office	EAS-15
	05/03	12/04	Supervisor of Mails (204B)	Orlando Main Post Office	EAS-15
	07/95	06/97	Supervisor of Mails (204B)	Bulk Mail Center, Orlando, FL	EAS-15
	07/95	06/97	Flow Control Operator	Bulk Mail Center, Orlando, FL	EAS-14
	07/95	06/97	Dock Clerk	Bulk Mail Center, Orlando, FL	PS-6
	07/95	06/97	Quality Control Clerk	Bulk Mail Center, Orlando, FL	PS-5

PS Form **991**, October 1993 (Page 1 of 5)

Nonpostal Positions

List permanent positions first, then temporary/detail assignments of 30 or more consecutive days. List in reverse chronological order. Use additional space below.

Ref. No.	Date (Mo./Yr.) From	Date (Mo./Yr.) To	Position Title	Grade or Salary	Name & Location of Organization
	11/99	06/00	Customer Account Representative	$50,000	GMC Credit Company, Miami, FL
	05/99	10/99	Wholesale Auditor	$48,000	GMC Credit Company, Miami, FL
	09/97	04/99	Assistant Customer Account Rep.	$45,000	GMC Credit Company, Miami, FL
	09/91	02/93	Stock Clerk	$8.00/hr	Best Buy, Miami, FL
	05/91	08/91	Soil Conservation Trainee	GS-4	U.S. Department of Soil & Water Conservation, Orlando, FL

Additional space for use in completing preceding information and listing any special assignments, projects, civic and professional organizations, awards, honors, special skills, etc.

Certificate of Appreciation, USPS, June 2004

Employee-of-the-Month (Tour I), Orlando Main Post Office, March 2004

Member of the Postmaster's Affirmative Action Committee, Orlando, FL

Member of the All-Services-Committee, U.S. Postal Service, Orlando, FL

Member of the Association of Master's of Business Administration, Executives, Inc., Washington, DC

Member of the University of Central Florida Alumni Chapter, Orlando, FL

Application must be received at vacancy office by closing date.

I hereby certify that the foregoing information is true, complete, and accurate, to the best of my knowledge and belief.

Signature of Employee	Date

☐ If you are applying for a specific position, complete pages 1-4 of this form and submit the completed form to your supervisor, who will complete the evaluation for each requirement. If you want a copy of the evaluation, check the box at left. If you are completing this form for another reason, disregard pages 3 and 4, unless otherwise instructed.

PS Form **991,** October 1993 *(Page 2 of 5)*

Statement of Qualifications	Name
	Hanson, Drake V.
Announcement Number	Position Applied For
Not Listed	Detail

Applicant position requirements are enumerated on the vacancy announcement. Enter the requirement in the space provided and explain your qualifications in reference to the requirement. A situation/task-action-result format for describing qualifications is recommended.

APPLICANT - COPY THIS PAGE. USE ONE PAGE PER REQUIREMENT/FACTOR.

Requirement/Factor   Computer Education

While completing my graduate and undergraduate degrees in Business Administration, I studied Java and Pearl programming languages and learned to write, document, debug, and input computer programs. Additionally, I used computer programs to solve practical business problems in my Quantitative Analysis course. Because of my technical expertise, I was detailed to work in two computer operator jobs for the U.S. Postal Service.

Most recently, I utilized my computer knowledge as a Supervisor of Flat Sorter Machines changing disks and programs, keypunching commands, and generating statistical summaries on my operations. In a previous job I excelled as a Flow Control Operator operating a computerized "command center" which controlled all keying stations and ran edit checks on the automatic data processing equipment. On my own initiative, I utilized my knowledge of Microsoft Excel to develop spreadsheets that were used to identify potential problem areas.

In my spare time, I am continuously seeking new opportunities for expanding my computer knowledge. For example, I am currently taking selective coursework in a non-degree-granting program at Bristol Technical Community College. Currently I am refining my computer knowledge in a course related to Web programming. It is my hope to put this state-of-the-art knowledge to work for the USPS.

Reference Number	Reference Name & Phone Number *(For use of review committee & selector)*

PS Form **991**, October 1993 *(Page 3 of 5)*

Requirements Page __1__ of __3__

Statement of Qualifications	Name Hanson, Drake V.
Announcement Number Not Listed	Position Applied For Detail

Applicant position requirements are enumerated on the vacancy announcement. Enter the requirement in the space provided and explain your qualifications in reference to the requirement. A situation/task-action-result format for describing qualifications is recommended.

APPLICANT - COPY THIS PAGE. USE ONE PAGE PER REQUIREMENT/FACTOR.

Requirement/Factor   On-the-Job Training and Experience

I have acquired excellent computer operator and data entry skills through intensive on-the-job training and work experience during my seven years of employment with the U.S. Postal Service and while working with GMC Credit Company for three years.

Because of my technical expertise, I was detailed to work in two computer operator jobs for the U.S. Postal Service. Most recently, I worked as a Supervisor of Flat Sorter Machines changing disks and programs, keypunching commands, and generating statistical summaries on my operations. In a previous job, I was a Flow Control Operator operating a "command center" which controlled all keying stations and ran edit checks on the automatic data processing equipment.

In several earlier jobs, I developed superior data entry skills while inputting various kinds of numerical and alphabetical data. As a Customer Account Representative for GMC Credit Company, I input customer account information into a teletype machine which produced delinquency ratio reports. I worked at the following data entry jobs for the U.S. Postal Service: Flat Sorter Operator, Quality Control Clerk, Non-zip Operator, Parcel Post Operator, Sack Sorter Operator. These jobs required absolute accuracy in the inputting of such data as zip codes, streets and corresponding states, city schemes, and data collected from other machines.

As a Flat Sorter Operator, I completed 100 hours of training in less than 3/4 the usual time and then volunteered to train others for this job. I consistently maintained a 95% accurate ratio. As a Parcel Post Operator and Sack Sorter Operator, I achieved rare 98% accurate rates at speeds of 60 and 35 items per minute respectively.

Reference Number	Reference Name & Phone Number (For use of review committee & selector)

PS Form **991,** October 1993 (Page 3 of 5)

68 Part Two: The 991 and the Statement of Qualifications

Statement of Qualifications	Name
	Hanson, Drake V.

Announcement Number	Position Applied For
Not Listed	Detail

Applicant position requirements are enumerated on the vacancy announcement. Enter the requirement in the space provided and explain your qualifications in reference to the requirement. A situation/task-action-result format for describing qualifications is recommended.

APPLICANT - COPY THIS PAGE. USE ONE PAGE PER REQUIREMENT/FACTOR.

Requirement/Factor Other Pertinent Information

I have refined my supervisory and management abilities while managing personnel and assets in the U.S. Postal Service jobs as Officer-in-Charge, Supervisor-of-Mails, and Supervisor of Flat Sorter Machines. I was selected as Officer-in-Charge (temporary Postmaster) for the Miami Main Post Office in 2004 until a new Postmaster was appointed. I supervised and scheduled five employees and managed all daily operations. In the Supervisor-of-Mails position, I supervised 25 personnel in a large technical operation, staffing each keying station based on the projected volume of mail for that shift. While the Supervisor of Flat Sorter Machines, I effectively supervised 15 data entry and mail processing personnel.

I have been recognized for my outstanding leadership, dedication, and job performance by these U.S. Postal Service awards and honors:

Certificate of Appreciation-June 2004
Employee of the Month-March 2004
Candidate, U.S. Postal Service Management Associate Program-August 2003
    (I was one of only 20 people selected as candidates out of the entire Florida Region.)

Reference Number	Reference Name & Phone Number (For use of review committee & selector)

PS Form **991**, October 1993 (Page 3 of 5)   Requirements Page 3 of 3

Applicant Information

Name (Last, First, MI) Wright, Candice L.		Title of Present Position MPLSM Operator			
Mailing Address 1110 1/2 Hay Street Fayetteville, NC 28305		Name and Location of Employing Office 483 Main Post Drive Anchorage, AK			
Home Phone (Area Code) (910) 483-6611	Work Phone (Area Code/PEN) (910) 483-6611	Social Security Number 111-22-3333	Grade L-6		Years of Service 1 yr., 9 mos.

Information About Vacant Position

Vacancy Announcement Number Not Listed	Closing Date Until Filled	Position Applied For Initial Level Supervisor	Grade
Name of Vacancy Office Anchorage Main Post Office		Location of Vacancy Office 483 Main Post Drive, Anchorage, AK	

Education/Training

Ref. No.	Date (Mo./Yr.) From	Date (Mo./Yr.) To	Name of Educational Institution (Address Not Required)	Major Fields of Study	No. of Credits (Hours) Semester	No. of Credits (Hours) Quarter	Type of Degree	Date
	09/92	06/93	University of Alaska Anchorage	Operating Room Technician		40	Certif.	
	06/91	06/93	University of Alaska Anchorage	Nursing		68	Certif. (LPN)	
	09/89	06/91	High School Mt. McKinley High School					

Ref. No.	From	To	Name of Postal or Other Training Facility	Course Name
	02/04	07/04	Anchorage Main Post Office	MPLSM Operator Training
	06/99	06/99	Fort Drum, NY, Post Office	Mail Clerk (Company) Training

Postal Positions

List permanent positions first, then temporary/detail assignments of 30 or more consecutive days.
List in reverse chronological order. Use additional space on page 2.

Ref. No.	Date (Mo./Yr.) From	Date (Mo./Yr.) To	Position Title	Name & Location of Organization	Grade
	08/04	Present	Mail Processing Letter Machine Operator (MPLSM)	Main Post Office Anchorage, AK	L-6
	07/04	08/04	PTF MPLSM	Main Post Office Anchorage, AK	L-5

PS Form **991,** October 1993 (Page 1 of 5)

Nonpostal Positions

List permanent positions first, then temporary/detail assignments of 30 or more consecutive days. List in reverse chronological order. Use additional space below.

Ref. No.	Date (Mo./Yr.) From	Date (Mo./Yr.) To	Position Title	Grade or Salary	Name & Location of Organization
	08/02	08/04	LPN	GS-4	Richardson Army Medical Hospital, Fort Richardson, AK
	02/01	08/02	Medical Specialist	E-3	HHC, 82d Airborne Division, Fort Bragg, NC
	06/00	02/01	Tamms Clerk	E-2	HHC, 82d Airborne Division, Fort Bragg, NC
	04/00	06/00	Supply Clerk	E-2	HHC, 82d Airborne Division, Fort Bragg, NC
	02/99	04/00	Medical Specialist	E-2	HHC, 82d Airborne Division, Fort Bragg, NC
	02/99	02/99	Clerk Typist	E-1	Receiving Station, Fort Drum, NY

Additional space for use in completing preceding information and listing any special assignments, projects, civic and professional organizations, awards, honors, special skills, etc.

SPECIAL ASSIGNMENTS
Blood Drive, 82d Airborne Division, Fort Bragg, NC
CPR Class, Richardson Army Medical Hospital, Fort Richardson, AK

CIVIC WORK
Candystriper (volunteer), Alaska Native Medical Center, Anchorage, AK
Secretary, Christian Youth Services

AWARDS
Certificate of Appreciation, Blood Drive, 2000
Letter of Commendation, LTC Crane, Medical Battalion Aid Station, 1999

SPECIAL SKILLS
Typing; shorthand, Spanish language; nursing (LPN); operating room technician; monogramming; sewing

Application must be received at vacancy office by closing date.

I hereby certify that the foregoing information is true, complete, and accurate, to the best of my knowledge and belief.

Signature of Employee	Date

☐ If you are applying for a specific position, complete pages 1-4 of this form and submit the completed form to your supervisor, who will complete the evaluation for each requirement. If you want a copy of the evaluation, check the box at left. If you are completing this form for another reason, disregard pages 3 and 4, unless otherwise instructed.

PS Form **991,** October 1993 *(Page 2 of 5)*

Statement of Qualifications	Name
	Wright, Candice L.

Announcement Number	Position Applied For
Not Listed	Initial Level Supervisor

Applicant position requirements are enumerated on the vacancy announcement. Enter the requirement in the space provided and explain your qualifications in reference to the requirement. A situation/task-action-result format for describing qualifications is recommended.

APPLICANT - COPY THIS PAGE. USE ONE PAGE PER REQUIREMENT/FACTOR.

Requirement/Factor   Leadership

While serving as a Medical Specialist in the U.S. Army, I was chosen to lead and guide approximately 80 soldiers (male and female) in all areas of medical care on a joint exercise to the Middle East. During that two-month assignment, I planned, organized, and requested supplies for sick call hours and set up an aid station while also developing, conducting, and supervising classes in these and other areas: maintaining safety and cleanliness in our new surroundings; what to look out for and how to be cautious of poisonous habitat and animals; what not to eat and drink; treatment and care of injuries; steps to avoid illnesses, and other matters.

While serving as the Medic in charge of my company, I demonstrated my decision-making and leadership abilities by quickly responding to an emergency situation in which jet fuel had entered a soldier's eyes. I made the immediate decision to flush his eyes, thereby relieving him from pain. Later I received a prestigious medal recognizing my leadership during an emergency, and physicians credited me with saving the sight of this soldier.

Reference Number	Reference Name & Phone Number (For use of review committee & selector)

PS Form **991,** October 1993 (Page 3 of 5)

Applicant position requirements are enumerated on the vacancy announcement. Enter the requirement in the space provided and explain your qualifications in reference to the requirement. A situation/task-action-result format for describing qualifications is recommended.

APPLICANT - COPY THIS PAGE. USE ONE PAGE PER REQUIREMENT/FACTOR.

Requirement/Factor   Other Pertinent Information

As a Candystriper for three years at Alaska Native Medical Center in Anchorage, AK, I had the opportunity to work with people from a variety of backgrounds (ethnic, religious, economic, and otherwise). I refined my skills in communicating more effectively, openly, and frankly. I learned that when you are straightforward and show empathy to people's feelings, you are better able to motivate them.

High school provided me with multiple opportunities through which to refine my leadership skills. While in high school, I lettered in three sports--soccer, tennis, and basketball--and I was named the Most Valuable Player of my basketball team during my senior year. I also expressed my leadership ability while playing a key role in organizing and implementing numerous community service projects including a project to benefit the Girls and Boys Homes, a project to benefit the victims of 9/11, and a project to support the children of prisoners.

Reference Number	Reference Name & Phone Number (For use of review committee & selector)

PS Form **991**, October 1993 (Page 3 of 5)

Government Jobs Series edited by Anne McKinney **73**

Applicant Information

Name *(Last, First, MI)* Creasey, Molly A.	Title of Present Position Associate Office Coordinator
Mailing Address 1110 1/2 Hay Street Fayetteville, NC 28305	Name and Location of Employing Office 987 Postman Lane Boston, MA

Home Phone *(Area Code)* (910) 483-6611	Work Phone *(Area Code/PEN)* (910) 483-6611	Social Security Number 012-34-5678	Grade EAS-17	Years of Service 24 years

Information About Vacant Position

Vacancy Announcement Number Not Listed	Closing Date 06/04/2004	Position Applied For Postmaster	Grade EAS-18
Name of Vacancy Office Boston Main Post Office		Location of Vacancy Office 987 Postman Lane, Boston, MA	

Education/Training

Ref. No.	Date (Mo./Yr.) From	To	Name of Educational Institution *(Address Not Required)*	Major Fields of Study	No. of Credits *(Hours)* Semester	Quarter	Type of Degree	Date
1-	1991	1993	Bunker Hill Community College	Postal History/Finance & Mail Processing	9			
2-	1974	1975	Boston University	Retail Merchandising	15			
3-	09/67	05/71	High School M.M. Jeremy High School					

Ref. No.	From	To	Name of Postal or Other Training Facility	Course Name
4-	03/01	03/01	PEDC Boston, MA	Associate Office Coordinator
5-	05/96	05/96	Management Academy, Boston, MA	Management Skills for Supervisors
6-	02/95	02/95	PEDC Boston, MA	Programmable Calculator-Window Clerks
7-	02/94	02/94	PEDC Boston, MA	Injury Compensation Program
8-	09/93	09/93	PEDC Worcester, MA	Delivery Service Supervisor Training
9 -	08/93	09/93	Management Academy, Boston, MA	Station Branch Manager Training
10-	03/93	03/93	Management Academy, Boston, MA	Window Service Coordinator

Postal Positions

List permanent positions first, then temporary/detail assignments of 30 or more consecutive days.
List in reverse chronological order. Use additional space on page 2.

Ref. No.	Date (Mo./Yr.) From	To	Position Title	Name & Location of Organization	Grade
11-	02/00	Present	Associate Office Coordinator	USPS, Boston, MA	EAS-17
12-	06/95	02/00	Manager, PEDC	USPS, Boston, MA	EAS-17
13-	02/94	06/95	Superintendent Window Services	USPS, Boston, MA	EAS-16
14-	02/92	02/94	Management Trainee	USPS, Cambridge, MA	EAS-14
15-	01/91	02/92	Postmaster	USPS, Cambridge, MA	EAS-15
16-	03/87	01/91	Distribution/Window Clerk	USPS, Boston, MA	PS-05
17-	12/86	03/87	Distribution Clerk	USPS, Boston, MA	PS-05
18-	06/84	12/86	Finance Clerk	USPS, Boston, MA	PS-03
19-	04/81	06/84	Distribution/Window Clerk	USPS, Springfield, MA	PS-05
20-	11/78	04/81	Distribution Clerk DETAILED ASSIGNMENTS	USPS, Cambridge, MA	PS-05
21-	09/00	07/01	Acting Station Manager	USPS, Boston, MA	EAS-19
22-	03/93	07/93	Customer Service Representative	USPS, Cambridge, MA	EAS-14
23-	06/92	09/92	Officer-in-Charge	USPS, Cambridge, MA	EAS-18
24-	05/90	01/91	Officer-in-Charge	USPS, Boston, MA	NCD-13

PS Form **991,** October 1993 *(Page 1 of 5)*

Nonpostal Positions

List permanent positions first, then temporary/detail assignments of 30 or more consecutive days. List in reverse chronological order. Use additional space below.

Ref. No.	Date (Mo./Yr.) From	To	Position Title	Grade or Salary	Name & Location of Organization
25-	03/79	07/86	Supply Clerk	$8,000	Facilities Engineers, Fort Bragg, NC
26-	05/76	11/78	Seamstress	$5,000	Alice Alterations, New York, NY
27-	02/74	05/76	Clerk	$4,500	Sweeney Cleaners, New York, NY
28-	05/71	02/74	Fountain Clerk	$3,500 + tips	So Gun Restaurant, Chicago, IL

Additional space for use in completing preceding information and listing any special assignments, projects, civic and professional organizations, awards, honors, special skills, etc.

SPECIAL ASSIGNMENTS
    CFS Coordinator, 1997
    STS Human Relation/Administration, Instructor
    Suggestion Program Administrator
    EI/QWL Coordinator/Recorder, MSC

CIVIC AND PROFESSIONAL ORGANIZATIONS

Executive Board Member, Postal Credit Union	2002-present	Lay Leader John F. Kennedy	1999-present
Vice President, Neighborhood Watch Program	2002-present	NAPS State President	1998-99
A-Plus Chapter Chairperson	2002-present	NAPS Vice President	1998-99
President, Neighborhood Watch Program	2001-02	NAPS Area Vice President	1998-99
Chairman, Supervisory Committee Postal Credit Union	2000-02	Vice President, Moore County Professional Women	1991
		Secretary, Women's Advisory	1987-99
		Secretary, NCO Wive's Club	1987-90
		Secretary, PTA Bowley Element	1987-89

AWARDS
    Prize in Performance Award, Bronze & Silver, 2003
    Special Achievement Award, 1999-2001
    Affirmative Action Spotlight Award, 1999
    Outstanding Merit Evaluation, 1998, 2001-2002

Application must be received at vacancy office by closing date.

I hereby certify that the foregoing information is true, complete, and accurate, to the best of my knowledge and belief.

Signature of Employee	Date

☐ If you are applying for a specific position, complete pages 1-4 of this form and submit the completed form to your supervisor, who will complete the evaluation for each requirement. If you want a copy of the evaluation, check the box at left. If you are completing this form for another reason, disregard pages 3 and 4, unless otherwise instructed.

PS Form **991,** October 1993 *(Page 2 of 5)*

Statement of Qualifications	Name
	Creasey, Molly A.

Announcement Number	Position Applied For
Not Listed	Postmaster

Applicant position requirements are enumerated on the vacancy announcement. Enter the requirement in the space provided and explain your qualifications in reference to the requirement. A situation/task-action-result format for describing qualifications is recommended.

APPLICANT - COPY THIS PAGE. USE ONE PAGE PER REQUIREMENT/FACTOR.

Requirement/Factor   Decision Making/Problem Analysis

Shortly after being detailed to the Bunker Hill Branch Post Office, I recognized several priority problems that needed immediate attention--namely morale, safety, overtime usage, productivity, and customer relations. I began by involving the complete work force and opened lines of communication between management and craft. During our weekly talks, we openly shared our opinions about our organization's weaknesses and strengths. As we built respect and trust for each other, morale improved. This led to a shared commitment to work on the problems through teamwork.

For example, we monitored the overtime by challenging the use of 3996 and conducted street observation. This analysis led to a reduction in overtime. Secondly, we initiated a safety awareness campaign through employee participation and a daily "safety tip" communication. Third, numerous suggestions were made regarding how to boost customer satisfaction, and a protocol was developed so that customer complaints were handled in timely manner by phone and in person as they were registered.

Among accomplishments we achieved were: (1) reduced overtime by 13% over SP/Y; (2) improved DEA by 2% over SP/Y; (3) accident-free for PQ III FY 89; (4) improved appearance of office with a major clean-up effort; (5) improved customer relations by providing prompt and courteous attention to the resolution of complaints; and (6) established an EI/QWL team and initiated projects that were beneficial to all employees.

Reference Number	Reference Name & Phone Number *(For use of review committee & selector)*

Statement of Qualifications	Name
	Creasey, Molly A.

Announcement Number	Position Applied For
Not Listed	Postmaster

Applicant position requirements are enumerated on the vacancy announcement. Enter the requirement in the space provided and explain your qualifications in reference to the requirement. A situation/task-action-result format for describing qualifications is recommended.

APPLICANT - COPY THIS PAGE. USE ONE PAGE PER REQUIREMENT/FACTOR.

Requirement/Factor   Budget Operations

During my tenure as Postmaster, 1991-92, I was able to prepare and remain within the budget after a drastic reduction of thirty hours weekly from the previous year. I planned and managed daily and, as a result, I remained within my budget during the entire Postmastership.

As Superintendent of Windows Service, I supervised 13 clerks and 1 SSPC. Between AP 5 and AP 13 FY 93, I reduced the clerks' overtime usage by 10% and managed the budget with a minimum overrun while manually maintaining the accountable paper stock in excess of one million dollars. I prepared the annual budget for the Main Postal Employees Development Center (PEDC) and two mini PEDC sites, which resulted in meeting planned goals for the five years I was manager. Among accomplishments we achieved were: (1) reduced overtime by 13% over SP/Y; (2) improved DEA by 2% over SP/Y; (3) accident-free for PQ III FY 89; (4) improved appearance of office with a major clean-up effort; (5) improved customer relations by providing prompt and courteous attention to the resolution of complaints; and (6) established an EI/QWL team and initiated projects that were beneficial to all employees.

As associate office coordinator, I have assisted in the preparation of the MSC FY budget. The budget hours are spread to the various LDCs. Once the budgeted hours are awarded to the 169 associate offices, I review weekly flash and NWRs to access the associate office performance in OT, DCEN, 2L, and accident. I monitor work hours and expenditures with follow-ups to offices that might be experiencing difficulty in managing their budget. I take pride in the fact that I have spent many additional hours of my time training and counseling junior employees so that the financial and budgeting goals of the USPS could be achieved.

Reference Number	Reference Name & Phone Number *(For use of review committee & selector)*

Government Jobs Series edited by Anne McKinney **77**

Statement of Qualifications	Name Creasey, Molly A.
Announcement Number Not Listed	Position Applied For Postmaster

Applicant position requirements are enumerated on the vacancy announcement. Enter the requirement in the space provided and explain your qualifications in reference to the requirement. A situation/task-action-result format for describing qualifications is recommended.

APPLICANT - COPY THIS PAGE. USE ONE PAGE PER REQUIREMENT/FACTOR.

Requirement/Factor   Planning and Scheduling of Work

During my tenure at Bunker Hill Station, I recognized that approximately 30% of the mail volume was arriving on the first mode of transportation. Most of the carriers would complete their mail and we were faced with downtime. After observing this problem, we changed some carriers' schedules on an approximately 30-minute temporary basis, which gave us the window of operation we needed to be effective.

As PEDC Manager, it was necessary to change the schedule of a training technician from a Sunday, Monday/Sunday non-schedule to a rotating Saturday, Sunday/Sunday, Monday. This change provided availability for the training section and often eliminated overtime on Mondays. Throughout my management positions, I have been successful in planning and scheduling my operation to provide the most cost-effective results.

As Superintendent of Windows Service, I refined my ability to plan and schedule work as I supervised 13 clerks and 1 SSPC. Between AP 5 and AP 13 FY 93, I reduced the clerks' overtime usage by 10% and managed the budget with a minimum overrun while manually maintaining the accountable paper stock in excess of one million dollars. I prepared the annual budget for the Main Postal Employees Development Center (PEDC) and two mini PEDC sites, which resulted in meeting planned goals for the five years I was manager. Among accomplishments we achieved were: (1) reduced overtime by 13% over SP/Y; (2) improved DEA by 2% over SP/Y; (3) accident-free for PQ III FY 89; (4) improved appearance of office with a major clean-up effort; (5) improved customer relations by providing prompt and courteous attention to the resolution of complaints; and (6) established an EI/QWL team and initiated projects that were beneficial to all employees.

Each management assignment has been a challenge and experience which enabled me to manage each operation with positive results. I maintain quantity and quality in my work performance. I am a self-starter with motivation and a combination of skills that enables me to challenge my own capabilities in performing excellently. I feel my eagerness to learn, my positive attitude, my communication and human relations skills will enable me to provide positive results in any assignment.

Reference Number	Reference Name & Phone Number (For use of review committee & selector)

PS Form **991,** October 1993 (Page 3 of 5)

Applicant position requirements are enumerated on the vacancy announcement. Enter the requirement in the space provided and explain your qualifications in reference to the requirement. A situation/task-action-result format for describing qualifications is recommended.

APPLICANT - COPY THIS PAGE. USE ONE PAGE PER REQUIREMENT/FACTOR.

Requirement/Factor   Safety and Health

My personal postal career of twenty-five years has not been blemished by a motor vehicle or industrial accident. During my various stages of management, I have been successful in promoting safety awareness through safety talks, vehicle checks, driver observation, practicing good housekeeping, and leading by example.

Accident prevention measures were taken which resulted in no accidents for two PQs at the Bunker Hill Station, 0% accidents during my five years of Manager PEDC, and an accident-free record both during my postmastership and as Superintendent of Window Services. Our record was measured by the safety knowledge and individual responsibility of each employee in relationship to an efficient and effective operation.

Safety programs I developed and implemented have been adopted for use at various other facilities nationwide.

| Reference Number | Reference Name & Phone Number (For use of review committee & selector) |
| | |

Announcement Number	Position Applied For
Not Listed	Postmaster

Applicant position requirements are enumerated on the vacancy announcement. Enter the requirement in the space provided and explain your qualifications in reference to the requirement. A situation/task-action-result format for describing qualifications is recommended.

APPLICANT - COPY THIS PAGE. USE ONE PAGE PER REQUIREMENT/FACTOR.

Requirement/Factor   Customer and Community Relations

Each management position I have held required communicating information to the internal and external customer. During my detail at the Bunker Hill Branch, our customer relations improved through prompt responses to verbal and written communication. As associate office coordinator, I respond to complaints on misdelivery of mail, Congressionals, late mail arrival, and other customers' basic needs. I respond to customers tactfully with a positive attitude and an image of professionalism.

Shortly after being detailed to the Bunker Hill Branch Post Office, I recognized several priority problems that needed immediate attention--namely morale, safety, overtime usage, productivity, and customer relations. I began by involving the complete work force and opened lines of communication between management and craft. During our weekly talks, we openly shared our opinions about our organization's weaknesses and strengths. As we built respect and trust for each other, morale improved. This led to a shared commitment to work on the problems through teamwork.

Numerous suggestions were made regarding how to boost customer satisfaction, and a protocol was developed so that customer complaints were handled in timely manner by phone and in person as they were registered. Our success at Bunker Hill Post Office was widely communicated within the USPS, and we were described as a "model of customer responsiveness" by a prominent USPS newsletter.

Reference Number	Reference Name & Phone Number (For use of review committee & selector)

PS Form **991,** October 1993 (Page 3 of 5)

Statement of Qualifications	Name
	Creasey, Molly A.
Announcement Number	Position Applied For
Not Listed	Postmaster

Applicant position requirements are enumerated on the vacancy announcement. Enter the requirement in the space provided and explain your qualifications in reference to the requirement. A situation/task-action-result format for describing qualifications is recommended.

APPLICANT - COPY THIS PAGE. USE ONE PAGE PER REQUIREMENT/FACTOR.

Requirement/Factor   Labor Relations

During each management assignment, I have used my fair supervisory style as well as my warmth towards other to resolve a variety of labor problems. I have encouraged employee/management participation, discussed and resolved most grievances internally, and shared postal information weekly with employees. All those approaches decreased friction, improved understanding of USPS policies, and reduced labor problems. I am familiar with the national and local agreements pertaining to policy and procedures; however, I would welcome an opportunity to train in contract negotiation, which would enhance my present knowledge and skills.

During my working career, I have volunteered for every training opportunity designed to improve my knowledge of human relations and labor relations. For example, I volunteered to participate in an unofficial study in 2004 designed to explore labor attitudes towards management.

On two different occasions, I have received awards recognizing my communication and negotiation skills in labor disputes. In 2003, I utilized my communication skills in resolving a dispute between a manager and a postal associate over overtime hours. I worked through the proper union officials and the matter was effectively mediated. In 2002, a pregnant postal employee challenged USPS policies toward pregnancy leave. On my own initiative, I worked closely with this employee and counseled her, with the result that she gained an understanding of USPS regulations and developed a maternity leave plan that would work for her family and for the USPS.

I have discovered that strong communication skills are frequently the key to resolving labor problems. I believe wholeheartedly in the fairness and generosity of the USPS system, so it has been my pleasure to enthusiastically present USPS policies and procedures so that employees will appreciate the reasoning behind USPS guidelines.

Reference Number	Reference Name & Phone Number *(For use of review committee & selector)*

Statement of Qualifications	Name
	Creasey, Molly A.
Announcement Number	Position Applied For
Not Listed	Postmaster

Applicant position requirements are enumerated on the vacancy announcement. Enter the requirement in the space provided and explain your qualifications in reference to the requirement. A situation/task-action-result format for describing qualifications is recommended.

APPLICANT - COPY THIS PAGE. USE ONE PAGE PER REQUIREMENT/FACTOR.

Requirement/Factor   Equal Employment Opportunity

I fully understand the AA/EEO policy and its responsibility, and I offer a reputation as a manager who can fairly and consistently apply the equal opportunity guidelines of the USPS. I am often utilized on Candidate Evaluation Boards and Promotion Boards, and participation on those boards require fair application of equal opportunity principles and an understanding of promotion guidelines. One of my duties as an associate office coordinator is monitoring the performance and assessing annual merit evaluations for Level 15-and-below Postmasters. I have been credited with making decisions that led to improved job satisfaction among employees and a higher level of approval by union officials.

On two different occasions, I have received awards recognizing my communication and negotiation skills related to equal employment opportunity. In 2004, I utilized my communication skills in resolving a dispute between a manager and a postal associate over alleged favoritism in job assignment. I worked through the proper union officials and the matter was effectively mediated. In 2002, a postal employee challenged USPS equal employment guidelines as they related to the management intern program. On my own initiative, I worked closely with this employee and counseled her, with the result that she gained an understanding of USPS regulations and developed a plan that would eventually make her eligible for the management intern program.

I have discovered that strong communication skills are frequently the key to resolving equal employment opportunity issues. Throughout my management career, I have gained respect for the equal opportunity opportunities at the USPS, and it has been my pleasure to aggressively market those opportunities to deserving employees and ensure their maximum understanding of those equal opportunity options.

Reference Number	Reference Name & Phone Number *(For use of review committee & selector)*

PS Form **991,** October 1993 *(Page 3 of 5)*

Statement of Qualifications	Name
	Creasey, Molly A.

Announcement Number	Position Applied For
Not Listed	Postmaster

Applicant position requirements are enumerated on the vacancy announcement. Enter the requirement in the space provided and explain your qualifications in reference to the requirement. A situation/task-action-result format for describing qualifications is recommended.

APPLICANT - COPY THIS PAGE. USE ONE PAGE PER REQUIREMENT/FACTOR.

Requirement/Factor Employee Development

My primary responsibility as Manager of the Postal Employees Development Center was the training and development of hundreds of employees. I accomplished this task through: (1) new employee orientation, (2) developing employees under my supervision in their management roles, (3) conducting training classes and career awareness conferences, and (4) monitoring employees in their development. I have been instrumental in the training and growth of many different employees. As a result of that management position, I offer proven expert understanding of USPS postal policies regarding employee development and personnel classification.

I have received multiple awards recognizing my work in the area of employee development. In 2001, I spearheaded an effort to implement a new program within the USPS designed to accelerate employee development. In 2002, new management internship policies were introduced within USPS that were widely misunderstood by the majority of full-time employees. On my own initiative, I worked closely with union officials and managers to troubleshoot the implementation of this program, with the result that the management intern program is now widely accepted and praised within the internal culture.

Perhaps the greatest measure of my success in the area of Employee Development is the recognition I received in 2001 from union officials for my "exemplary leadership in the area of employee development." I was named the "Top Notch Manager" by a vote of union personnel because of my work in the area of employee development.

Reference Number	Reference Name & Phone Number *(For use of review committee & selector)*

PS Form **991**, October 1993 *(Page 3 of 5)*

Applicant Information

Name (Last, First, MI)	Title of Present Position
Novak, Agnes B.	MPLSM Operator

Mailing Address	Name and Location of Employing Office
1110 1/2 Hay Street Fayetteville, NC 28305	1110 Postmark Drive Dallas, TX

Home Phone (Area Code)	Work Phone (Area Code/PEN)	Social Security Number	Grade	Years of Service
(910) 483-6611	(910) 483-6611	000-11-2222	L-6	2 yrs., 7 mos.

Information About Vacant Position

Vacancy Announcement Number	Closing Date	Position Applied For	Grade
Not Listed	08/01/2001	Officer-in-Charge	EAS-13

Name of Vacancy Office	Location of Vacancy Office
Dallas Main Post Office	1110 Postmark Drive

Education/Training

Ref. No.	From (Mo./Yr.)	To (Mo./Yr.)	Name of Educational Institution (Address Not Required)	Major Fields of Study	No. of Credits (Hours) Semester	No. of Credits (Hours) Quarter	Type of Degree	Date
	01/97	05/98	Southern Methodist University	Computer Programming		12	Part-time	
	09/89	05/92	The University of North Carolina at Chapel Hill	Business Education	68			
	09/86	6/89	High School Dannon High School					

Ref. No.	From	To	Name of Postal or Other Training Facility	Course Name
	03/01	03/01	Dallas, TX, MSC	Supervisory Basic-Human Relations/Admin. Cert.
	03/01	03/01	Houston, TX	Career Awareness Conference
	Incomplete		Dallas, TX, MSC (PEDC)	Administrative Management for Postmasters
	10/00	10/00	Southern Methodist University	Sign Language I
	09/99	09/99	Dallas, TX	Career Awareness

Postal Positions

List permanent positions first, then temporary/detail assignments of 30 or more consecutive days. List in reverse chronological order. Use additional space on page 2.

Ref. No.	From (Mo./Yr.)	To (Mo./Yr.)	Position Title	Name & Location of Organization	Grade
	09/98	Present	Mail Processing Letter Machine Operator (MPLSM)	Main Post Office Dallas, TX	L-6
	10/00	Pres.	Supervisor Mails (204B)	Lone Star Post Office	L-15
	10/00	Pres.	Supervisor Mails (204B)	Main Post Office	L-16
			DETAIL POSITIONS		
	06/00	09/00	Finance Clerk Supervisor OER Level 5	Finance, Main Post Office	L-6

PS Form **991,** October 1993 *(Page 1 of 5)*

Nonpostal Positions

List permanent positions first, then temporary/detail assignments of 30 or more consecutive days. List in reverse chronological order. Use additional space below.

Ref. No.	Date (Mo./Yr.) From	Date (Mo./Yr.) To	Position Title	Grade or Salary	Name & Location of Organization
	01/98	06/00	Clerk Typist	GS2/5	AG, ID Card Facility, Fort Hood, TX
	08/97	01/98	Supply Clerk	GS3	Supply Division, Fort Hood, TX
	09/95	08/97	Education Specialist	GS3/4	USARB, Fort Bragg, NC
	05/94	09/95	Clerk (Administration)	GS3	Admin. Services Division, Fort Bragg, NC
	12/93	05/94	Supply Clerk	GS3	DIO Supply Division, Fort Lewis, WA
	01/93	12/93	Payroll Clerk (Typing)	GS3	Facility Engineer, Fort Lewis, WA
	07/92	01/93	Dispatcher/Jailer	N/A	Durham County Sheriff Department, Durham, NC

Additional space for use in completing preceding information and listing any special assignments, projects, civic and professional organizations, awards, honors, special skills, etc.

SPECIAL ASSIGNMENTS
Fast Track Management
Member of Women's Advisory Council
Initial Level Supervisor Program

COMPUTER AND OFFICE SKILLS
Proficient with Microsoft Word, Access, and Excel
Fast and accurate typist: 60 wpm
Outstanding organizational skills in office environments

CIVIC
Volunteer for Cumberland County Schools
Member, Non-Commissioned Officer's Wives Club
Choir Director
Fundraiser, Team Leader for the March of Dimes

SPECIAL PROJECTS
Youth Counselor for the Organization for Youth Development (OYD)
Coordinator for Tutorial Program for OYD

AWARDS
Certificate of Appreciation-March of Dimes, 2001
Letter of Appreciation-Organization for Youth Development, 2000-01
Letter of Commendation-GS COL George Tucker, Directorate of Industrial Operations, 1997
Letter of Commendation-Dr. Francis Sweeney, PhD Education, 1996

Application must be received at vacancy office by closing date.

I hereby certify that the foregoing information is true, complete, and accurate, to the best of my knowledge and belief.

Signature of Employee	Date

☐ If you are applying for a specific position, complete pages 1-4 of this form and submit the completed form to your supervisor, who will complete the evaluation for each requirement. If you want a copy of the evaluation, check the box at left. If you are completing this form for another reason, disregard pages 3 and 4, unless otherwise instructed.

PS Form **991**, October 1993 *(Page 2 of 5)*

Statement of Qualifications	Name
	Novak, Agnes, B.

Announcement Number	Position Applied For
Not Listed	Officer-in-Charge

Applicant position requirements are enumerated on the vacancy announcement. Enter the requirement in the space provided and explain your qualifications in reference to the requirement. A situation/task-action-result format for describing qualifications is recommended.

APPLICANT - COPY THIS PAGE. USE ONE PAGE PER REQUIREMENT/FACTOR.

Requirement/Factor   Personnel Training

As Education Specialist for the U.S. Army Retraining Brigade, I planned and scheduled classes for trainees preparing for the General Equivalency and General Aptitude test. My duties included scheduling classes and exams within an eight-week cycle period. My facility accommodated 180 trainees per cycle. I instructed 40 students per class in basic skills (Math, English, Reading, Science, Social Studies). I administered GED and GT tests and was responsible for the security of all testing materials. At the completion of the five phases of GED Exam, I graded tests and submitted scores for diplomas from the trainee's home state. I assisted students in preparing for the College Level Entry Program (CLEP). While in this position, I advised military trainees of educational benefits and entitlements under discharges other than honorable. This required me to obtain a general knowledge of the postal examination and selection process as it applies to the Veteran, Disabled Veteran, and Active Duty Personnel.

Other pertinent information: My work as a Youth Counselor has given me the opportunity to plan and coordinate several projects that were very successful. I am responsible for planning, scheduling, and budgeting for the Tutorial Program designed to help problem students. This requires me to obtain support from teachers, retired teachers, and aides. In that capacity, I am responsible for obtaining a building to be utilized for tutoring sessions, and I also handle the scheduling of students according to their needs and availability of the instructors.

A Letter of Commendation dated 2004 described me an "an outstanding communicator with a gift for training and motivating others."

Reference Number	Reference Name & Phone Number (For use of review committee & selector)

PS Form **991**, October 1993 (Page 3 of 5)

Requirements Page _1_ of _2_

Statement of Qualifications	Name
	Novak, Agnes B.

Announcement Number	Position Applied For
Not Listed	Officer-in-Charge

Applicant position requirements are enumerated on the vacancy announcement. Enter the requirement in the space provided and explain your qualifications in reference to the requirement. A situation/task-action-result format for describing qualifications is recommended.

APPLICANT - COPY THIS PAGE. USE ONE PAGE PER REQUIREMENT/FACTOR.

Requirement/Factor   Personnel Supervision

As Supervisor, Mails, I supervise a large number of employees who cancel, case, and dispatch the mail. My responsibilities include the staffing of work room areas to assure maximum productivity and timely dispatch of mail. While managing up to 25 employees, I instruct and mentor new employees. Several times during the tour I count the mail on the floor to determine a completion time for outgoing operations.

My duties include ensuring that all employees are adherent to safety policies. I maintain a comfortable working relationship filled with mutual respect with all employees and staff, and I make a conscious effort to create a comfortable work environment.

My practices related to EEO policies and my strong communication skills have in some instances served to alleviate problems that might have otherwise been serious. My extensive training related to Affirmative Action projects and the Women's Advisory Program have enhanced my knowledge of EEO practices and policies. Recently I completed a Human Relations class that included a detailed analysis of Equal Employment Opportunity policies.

In all evaluations of my performance, I have received the highest ratings of my performance in the area of personnel management. I have been described in writing as "a fair and compassionate supervisor who strives to create the highest morale among employees."

Reference Number	Reference Name & Phone Number (For use of review committee & selector)

PS Form **991**, October 1993 (Page 3 of 5)

Applicant Information

Name (Last, First, MI)	Title of Present Position
Novak, Agnes B.	Supervisor of Mails

Mailing Address	Name and Location of Employing Office
1110 1/2 Hay Street Fayetteville, NC 28305	1110 Postmark Drive Dallas, TX

Home Phone (Area Code)	Work Phone (Area Code/PEN)	Social Security Number	Grade	Years of Service
(910) 483-6611	(910) 483-6611	000-11-2222	EAS-18	6 years

Information About Vacant Position

Vacancy Announcement Number	Closing Date	Position Applied For	Grade
199009	08/02/2004	Postmaster	EAS-13

Name of Vacancy Office	Location of Vacancy Office
Dallas Main Post Office	1110 Postmark Drive, Dallas TX

Education/Training

Ref. No.	Date (Mo./Yr.) From	Date (Mo./Yr.) To	Name of Educational Institution (Address Not Required)	Major Fields of Study	No. of Credits (Hours) Semester	No. of Credits (Hours) Quarter	Type of Degree	Date
1-	03/02	12/03	Southern Methodist University	Real Estate Fund.		4	N/A	
2-	03/02	12/03	Southern Methodist University	Real Estate Math		2	N/A	
3-	01/97	05/98	Southern Methodist University	Computer Programming		12	N/A	
4-	09/89	05/92	The University of North Carolina at Chapel Hill	Business Education	68		N/A	
5-	09/86	6/89	High School Dannon High School					

Ref. No.	From	To	Name of Postal or Other Training Facility	Course Name
6-	07/04	07/04	Dallas, TX, MSC	Administrative Management for Postmasters
7-	04/04	04/04	Houston, TX	Safety/Accident
8-	03/04	03/04	Dallas, TX, MSC (PEDC)	Supervisory Training System
9-	08/02	08/02	Southern Methodist University	Career Awareness Conference
10-	09/01	09/01	Dallas, TX	Supervisory, Basic Human Relations/Admin.
11-	10/00	01/01	Southern Methodist University	Sign Language I

Postal Positions

List permanent positions first, then temporary/detail assignments of 30 or more consecutive days.
List in reverse chronological order. Use additional space on page 2.

Ref. No.	Date (Mo./Yr.) From	Date (Mo./Yr.) To	Position Title	Name & Location of Organization	Grade
12-	04/03	Present	Supervisor of Mails	Main Post Office, Dallas, TX	EAS-15
13-	09/98	04/03	MP Letter Sorting Machine Oper. DETAILS	Main Post Office	L-6
14-	06/04	Pres.	Supervisor Contact for Special Delivery Carriers	Main Post Office	EAS-15
15-	04/04	07/04	Tour Superintendent Relief	Lone Star Branch Post Office	EAS-18
16-	07/02	08/02	Officer-in-Charge	Main Post Office	EAS-13
17-	10/00	04/03	Supervisor Trainee OCR/BCS, LSM, Platform, and Outgoing Manual Oper.	Main Post Office	EAS-15
18-	06/00	09/00	Finance Clerk	Finance, Main Post Office	L-6

PS Form **991,** October 1993 (Page 1 of 5)

Nonpostal Positions

List permanent positions first, then temporary/detail assignments of 30 or more consecutive days. List in reverse chronological order. Use additional space below.

Ref. No.	Date (Mo./Yr.) From	Date (Mo./Yr.) To	Position Title	Grade or Salary	Name & Location of Organization
19-	01/98	09/98	Clerk Typist	GS2/5	AG, ID Card Facility, Fort Hood, TX
20-	08/97	01/98	Supply Clerk	GS3	Supply Division, Fort Hood, TX
21-	09/95	08/97	Education Specialist	GS3/4	Admin. Services Division, Fort Bragg, NC
22-	10/93	12/93	Payroll Clerk	GS3	Facility Engineer, Fort Lewis, WA
23-	07/92	01/93	Dispatcher/Jailer	N/A	Durham County Sheriff Department, Durham, NC

Additional space for use in completing preceding information and listing any special assignments, projects, civic and professional organizations, awards, honors, special skills, etc.

VOLUNTEER WORK
Volunteer Teacher's Aide/Test Monitor, 09/96-08/97
Budget Director, Organization of Youth Development, 10/01-11/03

SPECIAL ASSIGNMENTS
Director At Lodge, Women's Advisory Council

AWARDS
Certificate of Appreciation, Jeff Martin, Postmaster, Dallas MSC
Certificate of Appreciation, Affirmative Action Director, Texas Division
Certificate of Appreciation, Cynthia Depps, OIC, Dallas MSC
Certificate of Appreciation, Savings Bond Campaign Coordinator
Certificate of Appreciation, March of Dimes
Letter of Commendation, GS COL Jerome Wahl, Directorate of Industrial Operations
Letter of Commendation, Dr. William E. Lockhart, PhD Education
Letter of Commendation, Fort Bragg, NC

CIVIC
Member, Non-Commissioned Officer's Wives Club
Choir Director
Fund Director

COMPUTERS
Proficient with Excel, Access, Word, and other popular software programs

Application must be received at vacancy office by closing date.

I hereby certify that the foregoing information is true, complete, and accurate, to the best of my knowledge and belief.

Signature of Employee	Date

☐ If you are applying for a specific position, complete pages 1-4 of this form and submit the completed form to your supervisor, who will complete the evaluation for each requirement. If you want a copy of the evaluation, check the box at left. If you are completing this form for another reason, disregard pages 3 and 4, unless otherwise instructed.

PS Form **991**, October 1993 *(Page 2 of 5)*

Statement of Qualifications	Name
	Novak, Agnes B.

Announcement Number	Position Applied For
199009	Postmaster

Applicant position requirements are enumerated on the vacancy announcement. Enter the requirement in the space provided and explain your qualifications in reference to the requirement. A situation/task-action-result format for describing qualifications is recommended.

APPLICANT - COPY THIS PAGE. USE ONE PAGE PER REQUIREMENT/FACTOR.

Requirement/Factor   Decision Making/Problem Analysis

During my tour as Officer-in-Charge at Dallas P.O., I received a customer complaint concerning mis-sent mail in her P.O. Box. I established a color-coded system for the box section and updated P.O. Box rent applications. This system enabled us to identify new box holders, box holders receiving mail in two or more names, and box holders receiving weekly/daily publications. This resulted in my being able to case the box section faster and more efficiently. I was later commended on our service by the same customer.

While in the position of Officer-in-Charge, I constantly sought ways to increase revenue and reduce work hours. I observed my customers' buying habits and determined that stamp book vending and the promotion of Priority and Express mail would be essential in accomplishing that goal. I requested and obtained the stamp vending. During this time I seized every opportunity to make my customers aware of the advantage of these services. This resulted in an increase of revenue and a positive reflection in terms of budget and work hours.

Reference Number	Reference Name & Phone Number *(For use of review committee & selector)*
12 & 16	Ms. Tamira Jones, Associate Office Coordinator phone (910) 483-6611

PS Form **991**, October 1993 *(Page 3 of 5)*   Requirements Page __1__ of __4__

Statement of Qualifications	Name
	Novak, Agnes B.
Announcement Number	Position Applied For
199009	Postmaster

Applicant position requirements are enumerated on the vacancy announcement. Enter the requirement in the space provided and explain your qualifications in reference to the requirement. A situation/task-action-result format for describing qualifications is recommended.

APPLICANT - COPY THIS PAGE. USE ONE PAGE PER REQUIREMENT/FACTOR.

Requirement/Factor   Customer and Community Relations

In my current position, I often encounter customers who need assistance or information on postal policies or preparation of mail. I have often been commended by customers on my willingness to assist and provide information. I find that when dealing with an angry customer in particular, just my courtesy and acknowledgement of the problem eases the tension and expedites the finding of a solution.

Such a situation occurred in June 2003, when I used my tact and problem-solving skills to resolve a customer's problem. The problem encountered by an established 25-year-old business was that its mail was being returned to senders, even though the customer's address had not changed in 25 years. That meant that the customer's checks from its own customers were not being received, so of course the USPS customer was distressed and angry since its revenue stream was interrupted. I immediately involved technical personnel who researched the problem, and it was discovered that "faceless" and newly installed computer equipment was seeking an additional address item "Suite C," as part of the address. I worked closely with the customer and encouraged the customer to add that address identification as part of its address, and I worked with new and casual carriers to alert them to the problem. The result was that the customer felt "listened to" and she appreciated the efforts of the USPS to remedy her problems.

During my assignment as Officer-in-Charge, I hosted a Tour of the Dallas Postal Facilities for Girl Scout Troup 427. During this tour, I explained postal operations and services available. I introduced the beginner's stamp collectors kit, and handed out brochures about Stamp Collecting. As a result, I received a letter of thanks from Troop Leader, Ms. Forbes.

Reference Number	Reference Name & Phone Number (For use of review committee & selector)
16	Mr. Bradley Smith, Finance Director phone (910) 483-6611

Statement of Qualifications	Name
	Novak, Agnes B.

Announcement Number	Position Applied For
199009	Postmaster

Applicant position requirements are enumerated on the vacancy announcement. Enter the requirement in the space provided and explain your qualifications in reference to the requirement. A situation/task-action-result format for describing qualifications is recommended.

APPLICANT - COPY THIS PAGE. USE ONE PAGE PER REQUIREMENT/FACTOR.

Requirement/Factor   Planning and Scheduling of Work

As Supervisor of Mails, I supervise up to 30 employees involved in performing multiple tasks under tight deadlines. I am responsible for the staffing of all manual operations of mail processing Tour III. During peaks periods of heavy mail flow, I staff areas to ensure maximum productivity and timely dispatch of mail. The result has been an even mail flow and a timely dispatch of manual mails.

One situation arose in March 2004 which tested my ability to plan and schedule work. There was a major power outage in March 2004 in our geographical area due to a major snow storm. Many regular employees were not able to come into work. I immediately conferred with my supervisor, and we were able to work with union officials to allow National Guard employees at the nearby National Guard facility to fill in for three days. This permitted an unusual solution for an atypical problem. A subsequent Letter of Appreciation praised my "ingenuity and resourcefulness in planning and scheduling work" for allowing the mail to be processed and delivered more or less on time, despite severe challenges and nearly arctic conditions.

Reference Number	Reference Name & Phone Number (For use of review committee & selector)	
15 & 12	Mr. Ted Cameron, Superintendent of Mail Processing	phone (910) 483-6611

PS Form **991,** October 1993 (Page 3 of 5)   Requirements Page __3__ of _4_

Statement of Qualifications	Name
	Novak, Agnes B.
Announcement Number	**Position Applied For**
199009	Postmaster

Applicant position requirements are enumerated on the vacancy announcement. Enter the requirement in the space provided and explain your qualifications in reference to the requirement. A situation/task-action-result format for describing qualifications is recommended.

APPLICANT - COPY THIS PAGE. USE ONE PAGE PER REQUIREMENT/FACTOR.

Requirement/Factor   Safety and Health

My position as Mail Processing Supervisor requires me to practice and enforce all safety procedures. I believe that accident prevention measures, such as reporting and correcting safety hazards on the spot is the most important factor in reducing accidents and injuries. I give weekly safety talks and ensure that my employees exercise good safety habits. As a result, accidents in my work area are decreasing.

There was one situation that occurred in June 2003 that created an opportunity for increased safety awareness. Shortly after the services of a new maintenance contractor were obtained, there were four instances of customers slipping on the foyer of the main post office. When we investigated the accidents, we discovered that the new maintenance contractor was not using non-slip wax, which was a requirement of the contract. We determined that the minority contractor had used the wrong kind of wax by accident, and with the blessing of the union we gave the contractor a second chance to improve her performance. The appreciative contractor modified its product line, and there were no more instances of safety hazards due to slippery floors. We were proud that we were able to handle this problem in such a way that customers and employees were safeguarded while no punitive action was required against the small business owner who valued her association with the post office.

Reference Number	Reference Name & Phone Number (For use of review committee & selector)
7	Mr. Ted Cameron, Tour Superintendent phone (910) 483-6611

PS Form **991**, October 1993 (Page 3 of 5)

Government Jobs Series edited by Anne McKinney 93

Applicant Information

Name *(Last, First, MI)*	Title of Present Position
Hughes, Michael	Supervisor, Mail's LSM

Mailing Address	Name and Location of Employing Office
1110 1/2 Hay Street Fayetteville, NC 28305	1110 Stamp Drive Missoula, MT

Home Phone *(Area Code)*	Work Phone *(Area Code/PEN)*	Social Security Number	Grade	Years of Service
(910) 483-6611	(910) 483-6611	000-00-0000	M-04	5 1/2 years

Information About Vacant Position

Vacancy Announcement Number	Closing Date	Position Applied For	Grade
05-05F	03/27/05	Supervisor, Customer Service	EAS-16

Name of Vacancy Office	Location of Vacancy Office
Missoula Main Post Office	1110 Stamp Drive, Missoula, MT

Education/Training

Ref. No.	Date (Mo./Yr.) From	To	Name of Educational Institution *(Address Not Required)*	Major Fields of Study	No. of Credits (Hours) Semester	Quarter	Type of Degree	Date
1-	06/99	03/00	University of Montana, Missoula	Public Administration		9		
2-	06/93	06/94	University of Montana, Missoula	Public Administration		9		
3-	06/87	06/90	High School P.P. Orange High School					

Ref. No.	From	To	Name of Postal or Other Training Facility	Course Name
4-	06/03	06/03	Missoula P & DC	Northwestern Quality Dispatch Training
5-	05/00	08/00	Missoula P & DC	Quality Management for Postmasters

Postal Positions

List permanent positions first, then temporary/detail assignments of 30 or more consecutive days. List in reverse chronological order. Use additional space on page 2.

Ref. No.	Date (Mo./Yr.) From	To	Position Title	Name & Location of Organization	Grade
6-	01/04	Present	Supervisor, Mail's LSM	Missoula Processing & Distribution Center, USPS	EAS-16
7-	10/03	01/04	Manager, Distribution Operations	Missoula Processing & Distribution Center, USPS	EAS-20
8-	08/03	10/03	Supervisor, Mail's Automation	Missoula Processing & Distribution Center, USPS	EAS-16
9-	06/01	08/03	Supervisor, Mail's Flat Sorting Machine	Missoula Processing & Distribution Center, USPS	EAS-16
10-	11/99	06/01	Supervisor, Mail's Platform 010 Operation	Missoula Processing & Distribution Center, USPS	EAS-16
11-	01/99	11/99	Mail Handler/Platform	Missoula Processing & Distribution Center, USPS	M-04

PS Form **991,** October 1993 *(Page 1 of 5)*

Nonpostal Positions

List permanent positions first, then temporary/detail assignments of 30 or more consecutive days. List in reverse chronological order. Use additional space below.

Ref. No.	Date (Mo./Yr.) From	Date (Mo./Yr.) To	Position Title	Grade or Salary	Name & Location of Organization
12-	01/97	01/99	Stocker	$8.00/hr	Target Stores, Missoula, MT
13-	06/95	07/96	Squad Leader	E-5	U.S. Army, Fort Lewis, WA
14-	02/94	05/95	Clerk	E-5	U.S. Army, Fort Lewis, WA
15-	07/91	09/94	Commander's Driver	E-4	U.S. Army, Fort Lewis, WA

Additional space for use in completing preceding information and listing any special assignments, projects, civic and professional organizations, awards, honors, special skills, etc.

16- Good Conduct Medal

17- Army Commendation Medal

18- Earned numerous Certificates of Achievement

19- Special Assignment: Haiti and Panama aircraft/rescue and clean up

20- I received a Letter of Appreciation from Plant Manager, Tangela Gibbons

21- I am currently a Big Brother helping disadvantaged youth

22- Am a member of Montana Statewide Lodge, #123

Application must be received at vacancy office by closing date.

I hereby certify that the foregoing information is true, complete, and accurate, to the best of my knowledge and belief.

Signature of Employee	Date

☐ If you are applying for a specific position, complete pages 1-4 of this form and submit the completed form to your supervisor, who will complete the evaluation for each requirement. If you want a copy of the evaluation, check the box at left. If you are completing this form for another reason, disregard pages 3 and 4, unless otherwise instructed.

Statement of Qualifications	Name Hughes, Michael
Announcement Number 05-05F	Position Applied For Supervisor, Customer Service, EAS-16

Applicant position requirements are enumerated on the vacancy announcement. Enter the requirement in the space provided and explain your qualifications in reference to the requirement. A situation/task-action-result format for describing qualifications is recommended.

APPLICANT - COPY THIS PAGE. USE ONE PAGE PER REQUIREMENT/FACTOR.

Requirement/Factor   Oral Communications

With the implementation of the RBCS mail flow, it became imperative that we increase the percentage of mail canceled everyday to 40%. It then became my job to inform and motivate my crew to achieve the desired cancellations rate by 1800.

To accomplish this mission, I held a service talk and informed my crew of the new goals and explained to them the new methodology that will be used to get the job done. I stressed the importance of gathering all raw mail from behind each star route as it arrives rather than staging the containers. I also identified the mail in a central location.

After the talk and the change in the way of identifying staging the raw mail, my crew achieved the 40% cancellations rate for two consecutive weeks. After the initial two weeks of the new cancellation program, there was some fluctuation in the obtainment of the 40% goal due to experimentation with manpower needs. However, the foundation was set to achieve the goal on a consistent basis, which is now the situation. This situation, task, action, and result took place as a result of effective oral communications which stimulated individual motivation as well as aggressive teamwork toward the task of accomplishment a goal.

Reference Number	Reference Name & Phone Number (For use of review committee & selector)
8	Ms. Caitlin Wall phone (910) 483-6611

PS Form **991**, October 1993 (Page 3 of 5)   Requirements Page __1_ of _9_

Statement of Qualifications	Name
	Hughes, Michael

Announcement Number	Position Applied For
05-05F	Supervisor, Customer Service, EAS-16

Applicant position requirements are enumerated on the vacancy announcement. Enter the requirement in the space provided and explain your qualifications in reference to the requirement. A situation/task-action-result format for describing qualifications is recommended.

APPLICANT - COPY THIS PAGE. USE ONE PAGE PER REQUIREMENT/FACTOR.

Requirement/Factor   Leadership

While detailed to the Supervisor of Distribution Operations position from June 2004 to September 2004, we were having trouble making timely dispatches from all machines in the automation area. This had the result of slowing down the processing of mail and creating bottlenecks in mail distribution.

While consulting with various technical experts, I examined possible causes to the problem and devised a new methodology that would solve the problem.

The new methodology ensured that, prior to each dispatch, the sweeper would pull the dispatch ten minutes before and stage it for the expediter.

Consequently, dispatch discipline improved and overnight ODIS scores for our neighboring MSC improved. On a subsequent formal performance evaluation, I was praised for my leadership in this highly technical area of postal operations, and I was cited for "common sense problem-solving and leadership."

Reference Number	Reference Name & Phone Number *(For use of review committee & selector)*
8	Ms. Caitlin Wall phone (910) 483-6611

PS Form **991,** October 1993 *(Page 3 of 5)*

Statement of Qualifications	Name
	Hughes, Michael
Announcement Number	Position Applied For
05-05F	Supervisor, Customer Service, EAS-16

Applicant position requirements are enumerated on the vacancy announcement. Enter the requirement in the space provided and explain your qualifications in reference to the requirement. A situation/task-action-result format for describing qualifications is recommended.

APPLICANT - COPY THIS PAGE. USE ONE PAGE PER REQUIREMENT/FACTOR.

Requirement/Factor   Human Relations

While detailed to the Supervisor of Distribution Operations position on the platform, I was confronted with a situation when an important task came up and a spontaneous job reassignment had to be made to cover the emergency.

I reassigned an employee to solve the problem; however, I failed to notify his group leader that I had reassigned him. As a result, the group leader became upset and accused the subordinate that I reassigned of being negligent and irresponsible. I immediately became aware that I had made a mistake by not informing the reassigned employee's group leader of his new status.

I immediately pulled both employees aside and apologized for not using the chain of command before making the reassignment. As a result of our conversation, it became apparent that this was a common occurrence that had caused problems in the past.

The result of the meeting was that a new awareness was created concerning the importance of using the chain of command in making personnel changes, and a better working environment was created. Since that time morale has improved, and there is a general consensus that everyone is "on the same wavelength" and committed to using the chain of command in making temporary changes in personnel assignments.

Reference Number	Reference Name & Phone Number *(For use of review committee & selector)*
10	Ms. Caitlin Wall and Mr. Neil Carter phone (910) 483-6611

PS Form **991**, October 1993 *(Page 3 of 5)*

Announcement Number	Position Applied For
05-05F	Supervisor, Customer Service, EAS-16

Applicant position requirements are enumerated on the vacancy announcement. Enter the requirement in the space provided and explain your qualifications in reference to the requirement. A situation/task-action-result format for describing qualifications is recommended.

APPLICANT - COPY THIS PAGE. USE ONE PAGE PER REQUIREMENT/FACTOR.

Requirement/Factor   Problem Analysis

On a reoccurring basis, we were finishing our 892 program well after our scheduled cut off time. The first thing I did was to analyze the mail flow to see what was causing the problem.

My investigation showed that the late allocation of Keyers by the Rec Site after 2250 was creating an avalanche of excessive 892 mail that could not be processed timely before cut off time on one DBCS. I decided that, in order to meet cut of time, I needed to start another DBCS at 2100. This adjustment allowed us to clear our volume by 22:30. It did, however, create more tied out bundles for the airlift sacks due to the fact that full trays were not created on second DBCS by the end of distribution. It did ensure, nevertheless, that all overnight surface mail was finalized by cut off time.

The final outcome of the decision was to have 892 mail distributed and ready for dispatch in a timely manner. This enhanced service standards not only for overnight delivery but also for two-day and three-day delivery.

Reference Number	Reference Name & Phone Number (For use of review committee & selector)
8	Ms. Caitlin Wall phone (910) 483-6611

Statement of Qualifications	Name
	Hughes, Michael

Announcement Number	Position Applied For
05-05F	Supervisor, Customer Service, EAS-16

Applicant position requirements are enumerated on the vacancy announcement. Enter the requirement in the space provided and explain your qualifications in reference to the requirement. A situation/task-action-result format for describing qualifications is recommended.

APPLICANT - COPY THIS PAGE. USE ONE PAGE PER REQUIREMENT/FACTOR.

Requirement/Factor   Decision Making

In June 2004, we were experiencing difficulties with not clearing the 971 mail in a timely manner. It was my responsibility to come up with a plan to identify how we could clear 971 OG efficiently.

I began by analyzing the flow of operations, and I walked the floor to make my own observations. I consulted with personnel as I made my own observations, and I made mathematical calculations using a stopwatch. I made the determination that, by better sequencing of operations, there would be a more efficient system.

I made the decision to start up the outgoing function and, by doing so, it allowed the letter sorting machine (LSM) to get their rejects earlier while also allowing us to clear my 971 operation earlier. In addition, the 892 outgoing operation was able to receive mail in a timely fashion.

As a result of this decision and this newly adopted procedure, we have been meeting our clearance time. Furthermore, two-day state mail and surface dispatch has vastly improved. I submitted a formal suggestion through our employee suggestion program, and several other post offices have contacted me to say that they encountered identical experiences and utilized my decision-making approach to solve their problems.

Reference Number	Reference Name & Phone Number (For use of review committee & selector)
8	Ms. Caitlin Wall phone (910) 483-6611

PS Form **991**, October 1993 (Page 3 of 5)

100 Part Two: The 991 and the Statement of Qualifications

Statement of Qualifications	Name
	Hughes, Michael
Announcement Number	Position Applied For
05-05F	Supervisor, Customer Service, EAS-16

Applicant position requirements are enumerated on the vacancy announcement. Enter the requirement in the space provided and explain your qualifications in reference to the requirement. A situation/task-action-result format for describing qualifications is recommended.

APPLICANT - COPY THIS PAGE. USE ONE PAGE PER REQUIREMENT/FACTOR.

Requirement/Factor   Written Communications

Under the tutelage of the Manager of Distribution Operations and Plant Manager, I have refined skills in all types of postal report writing, including ODIS, Service Performance, and Bin Analysis as well as various other types of reports. In addition, I have the opportunity to utilize my written communication skills while filling out the PS 991 and the OF 612. I feel that my skills in this area are indicative of my potential in this area.

During my five years as an Acting Supervisor, I supervised each operation and submitted accurate reports on a daily basis. On a formal performance evaluation, I was commended for my excellent spelling and grammar skills as reflected in my report writing.

On numerous occasions, I have drafted correspondence for the Manager of Distribution Operations and the Plant Manager. I have become skilled in preparing letters in response to customer complaints as well as Congressional inquiries. During a recent overhaul of the employee handbook, I was specially requested to assist in the rewriting of that important employee manual, and I served for 10 months on a six-person team that revised the handbook significantly.

Reference Number	Reference Name & Phone Number (For use of review committee & selector)
7	Ms. Caitlin Wall phone (910) 483-6611

Government Jobs Series edited by Anne McKinney **101**

Statement of Qualifications	Name
	Hughes, Michael

Announcement Number	Position Applied For
05-05F	Supervisor, Customer Service, EAS-16

Applicant position requirements are enumerated on the vacancy announcement. Enter the requirement in the space provided and explain your qualifications in reference to the requirement. A situation/task-action-result format for describing qualifications is recommended.

APPLICANT - COPY THIS PAGE. USE ONE PAGE PER REQUIREMENT/FACTOR.

Requirement/Factor __Mathematical Computations__

A part of my duties when supervising the ISS System is to keep a continuous count of my own time, the image generation rate of mail I am running, the amount of images on hand, and the keying rate of the DCOs at the Rec Center. In order to do this, I have to constantly calculate percentages and convert my finding into projections that allow me to process the mail by clearance time. To do this I keep a count of my script and meter volume and then multiply these different volumes by the image that will be generated. I then add this estimate to the images already in the system. Once I obtain this figure, I multiply the key rate of DCOs by the number of keyers I have allocated. By doing this, I get an idea of how long it would take me to process my on-hand volume and how much volume I will need to divert to downstream operations in order to meet my clearance time.

By using this procedure, I have been able to project my processing window accurately on a consistent basis. This has facilitated our ability to clear our mail in a timely fashion.

An example of the above was when I took over the buffer on the ISSs from Tour II. I had 38,348 images with the DCOs keying at 894 images per hour. I had 42 DCOs on the clock when I took over. This meant that in the next hour, if they maintained their keying rate, I could process 37,548 images per hour while the stage capacity in front of ISS was approximately 500 feet or approximately 125,000 pieces of script mail. Using image generation rate of 65%, I calculated that I could generate an additional 81,250 pieces of mail. By adding the buffer count to the projected images I came up with a total of 119,598 images and by simple arithmetic, I determined that I had a run time of three hours and eleven minutes. I added another twenty minutes run time to compensate for breaks by the DCOs, that gave me a total of three hours and thirty minutes run time. This told me that I could run to 1830 with-on hand volume at that time without having to divert to MPLSM.

In the fast-paced, high volume environment of the USPS, performing mathematical calculations quickly and accurately is a key to supervisory and managerial excellence, and I have been praised on formal evaluations for my strong mathematical abilities.

Reference Number	Reference Name & Phone Number (For use of review committee & selector)
8	Ms. Caitlin Wall phone (910) 483-6611

PS Form **991,** October 1993 (Page 3 of 5)

Statement of Qualifications	Name
	Hughes, Michael
Announcement Number	Position Applied For
05-05F	Supervisor, Customer Service, EAS-16

Applicant position requirements are enumerated on the vacancy announcement. Enter the requirement in the space provided and explain your qualifications in reference to the requirement. A situation/task-action-result format for describing qualifications is recommended.

APPLICANT - COPY THIS PAGE. USE ONE PAGE PER REQUIREMENT/FACTOR.

Requirement/Factor   Safety

Within a short period of time in September 2004, we had a rash of accidents concerning the proper usage of all purpose container. All of the accidents revolved around the proper securing of the top shelf and the proper closing and securing of the top gate.

On my own initiative, I organized and conducted a safety briefing on the proper usage of all purpose containers. I explained the importance of securing the top shelf in the "up" position by making sure that all restraints were used and properly seated to prevent the shelf from accidentally falling. I also stressed the point that the top gate should be securely seeded and checked before moving. I added that, if any of the safety devices were defective, the container would be tagged orange and put out of circulation until it was properly fixed by maintenance.

By monitoring the usage of all purpose containers and making on-the-spot corrections when they were discovered to be mishandled, I was able to eliminate all purpose container accidents under my supervision. After that situation occurred, I was asked to author a special Employee Bulletin advising employees of the specifics of this new tagging system.

Reference Number	Reference Name & Phone Number (For use of review committee & selector)
6-11	Ms. Caitlin Wall phone (910) 483-6611

PS Form **991,** October 1993 *(Page 3 of 5)*

Statement of Qualifications	Name Hughes, Michael
Announcement Number 05-05F	Position Applied For Supervisor, Customer Service, EAS-16

Applicant position requirements are enumerated on the vacancy announcement. Enter the requirement in the space provided and explain your qualifications in reference to the requirement. A situation/task-action-result format for describing qualifications is recommended.

APPLICANT - COPY THIS PAGE. USE ONE PAGE PER REQUIREMENT/FACTOR.

Requirement/Factor   Job Knowledge

Having worked for the U.S. Postal Service in excess of five years, I have gained valuable knowledge of many operations from an employee's perspective. I desired in-depth knowledge of every operation in the Missoula Processing Distribution for my personal fulfillment; therefore, I volunteered for the Supervisory Training Program (204B) and rapidly grasped the intricacies of the 010 and platform operations.

I asked for and received training on the flat sorter machine which enabled me to see the down flow from the flat's canceler; 010 Flats Operation; and the Bump table to the FSM and manual flats (060).

Next I received training as Letter Sorting Machine (LSM), Manual Operation and Automation Supervisor. Respectfully, after excelling as SDO of all Tour III operations, I requested training as a Manager, Distribution Operations, and performed well in this capacity on seven occasions when needed in the capacity.

I have become a vital member of the management trainee program and obtained valuable knowledge of goals and procedures of each area. I achieved a record setting volume as Automation SDO on October 2003, of 1,442,254 and on September 2003 we set a new record at 1,460,458, and the highest cancellation of 45% as 010 SDO. These accomplishments in addition to completion of every available course and classroom training, has given me many of the tools to excel as a full-time supervisor for the challenges of the USPS.

Reference Number	Reference Name & Phone Number *(For use of review committee & selector)*
8	Ms. Caitlin Wall (910) 483-6611

PS Form **991**, October 1993 *(Page 3 of 5)*

104 Part Two: The 991 and the Statement of Qualifications

Supervisory Evaluation for Initial-Level Supervisor Position	Name Hughes, Michael
Announcement Number 05-05F	Initial-Level Supervisor Position Supervisor, Customer Service, EAS-16

Requirement Oral Communications: Leadership: Human Relations: Problem Analysis: Decision Making: Written Communications: Mathematical Computations: Safety & Job Knowledge.

Employee Michael Hughes is an exemplary employee possessing above-average skills in communications, human relations, technical knowledge, and leadership. His work ethic and intensity sets him apart from the rest. He has the ability to quickly gain the respect of subordinates and is effective in delegating tasks to them. He has a thorough knowledge of mail processing techniques and mail flow.

Mr. Hughes' ability to lead would make him an effective supervisor in Distribution Operations or Customer Service. I highly recommend him on the basis of his strong oral communications skills, human relations ability, decision-making style, knowledge of safety and health practices, as well as his strong mathematical background.

Here is an example of a Supervisory Evaluation for Initial-Level Supervisor Position, which is one of the documents involved in internal promotion.

Ability Rating *(Check one)*	[X] Superior	[ ] Above Average	[ ] Basic

Signature of Supervisor	Date	Office Address	Phone No.
		1110 Stamp Drive Missoula, MT	(910) 483-6611
Printed Name & Position Caitlin Wall, Supervisor, District Operations			

PS Form **991,** October 1993 *(Page 4 of 5)*

Applicant Information

Name *(Last, First, MI)*	Title of Present Position
Pritchett, Matthew R.	Mail Handler

Mailing Address	Name and Location of Employing Office
1110 1/2 Hay Street Fayetteville, NC 28305	1110 Stamp Drive Phoenix, AZ

Home Phone *(Area Code)*	Work Phone *(Area Code/PEN)*	Social Security Number	Grade	Years of Service
(910) 483-6611	(910) 483-6611	987-65-4321	4	4 years

Information About Vacant Position

Vacancy Announcement Number	Closing Date	Position Applied For	Grade
Not Listed	06/04/2004	Supervisor, Mails	EAS-15

Name of Vacancy Office	Location of Vacancy Office
Phoenix Main Post Office	1110 Stamp Drive, Phoenix, AZ

Education/Training

Ref. No.	Date (Mo./Yr.) From	Date (Mo./Yr.) To	Name of Educational Institution *(Address Not Required)*	Major Fields of Study	No. of Credits (Hours) Semester	No. of Credits (Hours) Quarter	Type of Degree	Date
1-	06/04	Pres.	University of Phoenix	Business	6		BBA	12/04
2-	08/82	12/87	Arizona State University	Business	123			
3-	09/78	06/82	High School P.P. Orange High School					

Ref. No.	From	To	Name of Postal or Other Training Facility	Course Name
4-	06/90	07/90	Fort Bragg, NC	Combat Reconnaissance School
5-	07/89	09/89	Fort Benning, GA	Special Forces Officers School
6-	03/88	03/88	Fort Benning, GA	Officers Candidate School

Postal Positions

List permanent positions first, then temporary/detail assignments of 30 or more consecutive days.
List in reverse chronological order. Use additional space on page 2.

Ref. No.	Date (Mo./Yr.) From	Date (Mo./Yr.) To	Position Title	Name & Location of Organization	Grade
7-	03/04	Present	204-B Supervisor	Main Post Office, Phoenix, AZ	EAS-15
8-	11/03	Pres.	Crew Leader Saturdays & Holidays	Main Post Office	M-5
9-	10/01	Pres.	Mail Handler	Main Post Office	M-4
10-	06/00	10/01	Clerk	Tempe, AZ	PS-5

PS Form **991**, October 1993 *(Page 1 of 5)*

Nonpostal Positions

List permanent positions first, then temporary/detail assignments of 30 or more consecutive days. List in reverse chronological order. Use additional space below.

Ref. No.	Date (Mo./Yr.) From	Date (Mo./Yr.) To	Position Title	Grade or Salary	Name & Location of Organization
11-	10/97	06/00	Tire Builder	$15.00/hr	Goodyear Tires, Yuma, AZ
12-	10/95	01/98	Co-Chairman "QWL" Seminar	-0-	Goodyear Tires, Yuma, AZ
13-	10/94	08/97	Union Division Chairman	$13.00/hr	U.R.W. Local #123, Phoenix, AZ
14-	12/90	10/94	Low Angle Operator	$12.50/hr	Goodyear Tires, Yuma, AZ
15-	12/87	08/90	Captain-Highest Rank Held	O-3	U.S. Army
16-	08/82	12/87	Student	-0-	University of Phoenix, AZ
17-	08/79	04/80	Stocker	$5.00/hr	Wal-Mart, Phoenix, AZ

Additional space for use in completing preceding information and listing any special assignments, projects, civic and professional organizations, awards, honors, special skills, etc.

SPECIAL ASSIGNMENTS
Member, Goodyear Equal Employment Opportunity Committee
Member of Goodyear Tires Safety Committee
Initial Level Supervisor Program

COMPUTER AND OFFICE SKILLS
Proficient with Microsoft Word, Access, and Excel
Fast and accurate typist: 60 wpm

CIVIC
Volunteer for Phoenix County Schools
Member, Phoenix Council for Disabilities
Sunday School Teacher
Fundraiser, Team Leader for the American Cancer Society

SPECIAL PROJECTS
Youth Counselor for the Teens Against Unwanted Pregnancy
Volunteer with Reading is Fundamental Program

AWARDS
Certificate of Appreciation-American Cancer Society, 2003, 2004
Letter of Appreciation-Teens Against Unwanted Pregnancy, 2002

Application must be received at vacancy office by closing date.

I hereby certify that the foregoing information is true, complete, and accurate, to the best of my knowledge and belief.

Signature of Employee	Date

PS Form **991,** October 1993 *(Page 2 of 5)*

Statement of Qualifications	Name Pritchett, Matthew R.
Announcement Number Not Listed	Position Applied For Supervisor, Mails

Applicant position requirements are enumerated on the vacancy announcement. Enter the requirement in the space provided and explain your qualifications in reference to the requirement. A situation/task-action-result format for describing qualifications is recommended.

APPLICANT - COPY THIS PAGE. USE ONE PAGE PER REQUIREMENT/FACTOR.

Requirement/Factor   Oral Communications

The Goodyear Tire Company determined its 5% absenteeism rate was due to poor human relations. I was selected to co-chair a seminar program based on the "Quality of Work Life" concept in order to correct this deficiency. During a two year period I taught over 3,200 members of the hourly and salaried workforce the theories of Gregor, T.A. Farris, and others, thereby changing the behavior of the workforce. At termination, the absenteeism rate was 1.75%.

Having been a 204B Supervisor since 2003 and a Mail Handler from 2001, I have been commended for my strong oral communications skills as I have become knowledgeable of the operating procedures and goals of the Processing and Distribution Center and of the U.S. Postal Service. I am currently taking the home study course "Oral Communications for Supervisors" course 95-W-32 which is giving me more of an opportunity to become knowledgeable of postal service operating procedures and what is expected of supervisory personnel.

I also am a member of A+ (Afro-American Postal League United for Success), a program within the U.S. Postal Service designed to help employees promote corporate goals, mentor employees, foster communications within the postal system. In my spare time, I am a member of the Toastmasters Club, and I have given more than three dozen speeches as I have refined my skills within the professional environment of the Toastmasters Club.

Reference Number	Reference Name & Phone Number *(For use of review committee & selector)*
12	Mr. Fred Smith, Department Foreman phone (910) 483-6611

PS Form **991,** October 1993 *(Page 3 of 5)*

Announcement Number	Position Applied For
Not Listed	Supervisor, Mails

Applicant position requirements are enumerated on the vacancy announcement. Enter the requirement in the space provided and explain your qualifications in reference to the requirement. A situation/task-action-result format for describing qualifications is recommended.

APPLICANT - COPY THIS PAGE. USE ONE PAGE PER REQUIREMENT/FACTOR.

Requirement/Factor Leadership

As a proud member of the National Guard during the Middle East conflict, I was assigned to lead a non-English speaking battalion of Arabs into combat operations. My only means of communication were hand signals and eye contact. I trained this unit in immediate action drills for initial contact with opposing forces and established hand and arm signals for use in sustained encounters. The proficiency of my unit earned it two combat unit citations and I was awarded the Cross of Gallantry with Silver Star.

As a 204B Supervisor and Mail Handler, I direct or coordinate actions so that specific tasks or goals can be accomplished while supervising from seven to as many as 25 people in mail handling duties. I oversee a group of people whose goal every day is to process a large volume of outgoing second class mail which must be sorted into the correct containers and further sent on by truck or plane to other destinations. In this capacity I provide the leadership and example of how to get the work done most efficiency and to use time and not waste it in unnecessary activities. I also coordinate with other post offices and airport personnel and am familiar with what each employee does so that the work load is distributed properly and everything is done on time. One reason I was chosen for a supervisory role so soon in my career with the USPS was my ability to provide leadership to other employees regarding the necessity of working according to schedules and proper guidelines.

Reference Number	Reference Name & Phone Number (For use of review committee & selector)
5 & 16	CSM Mitchell, R.O.T.C. Instructor phone (910) 483-6611

PS Form **991**, October 1993 *(Page 3 of 5)*

Statement of Qualifications	Name
	Pritchett, Matthew R.

Announcement Number	Position Applied For
Not Listed	Supervisor, Mails

Applicant position requirements are enumerated on the vacancy announcement. Enter the requirement in the space provided and explain your qualifications in reference to the requirement. A situation/task-action-result format for describing qualifications is recommended.

APPLICANT - COPY THIS PAGE. USE ONE PAGE PER REQUIREMENT/FACTOR.

Requirement/Factor   Human Relations

_____

I was the 204-B platform supervisor. Two trailers arrived at the platform, one partially bedloaded, the other with roll-off equipment. Production priorities required their simultaneous unloading. The five-man platform crew stated that all five were needed to operate the trailer belt due to a prior practice safety agreement and a grievance would be filed if anyone was removed. I explained that the person inside the trailer could be observed by the reader, I could observe the individual performing roll-off, and one person on each side of the belt provided adequate safety. No grievance was filed and the trailers were off-loaded through the use of learned human relations techniques.

As a 204B Supervisor and Mail Handler, I demonstrate the ability to interact with others and to be tactful. I supervise from seven up to 25 people, deal on a regular basis with personnel from other post offices, and communicate with personnel from the airport while coordinating mail shipments. While ensuring that second class mail is sorted, prioritized, and prepared for transportation on from our regional center, one of my responsibilities is getting the most out of each employee. I must be tactful while disciplining employees for rules infractions and when counseling them one-on-one about their status and performance. I provide for fair distribution of the work load so that if an employee is slower at one task than another employee, I can move people around so that everyone understands that people's strong points are being considered in order to reach our goals and complete all tasks in a timely manner.

Reference Number	Reference Name & Phone Number *(For use of review committee & selector)*
12	Mr. Daniel Johnson, Tour Superintendent phone (910) 483-6611

Statement of Qualifications	Name: Pritchett, Matthew R.
Announcement Number: Not Listed	Position Applied For: Supervisor, Mails

Applicant position requirements are enumerated on the vacancy announcement. Enter the requirement in the space provided and explain your qualifications in reference to the requirement. A situation/task-action-result format for describing qualifications is recommended.

APPLICANT - COPY THIS PAGE. USE ONE PAGE PER REQUIREMENT/FACTOR.

Requirement/Factor   Problem Analysis

The Goodyear Tire Company Department 320 was experiencing overall low productivity. My assistance was requested to resolve the problem. I interviewed the work force, observed the operations, and gathered information on all three shifts. My analysis showed the poor air quality, a sustained 6-day work week, and no established goals were the major reason for the problem. An air filtration system was installed and it was agreed, if 1.2 million pounds of rubber remained in inventory, a work schedule modification would be made. Inventory was maintained and volunteer overtime performed Saturday work.

As a 204B Supervisor and Mail Handler at the Processing and Distribution Center, I have used my analytical and problem-solving skills to analyze problems and the work performance of from seven up to 25 employees and to find solutions. I have been effective in making decisions so that mail is routed correctly and on schedule while becoming familiar with every task carried out by the people under my supervision. For instance, by knowing each job as well as each person's strongest skills, I can move employees around and am authorized to place people in higher level tasks — such as placing a step 4 worker in a step 5 job — so that the work gets done and time is not wasted.

Reference Number	Reference Name & Phone Number *(For use of review committee & selector)*
1 & 6	Mr. Casey Usher, Department 320 Foreman phone (910) 483-6611

PS Form **991**, October 1993 *(Page 3 of 5)*

Statement of Qualifications	Name
	Pritchett, Matthew R.

Announcement Number	Position Applied For
Not Listed	Supervisor, Mails

Applicant position requirements are enumerated on the vacancy announcement. Enter the requirement in the space provided and explain your qualifications in reference to the requirement. A situation/task-action-result format for describing qualifications is recommended.

APPLICANT - COPY THIS PAGE. USE ONE PAGE PER REQUIREMENT/FACTOR.

Requirement/Factor   Decision Making

While serving as a Special Forces Officer in the Middle East, I was detailed Team Leader of a Special Operations Group. My mission was to perform operations in third countries. I developed plans, conducted mission training, and was then flown to a second friendly country. I evaluated intelligence, weather, and conducted overflights in order to select possible insertion and extraction locations within the operational area. I made all operational decisions after insertion into the third country and had operational control of all American aircraft in the air over the Middle East. My unit was never compromised or failed to complete a mission.

As a 204B Supervisor and Mail Handler, I develop and evaluate plans and take action to see that they are carried out each day. While supervising from seven up to 25 employees carrying out mail handling duties I see that outgoing second class mail is broken down and properly distributed. Each day is different because of the volume of mail going out and the number of people needed to carry out the process. I move employees into different tasks so that the work is done correctly. By knowing the functions and tasks needed in each job I can see if problems are occurring and move personnel around so that each job is taken care of.

Reference Number	Reference Name & Phone Number *(For use of review committee & selector)*
4	Mr. Roger Young, E. & L.R. phone (910) 483-6611

PS Form **991**, October 1993 *(Page 3 of 5)*

Statement of Qualifications	Name
	Pritchett, Matthew R.

Announcement Number	Position Applied For
Not Listed	Supervisor, Mails

Applicant position requirements are enumerated on the vacancy announcement. Enter the requirement in the space provided and explain your qualifications in reference to the requirement. A situation/task-action-result format for describing qualifications is recommended.

APPLICANT - COPY THIS PAGE. USE ONE PAGE PER REQUIREMENT/FACTOR.

Requirement/Factor   Written Communications

I have been detailed Crewleader of the 010 operation (with the acquiesce of more senior mail handlers) on Saturdays and holidays for over eight months. I have never failed to make 010 clearance. Mr. Turner requested information regarding how I eliminated bottlenecks in the operation. I provided Mr. Turner with a nine-page narrative with 11 attached diagrams explaining my analysis and 010 operating procedures. This document was tabbed, keyed, and referenced. Mr. Turner stated it was one of the most professionally done documents he had received as Manager of Human Resources.

As a 204B Supervisor and Mail Handler, I am the supervisor of from seven up to 25 employees, a number which varies from day to day depending on the volume of mail. I write regular reports and employee evaluations because of my responsibilities in discipline and counseling employees. I track manhours, breaks, lunches, sick leave, and vacation time.

Reference Number	Reference Name & Phone Number (For use of review committee & selector)
1 & 6	Mr. Gregory Turner, Manager of Human Resources phone (910) 483-6611

PS Form **991**, October 1993 (Page 3 of 5)

Statement of Qualifications	Name Pritchett, Matthew R.
Announcement Number Not Listed	Position Applied For Supervisor, Mails

Applicant position requirements are enumerated on the vacancy announcement. Enter the requirement in the space provided and explain your qualifications in reference to the requirement. A situation/task-action-result format for describing qualifications is recommended.

APPLICANT - COPY THIS PAGE. USE ONE PAGE PER REQUIREMENT/FACTOR.

Requirement/Factor   Mathematical Computations

While supervising the O.C.R. operation, I noticed the required production reporting forms were requesting two different methods of reporting operational time. My task was to determine the method endorsed by the finance department. On my nonscheduled day I met with Mr. Johnson, the individual receiving these reports in the finance department. He stated that my reports, filled out in hundredths of a minute, had been completed correctly. I am continuing to utilize the procedures advocated by the finance department. While working for the USPS, I have used basic mathematical skills to calculate such things as employee hours worked, vacation time and sick leave, as well as overtime hours and pay.

Throughout my service in the U.S. Army, I advanced to the rank of Captain, and it was a necessity that I demonstrate outstanding mathematical skills. I volunteered as an Income Tax Preparer in my spare time, and I utilized my strong mathematical skills to calculate tax payments. As a military officer, I became the "resident expert" on Excel software as I developed unique spreadsheets designed to monitor budgetary funds and track expenses. I trained junior military officers in the use of Excel and in the basics of financial management. Previously as a Business student at Arizona State University, I excelled in financial management courses including Managerial Accounting.

Reference Number	Reference Name & Phone Number (For use of review committee & selector)
1 & 3	Mr. David Johnson, Finance phone (910) 483-6611

PS Form **991**, October 1993 *(Page 3 of 5)*

Statement of Qualifications	Name
	Pritchett, Matthew R.

Announcement Number	Position Applied For
Not Listed	Supervisor, Mails

Applicant position requirements are enumerated on the vacancy announcement. Enter the requirement in the space provided and explain your qualifications in reference to the requirement. A situation/task-action-result format for describing qualifications is recommended.

APPLICANT - COPY THIS PAGE. USE ONE PAGE PER REQUIREMENT/FACTOR.

Requirement/Factor   Safety

In 2003 a new culling belt assembly was placed in operation. This assembly presented numerous safety hazards to include sharp edges and an open chainhousing. I reported these conditions to Mr. Cowley, supervisor. He stated that a way to remove the unsafe situation needed to be found. I discussed this hazard with the mailhandler culling crew and members of maintenance. All parties agreed the hazard could be eliminated by reversing the culling set-up and working the mail from the opposite side of the belt. This plan was implemented and the safety hazard removed. Having worked for the U.S. Postal Service since February 2003 and having rapidly advanced to a supervisory position, I have become knowledgeable of safety procedures in the workplace, of accident prevention and emergency procedures, and of what is necessary to keep the work place safe for all employees.

During my service in the U.S. Army, I was constantly aware of safety in the work place and of the special safety and emergency response requirements in an environment where there were numerous danger areas due to aircraft fuel, electronics equipment, and the potential for fires and accidents. I was always known for my insistence on enforcing safety procedures and policies and for training younger personnel in important actions and procedures. During my military career I was heavily involved in safety awareness and in ensuring compliance with all applicable rules and regulations.

Reference Number	Reference Name & Phone Number (For use of review committee & selector)
9	Mr. Joseph Cowley, Supervisor phone (910) 483-6611

PS Form **991**, October 1993 (Page 3 of 5)

Statement of Qualifications	Name Pritchett, Matthew R.
Announcement Number Not Listed	Position Applied For Supervisor, Mails

Applicant position requirements are enumerated on the vacancy announcement. Enter the requirement in the space provided and explain your qualifications in reference to the requirement. A situation/task-action-result format for describing qualifications is recommended.

APPLICANT - COPY THIS PAGE. USE ONE PAGE PER REQUIREMENT/FACTOR.

Requirement/Factor   Job Knowledge

I had not been trained for the Floor Supervision position when I was requested to perform this assignment by the Acting Tour Superintendent. I realized this position's task was to ensure that the mail was received, dispatched, and processed through the internal mail flow expeditiously. I achieved this by coordinating with supervisors in order to avoid potential sources of delay, i.e., I required oversized Mother's Day cards be pulled from the culling belt, cancelled, and sent immediately to the F.S.M. I ensured mail not read on the O.C.R. was sent to the L.S.M. in order to expedite the mail flow and not delay these operations. Our tour made plans and all mail was dispatched on time.

Reference Number	Reference Name & Phone Number (For use of review committee & selector)
7	Ms. Agnes B. Novak, Supervisor phone (910) 483-6611

PS Form **991**, October 1993 (Page 3 of 5)

Requirements Page 9 of 14

116 Part Two: The 991 and the Statement of Qualifications

Statement of Qualifications	Name
	Pritchett, Matthew R.

Announcement Number	Position Applied For
Not Listed	Supervisor, Mails

Applicant position requirements are enumerated on the vacancy announcement. Enter the requirement in the space provided and explain your qualifications in reference to the requirement. A situation/task-action-result format for describing qualifications is recommended.

APPLICANT - COPY THIS PAGE. USE ONE PAGE PER REQUIREMENT/FACTOR.

Requirement/Factor   Other Pertinent Information

In the preceding pages, position requirements were listed to which I have responded. As in most things, there are intangibles that require consideration. S.T.A.R. cannot measure of the sense of duty, responsibility, or character one develops when he is required to make decisions in combat situations. No questionnaire can measure the tenacity or integrity required to be promoted from Lieutenant to Captain within three years.

Nothing can rate morality or the code of ethics developed by being raised by a Baptist minister. These intangibles are not rated but are necessary. I was proud to serve my country as a military officer, and I subscribed to the highest code of ethics and morality as "an officer and a gentleman." I believe my job performance and life experience has prepared me for this position, and I offer a character and reputation that is of the highest calibre.

Reference Number	Reference Name & Phone Number *(For use of review committee & selector)*

Statement of Qualifications	Name Pritchett, Matthew R.
Announcement Number Not Listed	Position Applied For Supervisor, Mails

Applicant position requirements are enumerated on the vacancy announcement. Enter the requirement in the space provided and explain your qualifications in reference to the requirement. A situation/task-action-result format for describing qualifications is recommended.

APPLICANT - COPY THIS PAGE. USE ONE PAGE PER REQUIREMENT/FACTOR.

Requirement/Factor Oral Communications

The Goodyear Tire Company, Yuma Plant, determined that the high rates of absenteeism, tardiness, accidents, and grievances were the direct result of poor human relations. A two-day seminar program for all employees of the plant, based on the General Motors Town "Quality of Work Life" concept, was initiated. I was selected to co-chair the seminars.

I attended a two-week intensive training program and received instruction on the theories of Gregor, T. A. Farris, and others. The knowledge acquired from this training proved valuable initially in controlling a class of 30 hourly and salaried individuals. Because of my comprehension of these theories, I was able to effectively utilize factual persuasion to communicate these ideas and instructive information, thereby changing the behavior of the workforce.

The program lasted for two years. I had instructed over 3,200 salaried and hourly employees in human relations during this period. The absenteeism rate had been 5% at the program's inception and 1.75% at its termination. Grievances, accidents, and tardiness had also improved.

Reference Number	Reference Name & Phone Number *(For use of review committee & selector)*

PS Form **991,** October 1993 *(Page 3 of 5)*   Requirements Page <u>11</u> of <u>14</u>

<table>
<tr><td rowspan="2">Statement of Qualifications</td><td>Name</td></tr>
<tr><td>Pritchett, Matthew R.</td></tr>
<tr><td>Announcement Number</td><td>Position Applied For</td></tr>
<tr><td>Not Listed</td><td>Supervisor, Mails</td></tr>
</table>

Applicant position requirements are enumerated on the vacancy announcement. Enter the requirement in the space provided and explain your qualifications in reference to the requirement. A situation/task-action-result format for describing qualifications is recommended.

APPLICANT - COPY THIS PAGE. USE ONE PAGE PER REQUIREMENT/FACTOR.

Requirement/Factor   Leadership

My greatest leadership challenge was during the Middle East Conflict. I was assigned as Commanding Officer. The battalion consisted of 538 Arab soldiers, divided into three infantry company size units. Each company was commanded by an American senior N.C.O. My challenge was to lead these men into battalion size combat operations without the benefit of verbal communications.

I realized my unit was reading my facial expressions and body language for information and direction. This became my leadership tools. In order to utilize these tools, it was necessary for me to be in control of my emotions at all times. I was required to stand when engaging with opposing forces to enable the Arabs to see me. A frown, nod, arm, or hand gesture conveyed a command.

During a two-month operation, my three companies operated in unison. I was able to maintain control and command, under fire, and through the use of non-verbal communications.

While in the Middle East, I was assigned as the Team Leader of Reconnaissance Team. My mission was to perform functions in third countries for our government. I would develop a plan of operation to include tactics, personnel, equipment, and necessary supplies. After I had conducted mission training, we were flown to a second friendly country. During this period, I conducted aerial overflights to select possible insertion and extraction locations and evaluated intelligence and weather.

I made all operational decision after insertion into the third country, and on occasion, depending on the mission, had operational control of all American aircraft in the air over the Middle East.

<table>
<tr><td>Reference Number</td><td>Reference Name & Phone Number (For use of review committee & selector)</td></tr>
</table>

Government Jobs Series edited by Anne McKinney **119**

Statement of Qualifications	Name
	Pritchett, Matthew R.

Announcement Number	Position Applied For
Not Listed	Supervisor, Mails

Applicant position requirements are enumerated on the vacancy announcement. Enter the requirement in the space provided and explain your qualifications in reference to the requirement. A situation/task-action-result format for describing qualifications is recommended.

APPLICANT - COPY THIS PAGE. USE ONE PAGE PER REQUIREMENT/FACTOR.

Requirement/Factor Human Relations

In January 2004, I was acting as a mail crew leader. A mail handler approached me carrying two flat trays filled with postcards and asked if he could cancel them on the flier-canceling machine. A micro-mark canceling machine operator entered the conversation stating that he was supposed to run the postcards, that the cards had always been saved for him to run at the end of his tour, and that he needed them for his cancellation count.

I realized that I was dealing with a past practice situation that was delaying the mail. If I chose to change this practice, I would upset the status quo. I explained that by allowing the postcards to accumulate, we were delaying the mail. I advised him that we would not be serving our customers or our own best interest by this delay. The operator departed and the postcards were ran on the flier canceller. A short time later the operator asked me a question, unrelated to the postcards, in a friendly and courteous manner.

The utilization of the words "we" and "our" had made the operator a part of the solution. By explaining and advising rather than telling and directing, I had not positioned myself as an authority figure. A past practice had changed, the distribution of mail had been expedited, the operator had retained his dignity, and I had gained his willing cooperation due to the factual use of learned human techniques.

Reference Number	Reference Name & Phone Number *(For use of review committee & selector)*

PS Form **991**, October 1993 *(Page 3 of 5)*

Statement of Qualifications	Name
	Pritchett, Matthew R.

Announcement Number	Position Applied For
Not Listed	Supervisor, Mails

Applicant position requirements are enumerated on the vacancy announcement. Enter the requirement in the space provided and explain your qualifications in reference to the requirement. A situation/task-action-result format for describing qualifications is recommended.

APPLICANT - COPY THIS PAGE. USE ONE PAGE PER REQUIREMENT/FACTOR.

Requirement/Factor   Problem Analysis

While at Goodyear Tire Company, I was elected to the Local Union position of Division Chairman. The Department 320 Foreman informed me of productivity problems and asked for my assistance.

I asked each hourly employee for three items necessary to improve productivity. I had one-on-one private meetings with employees known to be chronic complaints. I was authorized to enter the plant on a 24-hour basis. I used this authorization to visit the other two shifts twice a week for over a month to make observations and collect information.

I found two common themes during my evaluation: (1) The air quality was terrible. Everyone looked as if they were coal miners and felt dirty. The pure carbon powder, used to decrease tire wear, was not being removed from the air. (2) The department had been on a six day work week for four years due to its inability to meet production requirements. With only one unscheduled day per week, some employees were attempting to put an entire weekend of fun into one day. This resulted in the 9% absenteeism rate on Saturdays. I organized my information and evaluation of the problem into a written report and gave an oral presentation to the plant, production, and department managers. The company invested over $250,000 in a vacuum system to remove the excess carbon powder from the air, and agreed, if 1.2 million pounds of rubber remained in inventory, adjustments could be made to the Saturday work schedule.

During the three months required to install the vacuum system, productivity increased. The department broke the existing industry record for poundage produced in a 24-hour period. Saturday work was reduced to one eight-hour shift, manned by volunteer time, and the Saturday absenteeism was reduced to less than 1%.

Reference Number	Reference Name & Phone Number *(For use of review committee & selector)*

In order to be considered for the job you want, you often must also demonstrate certain knowledge, skills, or abilities (KSAs). In other words, you need to also submit written narrative statements which microscopically focus on your particular knowledge, skill, or ability in a certain area. The next few pages are filled with examples of excellent KSAs. If you wish to see many other examples of KSAs, you may look for another book published by PREP: "Real KSAs--Knowledge, Skills & Abilities--for Government Jobs." Although you will be able to use the Federal Resume you prepare in order to apply for all sorts of jobs in the federal government, the KSAs you write are particular to a specific job and you may be able to use the KSAs you write only one time. If you get into the Civil Service system, however, you will discover that many KSAs tend to appear on lots of different job announcement bulletins. For example, "Ability to communicate orally and in writing" is a frequently requested KSA. This means that you would be able to use and re-use this KSA for any job bulletin which requests you to give evidence of your ability in this area.

What does "Screen Out" mean? If you see that a KSA is requested and the words "Screen out" are mentioned beside the KSA, this means that this KSA is of vital importance in "getting you in the door." If the individuals who review your application feel that your screen-out KSA does not establish your strengths in this area, you will not be considered as a candidate for the job. You need to make sure that any screen-out KSA is especially well-written and comprehensive.

How long can a KSA be? A job vacancy announcement bulletin may specify a length for the KSAs it requests. Sometimes KSAs can be 1-2 pages long each, but sometimes you are asked to submit several KSAs within a maximum of two pages. Remember that the purpose of a KSA is to microscopically examine your level of competence in a specific area, so you need to be extremely detailed and comprehensive. Give examples and details wherever possible. For example, your written communication skills might appear more credible if you provide the details of the kinds of reports and paperwork you prepared. KSAs are extremely important in "getting you in the door" for a federal government job. If you are working under a tight deadline in preparing your paperwork for a federal government position, don't spend all your time preparing the Federal Resume if you also have KSAs to do. Create "blockbuster" KSAs as well!

If you are lucky enough to get an interview, you need to understand that a post office interview is like any other interview. You are trying to sell yourself! Since it may have been a long time (months probably) between submitting your paperwork and interviewing for the job, it's wise to prepare for the interview by reading the KSAs you submitted.

The U.S. Postal Service may request that you demonstrate your knowledge, skills, or abilities by presenting your information within a precise framework referred to as "STAR." STAR stands for Situation, Task, Action, and Result, and you are asked to describe a situation or event in which you did, said, produced, or accomplished something which illustrated your level of proficiency related to that KSA. Postal Service KSAs based on the STAR format can be shorter than KSAs for other federal service jobs. Often a single incident will reveal your competence in a certain area. Remember here to be very detailed, and try to make sure that you clearly show the result you were able to achieve by your involvement in the situation or event you are describing. In KSAs for non-postal-service jobs, you often need to "translate" jargon into language that can be understood by others. For example, military professionals need to make sure that their experience is "translated" into terminology that civilians can understand. In the case of postal service KSAs, however, you are often writing about technical matters for an audience that is very familiar with the "language" of the postal service, so you can feel comfortable using technical terminology and acronyms.

EXAMPLE of a KSA

JOHN McMILLAN
SSN: 000-11-2222
204B SUPERVISOR/MAIL HANDLER, ANNOUNCEMENT #XYZ123

204B SUPERVISOR/
MAIL HANDLER,
Announcement
#XYZ123
KSA #1

KSA #1: ORAL COMMUNICATIONS: Ability to communicate information, instructions, or ideas orally in a clear and concise manner in individual or group situations.

From February 2004-present as a 204B Supervisor/Mail Handler at the Little Rock (AR) Processing and Distribution Center, I communicate on a regular and routine daily basis with from seven to 25 people who are under my direct supervision while on mail handling duties. I oversee activities as they break down, process, and sort mail at this main regional distribution center which covers the greater Little Rock area and give them verbal instructions so they understand what I am requesting them to do as I prioritize the work flow. In this job I have used my oral communication skills to counsel employees one-on-one and to reprimand any employee who is not pulling his fair share of the work load. I have become more effective in motivating people so that they are more productive and so that work is done according to union requirements and that time is not wasted. From May 2003 to February 2004 as a Mail Handler in the same facility and from February to May 2003 as a Trainee, I quickly learned that proper movement of the mail is the priority and was selected within six to eight months for a supervisory position. One reason I was chosen for a supervisory role so soon was my ability to communicate to other employees the necessity of working according to schedules and proper guidelines.

As a Manager and Cashier for a 7-11 convenience store in Conway, AR, from January 2002 to February 2003, I used my verbal communication skills while dealing with members of the public in a busy gas station-convenience store setting by answering their questions and assisting them with purchases.

Prior to 2002, I served in the U.S. Air Force for more than 20 years culminating in supervisory and leadership positions where my oral communication skills were demonstrated in numerous assignments as a training specialist and technical instructor. From 1989 until around March 1998, I was a supervisor and instructor in a qualification training program and provided formal classroom instruction as well as remedial tutoring for aircraft mechanics at Barksdale AFB, TN. On a formal evaluation in March of 1994, I was cited for my communication and leadership skills which resulted in a crew chief program rated as "second to none." On a 1991 annual evaluation of my performance as a Training Instructor, was cited for my ability to take complex tasks and break them into simple and understandable terms and for being named by students as one of the organization's most effective and respected instructors.

KSA #2: LEADERSHIP: Ability to direct or coordinate individual or group action in order to accomplish a task or goal.

From February 2004 to present as a 204B Supervisor and Mail Handler at the Little Rock Processing and Distribution Center, Little Rock, AR, I direct or coordinate actions so that specific tasks or goals can be accomplished while supervising from seven to as many as 25 people in mail handling duties. I oversee a group of people whose goal every day is to process a large volume of outgoing second class mail which must be sorted into the correct containers and further sent on by truck or plane to other destinations. In this capacity I provide the leadership and example of how to get the work done most efficiency and to use time and not waste it in unnecessary activities. I also coordinate with other post offices and airport personnel and am familiar with what each employee does so that the work load is distributed properly and everything is done on time. From May 2003 to February 2004 as a Mail Handler in the same facility and from February to May 2003 as a Trainee, I quickly learned that proper movement of the mail is the priority and was selected within six to eight months for a supervisory position. One reason I was chosen for a supervisory role so soon was my ability to communicate to other employees the necessity of working according to schedules and proper guidelines.

My earlier experience was focused on service in the U.S. Air Force up until 2002. During my more than 20 years in military service, I held numerous leadership roles where I was effective in directing or coordinating individual or group efforts toward reaching goals or completing tasks. In one of my last military assignments prior to retirement, I was credited with providing the leadership which led a training program to a 25% increase in the number of classes taught and to 100% of all students graduating for a full fiscal year. During my years as an aircraft mechanic and as an instructor I was selected for leadership roles and consistently evaluated as an "exceptionally effective leader."

EXAMPLE of a KSA

JOHN McMILLAN
SSN: 000-11-2222
204B SUPERVISOR/MAIL HANDLER, ANNOUNCEMENT #XYZ123

**204B SUPERVISOR/
MAIL HANDLER,
Announcement
#XYZ123
KSA #3**

KSA #3: HUMAN RELATIONS: Ability to interact tactfully and relate well with others.

As a 204B Supervisor and Mail Handler at the Little Rock Processing and Distribution Center, Little Rock, AR, I demonstrate the ability to interact with others and to be tactful. I supervise from seven up to 25 people, deal on a regular basis with personnel from other post offices, and communicate with personnel from the airport while coordinating mail shipments. One of my responsibilities while ensuring that second class mail is sorted, prioritized, and prepared for transportation on from our regional center is getting the most out of each employee. I must be tactful while disciplining employees for rules infractions and when counseling them one-on-one about their status and performance. I provide for fair distribution of the work load so that if an employee is slower at one task than another, I can move people around so that everyone understands that people's strong points are being considered in order to reach our goals and complete all tasks in a timely manner.

During my more than 20 years of service in the U.S. Air Force which ended with my retirement in 2001, as an instructor for technical courses, an aircraft mechanics, and in my last military assignments in mobility planning, I was always part of a team. Consistently cited for my leadership abilities, I often provided one-on-one counseling for personnel under my direct supervision and after reaching supervisory status early in my military career, provided human resources management while completing regular performance evaluations for each of the up to 46 people under my direct supervision. As a senior supervisory instructor, I also evaluated and critiqued the performance of instructors and tactfully made suggestions of ways they could increase their effectiveness.

KSA #4: PROBLEM ANALYSIS: Ability to analyze problems, work performance, suggestions, and complaints by listening, observing, gathering, organizing, and interpreting information.

Since February 1996 as a 204B Supervisor and Mail Handler at the Little Rock (AR) Processing and Distribution Center, I have used my powers of observation and listening skills to analyze problems and the work performance of from seven to 25 employees and to find solutions. I have been effective in making decisions so that mail is routed correctly and on schedule while becoming familiar with every task carried out by the people under my supervision. For instance, by knowing each job as well as each person's strongest skills, I can move employees around and am authorized to place people in higher level tasks — such as placing a step 4 worker in a step 5 job — so that the work gets done and time is not wasted.

During my more than 20 years of service in the U.S. Air Force which ended with my retirement in 2001, I was often involved in analyzing problems, work performance, and complaints while holding positions in mobility planning, technical instruction programs, and as an aircraft mechanic. From 1988 to 1998 I held leadership and supervisory roles and served as a technical instructor. One important example of how I used analytical and organizational skills was a 1996-97 project when I started with an empty building and took care of all the details which turned it into a functioning training headquarters operation with telephones, radios, audiovisual aids, and classroom furniture. I coordinated with other agencies, set up objectives and requirements, and determined the course of action that needed to be taken to ensure this project was staffed and ready for students on time.

EXAMPLE of a KSA

JOHN McMILLAN
SSN: 000-11-2222
204B SUPERVISOR/MAIL HANDLER, ANNOUNCEMENT #XYZ123

204B SUPERVISOR/ MAIL HANDLER, Announcement #XYZ123 KSA #5

KSA #5: DECISION MAKING: Ability to develop plans, evaluate their anticipated effectiveness, make decisions, and take appropriate action.

As a 204B Supervisor and Mail Handler at the Little Rock (AR) Processing and Distribution Center, I develop and evaluate plans and take action to see that they are carried out each day. While supervising from seven up to 25 employees carrying out mail handling duties I see that outgoing second class mail is broken down and properly distributed. Each day is different because of the volume of mail going out and the number of people needed to carry out the process. I move employees into different tasks so that the work is done correctly. By knowing the functions and tasks needed in each job I can see if problems are occurring and move personnel around so that each job is taken care of.

During my more than 20 years of service in the U.S. Air Force which ended with my retirement in 2001, I was often involved in analyzing problems, work performance, and complaints while holding positions in mobility planning, technical instruction programs, and as an aircraft mechanic. From 1988-98 I held leadership and supervisory roles and served as a technical instructor. One important example of how I used analytical and organizational skills was a 1996-97 project when I started with an empty building and took care of all the details which turned it into a functioning training headquarters operation with telephones, radios, audio-visual aids, and classroom furniture. I coordinated with other agencies, set up objectives and requirements, and determined the course of action that needed to be taken to ensure this project was staffed and ready for students on time.

JOHN McMILLAN
SSN: 000-11-2222
204B SUPERVISOR/MAIL HANDLER, ANNOUNCEMENT #XYZ123

KSA #6: WRITTEN COMMUNICATION: Ability to write letters, simple reports, and employee evaluations clearly and effectively and to complete standardized reporting forms accurately.

I have been a 204B Supervisor and Mail Handler at the Little Rock (AR) Processing and Distribution Center since February 2004. As the supervisor of from seven to 25 employees, a number which varies from day to day depending on the volume of mail, I write regular reports and employee evaluations because of my responsibilities in discipline and counseling employees. I track manhours, breaks, lunches, sick leave, and vacation time.

My written communication skills at writing letters, reports, and employee evaluations and in completing standardized reports were applied frequently during my more than 20 years serving in the U.S. Air Force. Approximately ten years of my military service was spent as a senior instructor for a skills qualification testing program. I wrote performance evaluations, maintained and updated lesson plans, developed training materials, supply and inventory control reports and documents and gained a strong base of experience in ensuring any written materials was clear, concise, and readily understandable.

EXAMPLE of a KSA

JOHN McMILLAN
SSN: 000-11-2222
204B SUPERVISOR/MAIL HANDLER, ANNOUNCEMENT #XYZ123

**204B SUPERVISOR/
MAIL HANDLER,
Announcement
#XYZ123
KSA #7**

KSA #7: MATHEMATICAL COMPUTATIONS: Ability to perform addition, subtraction, multiplication, and division with whole numbers, fractions, and decimals.

My ability to perform basic mathematical computations was most prominently applied while I was the Manager and Cashier at a 7-11 convenience store in Conway, AR, from January 2002 until February 2003, when I began working for the postal service. In a busy gas station-convenience store, I accepted cash and credit card payments and had to be able to quickly and accurately make change for customers.

Throughout my 20-year career in the U.S. Air Force and while working for the U.S. Postal Service from February 2003 until the present, I have used basic mathematics to calculate such things as employee hours worked, vacation time and sick leave, and to figure out how much overtime workers have built up.

KSA #8: SAFETY: Knowledge of safety procedures needed to ensure that safe working conditions are maintained, including knowledge of the procedures and techniques established to avoid injuries, and of normal accident prevention measures and emergency procedures.

Having worked for the U.S. Postal Service since February 2003 and having rapidly advanced to a supervisory position, I have become knowledgeable of safety procedures in the workplace, of accident prevention and emergency procedures, and of what is necessary to keep the work place safe for all employees.

During my more than 20 years of service in the U.S. Air Force I was constantly aware of safety in the work place and of the special safety and emergency response requirements in an environment where there were numerous danger areas due to aircraft fuel, electronics equipment, and the potential for fires and accidents. I was always known for my insistence on enforcing safety procedures and policies and for training younger personnel in important actions and procedures. During the early years of my military career I was an aircraft maintenance technician and was heavily involved in safety awareness and in ensuring compliance with all applicable rules and regulations.

KSA #9: JOB KNOWLEDGE: Knowledge of the operating procedures and the goal of the function to be supervised.

Having been a 204B Supervisor since February 2003, a Mail Handler from May 2003, and a Mail Handler Trainee from February to May 2003, I have become knowledgeable of the operating procedures and goals of the Little Rock Processing and Distribution Center and of the U.S. Postal Service. I am currently taking the home study course "Introduction to Postal Supervision" course 11561-00 which is giving me more of an opportunity to become knowledgeable of postal service operating procedures and what is expected of supervisory personnel. I also am a member of A+ (Afro-American Postal League United for Success), a program within the U.S. Postal Service designed to help employees promote corporate goals, mentor employees, foster communications within the postal system.

EXAMPLE of a KSA

DYLAN HANCOCK
SSN: 999-88-7777
ELECTRONIC TECHNICIAN, ANNOUNCEMENT #123XYZ

KSA #1: Knowledge of Windows NT Server.

As a U.S. Postal Service Electronic Technician, I have the working knowledge, skills, and abilities to work with operating systems to include the ability to work with Windows NT Server operating systems.

I have worked with Windows NT exclusive set of programs and interfaces which show remote access to the computer network. I know how to implement and use Windows NT Protocol. I have set up, forecast, and configured this operating system. I understand how the NT architecture and installation is used. I have full knowledge of how the Windows NT is designed, what conditions it works best with and the best installations procedures to use. I can manage the Windows NT files and run the applications. I have a working knowledge of day-to-day tasks of word processing, database management, spreadsheets, and computer networking.

As a result, I have the knowledge and educational background to work with many operating systems to include Windows NT Servers.

KSA #2: Ability to develop standards, processes and procedures in support of remote management and administration of Oracle databases for the USPS LAN platform. Includes, but not limited to: alerting mechanisms, system utilization, performance statistics and reporting, capacity planning, integrity monitoring; creation, population, maintenance, reorganization, backup, security, and recovery of databases.

As an Electronic Technician, I have a working knowledge and understanding of backup policies and procedures. I have backed up many operating systems' software. I have to regularly back up media from floppy drives and hard drives from disks and remove data to store the back up software in a safe place. Installed back ups as standby power supplies and uninterruptable power supplies. I have performed preventive and corrective maintenance on the operating system and peripheral devices. Preventive maintenance, I have to use the U.S. Postal Service method of disassembling and cleaning procedures. I have cleaned boards, connectors, and contacts, floppy drives, keyboards, mouses, and VDTs. I have worked on hard disk maintenance. I have used contact cleaner/lubricants, vacuum cleaners, brushes and swabs, and dusters. I have reseated socketed chips. Corrective maintenance, I have repaired power supplies, fans, and PC boards and PC ICS. Chips solder and resolder. Replaced cables and connectors and fuses. Used safety when working on the equipment and static maps. I have pulled many statistics and reports. Recovered lost databases when the IPSS system malfunctioned. I have never misused any security of any password such as giving one out. I use the USPS security accounts and policies on all operating systems, and security menu. I have used security administrators authority and category and classification. I worked with reorganization database management and utilization of storage space when it is degraded and wasteful of ongoing processing activity in database operations. Reorganized how data is stored and printed or displayed. To change the structure or contents of files, I have worked with creation dates and facilities programs, directories, files, keys, masks, and profiles. I have performed integrity monitoring, protection of systems, programs, and data form destruction and alteration. Worked with applications and system integrity. Performed work on CSU and DSU for LANS network.

As a result I have received training from Armstrong Atlantic State University, NRI Computers, and LANS support also many computer and software classes from the USPS Technical Training Center, Savannah, GA.

EXAMPLE of a KSA

DYLAN HANCOCK
SSN: 999-88-7777
ELECTRONIC TECHNICIAN, ANNOUNCEMENT #123XYZ

ELECTRONIC TECHNICIAN, ANNOUNCEMENT #123XYZ KSA #3

KSA #3: Ability to provide technical leadership of teams in the completion of time critical tasks.

As an Electronic Technician, I have provided technical leadership to my co-workers, supervisors, and managers.

I had to get the IPSS System up and running to process the mail to make the dispatch time at both the Savannah, GA, Processing & Distribution Center and the Savannah Remote Encoding Center. I informed the Electronic Technicians that they must observe all lights (LEDs) to the IPSS System. Each technician must have access to the main computer which is the alpha computer. Also access to the super monitor and report monitor. I informed the technician to check for loose cable connections in the IPSS System. I informed the technician if the hardware was okay to pull all the system reports. Then I informed the supervisor that it was okay to do a complete system shutdown and start up. The Electronic Technician got an okay from the supervisor. I proceeded to tell the Electronic Technician to do a cold/warm start on the upper bus to get rid of the software error. I had the technician to reconnect the site-to-site and I reconnected the VIP/VAP. The reason for doing the cold/warm complete system start up is to save the images at the P&DC side of operations. Once both the P&DC and the Remote Encoding Center were reconnected, the images I had at the REC when the P&DC side was down have to be sent back over to the P&DC for processing.

As a result the Electronic Technician at the Savannah P&DC Plant informed the supervisor that the IPSS System is up and running to process the mail without any plant failure. My sixteen (16) years in the U.S. Postal Service, my college education, as well as my U.S. Postal training has helped me to understand computers, computer programming, software, and hardware.

KSA #4: Ability to plan, design, develop, implement and support oracle database in a large, diverse, complex and widely distributed computing environment.

As an Electronic and Computer LAN Technician, I work with the planning, design, and the development of computer programming and many operating systems.

I have the knowledge to plan information in order to resolve problems in which I would rewrite the outlines as a list of individual program modules for the Program to Perform. Each program module will be considered individually and defined in detail separately from all other program modules. Then my outline will help me to place the program module in the correct order later. Once the module has been listed individually, I will add details to each program module by itself and each module will be a single logical unit within the entire program and can be defined as such. Later, the individual units will be put together again in the proper sequence. Once each module section of the program has been designed in detail, I will rewrite the solution procedure on a flow chart. The solution procedure will be presented in a format that will clearly show all the possible choices and decisions. I will then code the program into a series of instructions that the computer can understand and execute by using a computer language.

As a result, I have the knowledge to plan, design, develop, and work with many operating systems.

ELECTRONIC TECHNICIAN, ANNOUNCEMENT #123XYZ KSA #4

KSA #5: Ability to meet the varied and changing requirements of a large-scale mission critical production operations support environment.

I have worked in the USPS maintenance work force for 16 years.

Because I have worked in various positions in the postal service, I have demonstrated my ability to meet varied and changing requirements of a large-scale critical production operations support environment. My experience within the postal system has included custodial work, maintenance supervisor 204B, MPE Mechanic, and Electronic Technician. In the course of excelling in those varied positions, I have seen many changes and have been involved in many of the changes within the postal service. For example, the LSMs at one time were by far one of the better machines used to process the mail. Now, however, newer and better automation equipment processes the mail. I have also observed how the maintenance work force educated the electronics technicians to be better prepared to handle the new automation equipment and to understand the troubleshooting functions of that new equipment. In a similar manner, I have observed how the operation department is no longer complaining about better equipment to process the mail because, since new automated equipment came on line, the mail is being processed at an extremely high rate.

As a result of many such changes, the overall performance of all levels of the maintenance work force received training from MTSC and from the TTC to work on any type of automated equipment.

ELECTRONIC TECHNICIAN, ANNOUNCEMENT #123XYZ KSA #5

EXAMPLE of a KSA

DYLAN HANCOCK
SSN: 999-88-7777
ELECTRONIC TECHNICIAN, ANNOUNCEMENT #ABC123

ELECTRONIC TECHNICIAN, ANNOUNCEMENT #ABC123 KSA #1

KSA #1: Knowledge of maintenance support issues and technology for systems and equipment that support mail processing, customer services, and facility operations including safety and energy conservation practices.

In my experience as an Electronic Technician, I have acquired extensive knowledge of the technology that supports mail processing, and my background in maintenance enables me to understand the maintenance support issues related to such technology. I continue to enforce energy conservation principles by insisting that equipment and lights be turned off when not in use.

Throughout my career I have worked extensively ensuring that OSHA's strict rules and regulations are followed. Have served periodically as HAZMAT TAC Captain monitoring potential safety hazards and providing expertise regarding safety procedures during chemical spills.

As a U.S. Postal Service Electronic Technician, I have the working knowledge, skills, and abilities to work with operating systems to include the ability to work with Windows NT Server operating systems.

I have worked with Windows NT exclusive set of programs and interfaces which show remote access to the computer network. I know how to implement and use Windows NT Protocol. I have set up, forecast, and configured this operating system. I understand how the NT architecture and installation is used. I have full knowledge of how the Windows NT is designed, what conditions it works best with and the best installations procedures to use. I can manage the Windows NT files and run the applications. I have a working knowledge of day-to-day tasks of word processing, database management, spreadsheets, and computer networking.

As a result, I have the knowledge and educational background to work with many operating systems to include Windows NT Servers.

KSA #2: Ability to manage the planning of preventive and corrective maintenance and project work.

As a USPS Electronics Technician and MPE Mechanic, I have performed preventive maintenance to eliminate and also reduce the possibility of failure and the need for repairs on USPS machines. For example, I handled regular cleaning, lubrication, and servicing equipment in order to assure that equipment had adequate ventilation to avoid overheating. I also checked many cables and interconnections and I cleaned IPSS systems, MLOCRs, BCS, DBCS, LMSs, AFC and computers, VOTs, keyboards, and printers. In performing those mentioned cleaning and maintenance jobs, I used VOT cleaners and compressed air, alcohol, cotton swabs, and I assured that dust, dirt, paper scraps, and other debris which can often cause machine failure after building up in the equipment.

I have also used safety equipment and am knowledgeable of proper procedures for safeguarding and controlling the inventory of such equipment. Safety equipment I have used has included employee safety equipment. I have developed expert skills in lubricating mechanical devices with lubrication such as oil and grease on the shafts, gears, cams, and levers of the machines. I have checked to see that the interface cables are properly seated, and I know how to readjust the connections to assure that equipment is straight and secure in the socket. I have replaced belts on this equipment as well.

I also offer expertise in performing correction maintenance, and my troubleshooting skills are highly respected. When troubleshooting, I first identify the problem and then perform the actual repair that corrects the problem, which could be a mechanical, electronic, or user problem. The USPS has trained me to work both in the corrective and preventive maintenance areas. I then worked with other employees during projects in which we worked as a team to identify problem areas in order to have the system up and running with no delay in mail processing or delivery.

EXAMPLE of a KSA

DYLAN HANCOCK

SSN: 999-88-7777

ELECTRONIC TECHNICIAN, ANNOUNCEMENT #ABC123

KSA #3: Ability to evaluate the effectiveness of maintenance methods and procedures.

As a USPS Electronics Technician and MPE Mechanic, I have performed preventive maintenance to eliminate and also reduce the possibility of failure and the need for repairs on USPS machines. For example, I handled regular cleaning, lubrication, and servicing equipment in order to assure that equipment had adequate ventilation to avoid overheating. I also checked many cables and interconnections and I cleaned IPSS systems, MLOCRs, BCS, DBCS, LMSs, AFC and computers, VOTs, keyboards, and printers. In performing those mentioned cleaning and maintenance jobs, I used vacuum cleaners and compressed air, alcohol, cotton swabs, and I assured that dust, dirt, paper scraps, and other debris which can often cause machine failure after building up in the equipment.

I have also used safety equipment and am knowledgeable of proper procedures for safeguarding and controlling the inventory of such equipment. Safety equipment I have used has included employee safety equipment. I have developed expert skills in lubricating mechanical devices with lubrication such as oil and grease on the shafts, gears, cams, and levers of the machines. I have checked to see that the interface cables are properly seated, and I know how to readjust the connections to assure that equipment is straight and secure in the socket. I have replaced belts on this equipment as well.

I also offer expertise in performing correction maintenance, and my troubleshooting skills are highly respected. When troubleshooting, I first identify the problem and then perform the actual repair that corrects the problem, which could be a mechanical, electronic, or user problem. The USPS has trained me to work both in the corrective and preventive maintenance areas. I then worked with other employees during projects in which we worked as a team to identify problem areas in order to have the system up and running with no delay in mail processing or delivery.

DYLAN HANCOCK
SSN: 999-88-7777
ELECTRONIC TECHNICIAN, ANNOUNCEMENT #ABC123

KSA #4: Ability to develop and implement equipment logistics support plans.

I have monitored and evaluated and taken corrective action for performance of USPS systems and equipment such as the IPSS system, MLOCR, BCSs, DBCs, computers, printers, and AFC's equipment during the past 16 years that I have served the post office.

I will describe a situation in which my technical skills solved a major problem and resulted in the mail getting out on time despite a plant failure. Once I monitored the IPSS system when Savannah, GA P&DC could not connect their IPSS system to Savannah, GA Remote Encoding Center in order for the mail to be processed. In that situation, I evaluated the problem and I have found that the IPSS at the Savannah Remote Encoding Center was working efficiently. Then I went on to isolate the problem. I then evaluated that the Savannah, GA P&DC could not connect their site-to-site and also could not connect any of the ISSs. What I discovered is that the IPSS system had a fatal error message and the super monitor would not function, therefore causing a delay in the mail processing as well as a plant failure on the P&DC side. The corrective action I chose to take in that situation was to inform the supervisor and manager of the situation so that they would be fully informed. I also coordinated with the P&DC Electronic Technician so that the IPSS system would be back on line and so that the mail would get out on time. Then I disconnected the VIP/VAP and also informed the supervisor in order to assure good communication with the keyers at the remote site so that they could key the mail out while I worked on the P&DC problem. Then I proceeded by getting the superopa monitor back up, after which I effected a system shutdown and then a system startup which got rid of the software error. Subsequently, I took steps to get the software task ready. After that, I logged into both super and report monitors, performing a system startup using cold/warm to save the images and then reconnecting the ISSs and making a site/site and VIP/VAP connection, by which the mail processing was performed.

EXAMPLE of a KSA

DYLAN HANCOCK
SSN: 999-88-7777
ELECTRONIC TECHNICIAN, ANNOUNCEMENT #ABC123

ELECTRONIC TECHNICIAN, ANNOUNCEMENT #ABC123 KSA #5

KSA #5: Ability to prepare maintenance contract specifications, evaluate proposals, and ensure compliance with control specifications.

During the 16 years that I have worked for the postal system, I have been involved in the preparation and execution of maintenance contracts. While working in Atlanta, GA, I was an Electronic Technician and then as an Electronic Technician at the Savannah Remote Encoding facility, and also in Columbia, SC as a Detailed Electronic Technician and then as an MPE Mechanic in the Atlanta main post office. In those positions I prepared maintenance contract specifications, was involved in the evaluation of maintenance contract proposals, and also worked to ensure compliance with control specifications.

As an Electronic Technician, I have managed requested repair and maintenance work including evaluation of requests, work coordination, and monitoring of requests and coordination of work. I had to get the IPSS System up and running to process the mail to make the dispatch time at both the Savannah, GA, Processing & Distribution Center and the Savannah Remote Encoding Center. I informed the Electronic Technicians that they must observe all lights (LEDs) to the IPSS System. Each technician must have access to the main computer which is the alpha computer. Also access to the super monitor and report monitor. I informed the technician to check for loose cable connections in the IPSS System. I informed the technician if the hardware was okay to pull all the system reports. Then I informed the supervisor that it was okay to do a complete system shutdown and start up. The Electronic Technician got an okay from the supervisor. I proceeded to tell the Electronic Technician to do a cold/warm start on the upper bus to get rid of the software error. I had the technician to reconnect the site-to-site and I reconnected the VIP/VAP. The reason for doing the cold/warm complete system start up is to save the images at the P&DC side of operations. Once both the P&DC and the Remote Encoding Center were reconnected, the images I had at the REC when the P&DC side was down have to be sent back over to the P&DC for processing.

As a result the Electronic Technician at the Savannah P&DC Plant informed the supervisor that the IPSS System is up and running to process the mail without any plant failure. My sixteen (16) years in the U.S. Postal Service, my college education, as well as my U.S. Postal training has helped me to understand computers, computer programming, software, and hardware.

KSA #6: Ability to manage requested repair and maintenance work including evaluation of requests, work coordination, and monitoring of work.

As an Electronic Technician, I have managed requested repair and maintenance work including evaluation of requests, work coordination, and monitoring of requests and coordination of work.

I had to get the IPSS System up and running to process the mail to make the dispatch time at both the Savannah, GA, Processing & Distribution Center and the Savannah Remote Encoding Center. I informed the Electronic Technicians that they must observe all lights (LEDs) to the IPSS System. Each technician must have access to the main computer which is the alpha computer. Also access to the super monitor and report monitor. I informed the technician to check for loose cable connections in the IPSS System. I informed the technician if the hardware was okay to pull all the system reports. Then I informed the supervisor that it was okay to do a complete system shutdown and start up. The Electronic Technician got an okay from the supervisor. I proceeded to tell the Electronic Technician to do a cold/warm start on the upper bus to get rid of the software error. I had the technician to reconnect the site-to-site and I reconnected the VIP/VAP. The reason for doing the cold/warm complete system start up is to save the images at the P&DC side of operations. Once both the P&DC and the Remote Encoding Center were reconnected, the images I had at the REC when the P&DC side was down have to be sent back over to the P&DC for processing.

As a result the Electronic Technician at the Savannah P&DC Plant informed the supervisor that the IPSS System is up and running to process the mail without any plant failure. My sixteen (16) years in the U.S. Postal Service, my college education, as well as my U.S. Postal training has helped me to understand computers, computer programming, software, and hardware.

EXAMPLE of a KSA

DYLAN HANCOCK
SSN: 999-88-7777
ELECTRONIC TECHNICIAN, ANNOUNCEMENT #ABC123

KSA #7: Ability to manage the reporting of maintenance operational data.

As a 204B supervisor in the maintenance department, I have handed out work orders and route sheets for the MPE mechanics, electronics technicians, and custodians. When a work order is completed I would close that work order out and inform the other tours that the work order was completed. I am skilled at filing work orders away. When necessary, I have also turned work orders over to other tours when the employees could not complete the work order in a timely manner. Furthermore, I have taken proper action when the part needed to complete the repair was not in stock, and I am skilled at ordering parts for the equipment. I am experienced in handing out route sheets for work to be performed on maintenance equipment. During my 16 years in the maintenance department, I have completed route sheets, work orders, and ordered hundreds of parts for the maintenance equipment. The result of this experience was to help me develop expert knowledge of how to prepare and manage work orders, how to interpret and manage the reporting of preventive maintenance operational data, and how to manage all other aspects of the maintenance management system.

I have monitored and evaluated and taken corrective action for performance of USPS systems and equipment such as the IPSS system, MLOCR, BCSs, DBCs, computers, printers, and AFC's equipment during the past 16 years that I have served the post office. I will describe a situation in which my technical skills solved a major problem and resulted in the mail getting out on time despite a plant failure. Once I monitored the IPSS system when Savannah, GA P&DC could not connect their IPSS system to Savannah, GA Remote Encoding Center in order for the mail to be processed. In that situation, I evaluated the problem and I have found that the IPSS at the Savannah Remote Encoding Center was working efficiently. Then I went on to isolate the problem. I then evaluated that the Savannah, GA P&DC could not connect their site-to-site and also could not connect any of the ISSs. What I discovered is that the IPSS system had a fatal error message and the super monitor would not function, therefore causing a delay in the mail processing as well as a plant failure on the P&DC side. The corrective action I chose to take in that situation was to inform the supervisor and manager of the situation so that they would be fully informed. I also coordinated with the P&DC Electronic Technician so that the IPSS system would be back on line and so that the mail would get out on time. Then I disconnected the VIP/VAP and also informed the supervisor in order to assure good communication with the keyers at the remote site so that they could key the mail out while I worked on the P&DC problem. Then I proceeded by getting the superlopa monitor back up, after which I effected a system shutdown and then a system startup which got rid of the software error. Subsequently, I took steps to get the software task ready. After that, I logged into both super and report monitors, performing a system startup using cold/warm to save the images and then reconnecting the ISSs and making a site/site and VIP/VAP connection, by which the mail processing was performed.

As a result of my training as a 204B I have the ability and training to manage the maintenance department.

KSA #8: Ability to manage the work of people to meet organizational goals including organizing and structuring the work, establishing effective work relationships, and facilitating the flow of work-related information.

As a 204B Supervisor it was my sole responsibility to schedule employee workhours, I achieved and maintained the work of the custodians, MPE mechanics, and electronic technicians to perform the work that was assigned to them and to have the work completed by the end of their tour. I was able to establish an excellent relationship with my employees in order to meet the organizational goals. During the tour, employees worked under a system in which they would keep me informed about work that was to be done and I would then coordinate my own inspection of their work.

I performed these duties to the best of my ability while also completing PEDC courses I felt were necessary to help me improve my managerial skills. For example, I completed the PASS Program, Introduction to Postal Supervision, AM-PM Administrative Management for Postmasters, and Express Mail Manager Training.

The result of the extra training and 204B experience helped me refine my managerial skills and enabled my unit to receive excellent ratings while also helping me gain greater understanding of postal management.

EXAMPLE of a KSA

DYLAN HANCOCK
SSN: 999-88-7777
ELECTRONIC TECHNICIAN, ANNOUNCEMENT #ABC123

KSA #9: Ability to monitor, evaluate, and take corrective action for performance of systems and equipment.

I have monitored and evaluated and taken corrective action for performance of USPS systems and equipment such as the IPSS system, MLOCR, BCSs, DBCs, computers, printers, and AFC's equipment during the past 16 years that I have served the post office. I will describe a situation in which my technical skills solved a major problem and resulted in the mail getting out on time despite a plant failure. Once I monitored the IPSS system when Savannah, GA P&DC could not connect their IPSS system to Savannah, GA Remote Encoding Center in order for the mail to be processed. In that situation, I evaluated the problem and I have found that the IPSS at the Savannah Remote Encoding Center was working efficiently. Then I went on to isolate the problem. I then evaluated that the Savannah, GA P&DC could not connect their site-to-site and also could not connect any of the ISSs. What I discovered is that the IPSS system had a fatal error message and the super monitor would not function, therefore causing a delay in the mail processing as well as a plant failure on the P&DC side. The corrective action I chose to take in that situation was to inform the supervisor and manager of the situation so that they would be fully informed. I also coordinated with the P&DC Electronic Technician so that the IPSS system would be back on line and so that the mail would get out on time. Then I disconnected the VIP/VAP and also informed the supervisor in order to assure good communication with the keyers at the remote site so that they could key the mail out while I worked on the P&DC problem. Then I proceeded by getting the superlopa monitor back up, after which I effected a system shutdown and then a system startup which got rid of the software error. Subsequently, I took steps to get the software task ready. After that, I logged into both super and report monitors, performing a system startup using cold/warm to save the images and then reconnecting the ISSs and making a site/site and VIP/VAP connection, by which the mail processing was performed.

As a result of extensive training and 16 years of maintenance troubleshooting experience, I have developed the ability to monitor, evaluate, and take corrective action for performance of systems and equipment.

KSA #10: Ability to evaluate the overall performance level of the maintenance work force.

As a 204B Supervisor it was my sole responsibility to schedule employee work hours, I achieved and maintained the work of the custodians, MPE mechanics, and electronic technicians to perform the work that was assigned to them and to have the work completed by the end of their tour. I was able to establish an excellent relationship with my employees in order to meet the organizational goals. During the tour, employees worked under a system in which they would keep me informed about work that was to be done and I would then coordinate my own inspection of their work.

I performed these duties to the best of my ability while also completing PEDC courses I felt were necessary to help me improve my managerial skills. For example, I completed the PASS Program, Introduction to Postal Supervision, AM-PM Administrative Management for Postmasters, and Express Mail Manager Training.

The result of the extra training and 204B experience helped me refine my managerial skills and enabled my unit to receive excellent ratings while also helping me gain greater understanding of postal management.

I have worked in the maintenance work force for 16 years which included custodial, supervisory 204B maintenance, MPE mechanic, and Electronic Technician positions. Along the way I have seen many changes in the way in which the mail is processed, for example I have seen the installation of newer and better automation equipment, and I have observed the training of a better educated maintenance work force that is capable of operating, maintaining, and troubleshooting the new automation equipment. I have observed that the operations department is no longer complaining about better equipment needed to process the mail. With the new automated equipment that has been installed, the mail processing is at an all-time high and the overall performance of the maintenance work force, from custodial to electronics technicians, is truly outstanding.

As a result of extensive training and 16 years of experience in the maintenance work force, have developed an in-depth understanding of effective ways to evaluate the overall performance level of the maintenance work force.

EXAMPLE of a KSA

DYLAN HANCOCK
SSN: 999-88-7777
ELECTRONIC TECHNICIAN, ANNOUNCEMENT #PRP483

KSA #1: Knowledge of basic electromechanical and electronic principles as they apply to the operation of computer and mail processing equipment.

As a trained Electronic Technician and MPE Mechanic in automation mail processing equipment, RBCS and IPSS systems, and Remote Encoding Center, I have the working knowledge, skills, and abilities to work with many mail processing operating systems.

I have booted up, reset, and shut down many computers. I set the system time and date. I use the computers to aid me in my troubleshooting. I check for error messages to see what part of the machine needs servicing. I have backed up and restored the computer from and to tape and disk as well as loaded new software and sorted plans. I have used the menus to perform many computer operations. For example, to connect and disconnect from the remote site as well as to set ISS mail priority and connect and disconnect the ISSs and OSSs. I have completed system downloads and uploads from NDSS, created bit maps, loaded completed databases, saved complete databases, and edited files and created directories for sort plans. I have viewed image disks, tested image disks, formatted image disks, and verified image disks. I have removed and replaced computers. I have troubleshot and serviced many operating systems for the USPS.

As a result, as an Electronic Technician trained in every area of automation mail processing equipment and as an MPE Mechanic, I have worked on many computers and serviced these machines known as computers. Received training from the Technical Training Center in Savannah, GA, on these computers and machines.

KSA #2: Knowledge of the assembly and repair of mechanical and electromechanical devices.

As a USPS Electronics Technician and MPE Mechanic, I have assembled and repaired mechanical and electromechanical equipment.

I will describe a situation in which I have assembled and made repairs on the LSM machine. I have assembled and disassembled motor control circuits in the LSM to make repairs. I have disassembled and assembled the feeder table on the LSM and repaired the feeder belts and motors. I have disassembled and assembled pick off arms and repaired the pick off arms. I have disassembled and assembled the A and BC chains and repaired the A and BC chains. I have disassembled and assembled bin trips and repaired them so that the mail could fall in the right letter compartment so that the mail would not be missorted. I have disassembled and assembled letter carts and made repairs on the letter carts. I have also used safety equipment and am knowledgeable of proper procedures for safeguarding and controlling the inventory of such equipment. Safety equipment I have used has included employee safety equipment.

As a result, I have taken care of this mechanical and electromechanical machine that at one time was the backbone and elite of the USPS equipment.

EXAMPLE of a KSA

DYLAN HANCOCK
SSN: 999-88-7777
ELECTRONIC TECHNICIAN, ANNOUNCEMENT #PRP483

ELECTRONIC TECHNICIAN, ANNOUNCEMENT #PRP483 KSA #3

KSA #3: Knowledge of the operating characteristics of mail processing equipment, including OCR and bar code sorting equipment, image processing systems, remote computer reader, and specifications.

Throughout my career I have the working knowledge, skills, and abilities to work on the MLOCR and bar code sorting equipment, image processing systems, and the RCR equipment. I have received PEDC courses and teletraining on this equipment before I could be sent out to the Technical Training Center in Savannah, GA. I have performed preventive and corrective maintenance and project work on this automation equipment. I have troubleshot this equipment during maintenance windows and mail runs. I have kept this type of equipment running during mail processing. I have solved other electronic technical troubleshooting problems on this automation equipment. I have received many telephone calls from other processing and distribution center MDOs and electronic technicians to aid them in their troubleshooting to keep these machines up and running to get their dispatches out on time and to avoid plant failures. I also offer expertise in performing preventive and corrective maintenance and my troubleshooting skills are highly respected. When troubleshooting, I first identify the problem and then perform the actual repair that corrects the problem. I have trained other electronic technicians on this automation equipment.

As a result, the USPS has trained me to work on mail processing automation equipment and to let me work on the equipment to gain my knowledge to keep these machines up and running and to get the mail out with no delay in mail processing or delivery.

148 Part Three: STARs and KSAs for U.S. Postal Service Jobs

KSA #4: Ability to use electromechanical and electronic inspection and measuring tools and equipment including voltmeters, tachometers, micrometers, oscilloscopes, ethernet, and RS-232 analyzers.

As a USPS Electronics Technician and MPE Mechanic, I performed inspections and troubleshooting on electromechanical and electronic equipment such as the IPSS system, MLOCRs, BDCs, DBSs, computers, and peripherals, I have used test equipment and measuring tools and tachometers, micrometers, ethernet, and RS-232 analyzers to troubleshoot USPS equipment during the 16 years that I served in the USPS.

I have identified, recognized, and corrected faulty USPS machines as mentioned above and determined the corrective measures required for USPS machines. I have used multimeters to measure values of voltage, current, and resistance AC and DC circuits. When troubleshooting USPS machines, the voltmeter would be on the correct range and setting and connected parallel in the circuit that is under test. When troubleshooting the faulty machine, the voltmeter is used to check for a low voltage reading and for correct voltage reading. If the voltage reading on the machine is not correct I would check that part of the machine for loose connections or missing wiring and for defective components. I would replace or remove the connection of defective components and have the employees clear the machine for safety and restart the machine to see if it will work. If not, I would continue troubleshooting the equipment until it is up and running. Once completed I would turn the equipment over to operations, turn off my voltmeter and put it in a safe place like my tool box. I have used the tachometer to measure for the correct belt speed to avoid jams and faults on USPS equipment and to make adjustments on belts for the correct speed using the tachometer.

In my experience as an Electronic Technician, I have acquired extensive knowledge working with the oscilloscope and the dual-trace oscilloscope. I use the oscilloscope to look at many signals such as analog and digital wave forms in which the voltmeter would not give me a visual image of these signals. I have worked with the oscilloscope to measure the pulse on postal equipment such as tach faults or to observe wave forms to a constant frequency and shape. To monitor the output signal of a digital clock or square wave generator as well as constant pulse train. To measure the duration of each cycle of the wave form, the width of each pulse, and the amplitude of the pulses, and timing of signals, and phase angles on postal equipment such as the feeder, reader area and SDPV area and ISPs and PC70/80 and the PC70 machines.

I installed ethernet cables and transceivers for the IPSS system and connected ethernet for trunk lines. Troubleshot defective ethernet cable and transceivers. Replaced ethernet cables and transceiver for the IPSS system. Worked with the RS-232 analyzers for the IPSS system. Used micrometers to measure threaded screws used on postal machines.

As a result, I have acquired extensive knowledge working with test equipment such as voltmeters, tachometers, micrometers, and oscilloscopes as well as the ethernet, RS-232 analyzers, and many measuring tools on electromechanical and electronic equipment for the USPS. I received training from USPS P&DC and the Technical Training Center in Savannah, GA. I have an associate's degree from the Armstrong Atlantic State University in Electronics and have attended NRI School of Electronics.

EXAMPLE of a KSA

SSN: 999-88-7777

ELECTRONIC TECHNICIAN, ANNOUNCEMENT #PRP483

ELECTRONIC TECHNICIAN, ANNOUNCEMENT #PRP483 KSA #5

KSA #5: Ability to evaluate technical information and data to identify system performance deficiencies and recommend remedial action.

As a U.S. Postal Service Electronic Technician and MPE Mechanic, I have the working knowledge, skills, and abilities to work with technical information and data, MS manuals, and technical drawings to include diagrams, schematics, flow charts, blueprints, and hand outs to solve malfunctions and take corrective actions on USPS postal machine equipment.

I have used technical information as mentioned to troubleshoot the IPSS system, MLOCRs, BCS, DBCS, AFC and computers and their peripheral devices. I have used MS manuals to troubleshoot the feeder/reader and sorting areas of these machines when they malfunctioned and the SDPV area. Working on the IPSS system I used schematics, diagrams, and hand outs to solve technical deficiencies; used flow charts to solve problems on computers and their peripheral devices. Also used flow charts and hand outs to solve problems on the MLOCRs, BCS, DBCS, and AFC equipment and read flow charts for programming concepts.

I also offer expertise in performing corrective maintenance and my troubleshooting skills are highly respected. When troubleshooting, I first identify the problem and then perform the actual repair that corrects the problem and which could be mechanical, electrical or a user problem.

As a result, the U.S. Postal Service trained me to work with technical manuals and to troubleshoot postal equipment and to correct malfunctions on their equipment. I have also received a college degree in Electronics in which was included using technical information and corrective action, also my NRI training helped me to understand technical drawings, manuals, and flow charts.

150 Part Three: STARs and KSAs for U.S. Postal Service Jobs

DYLAN HANCOCK
SSN: 999-88-7777
ELECTRONIC TECHNICIAN, ANNOUNCEMENT #PRP483

KSA #6: Ability to review and analyze mail processing systems functions and recommend performance improvements.

In my experience as an Electronic Technician, I have received extensive knowledge of the technology that supports mail processing and my background in maintenance enables me to understand the maintenance support issues of reviewing and analyzing mail processing equipment and also to make improvements on automation equipment.

I have analyzed and made improvements on the IPSS system. I have noticed that during mail run and dispatch times that when the MLOCR is in the ISS mode, one of the ISSs have faulted out and that every ISS on that line would stop operating. Then the other ISSs that are not on that line will stop operating. The improvement was that when one ISS on a certain line faulted out, that machine was disconnected from the IPSS system. Then that machine was disconnected from the OCR by placing the ISS mode switch to the regular OCR mode. Then I troubleshot that machine only and kept the other machines in the ISS mode to process the mail for dispatch. Once that OCR was back on line, it was reconnected to the IPSS system and switched back to the ISS mode and processed that mail for dispatch time.

As a result, every IPSS system plant was made aware of this problem and could solve this type of problem and the mail would get out without a plant failure.

EXAMPLE of a KSA

DYLAN HANCOCK
SSN: 999-88-7777
ELECTRONIC TECHNICIAN, ANNOUNCEMENT #PRP483

**ELECTRONIC
TECHNICIAN,
ANNOUNCEMENT
#PRP483
KSA #7**

KSA #7: Ability to plan, organize, and manage multiple projects with contractors and postal employees across functional groups.

During the 16 years I have worked for the U.S. Postal Service, I have been involved in the preparation and execution of maintenance contracts. While working in Atlanta, GA, I was an Electronic Technician and then an Electronic Technician at the Savannah Remote Encoding Center, and also in Columbia, SC, as a Detailed Electronic Technician. In these positions I prepared maintenance contract specifications, was involved in the evaluation of maintenance contract proposals, and also worked to ensure compliance with control specifications.

As an Electronic Technician I have managed requested repair and maintenance work including evaluation of requests, work coordination, and monitoring of requests and coordination of work. I had to get the IPSS system up and running to process the mail to make the dispatch time at both the Savannah, GA, Processing and Distribution Center and the Savannah Remote Encoding Center. I informed the Electronic Technicians that they must observe all lights (LEDs) to the IPSS system. The technicians must have access to the main computer which is the alpha computer and also must have access to the super monitor and report monitor. I informed the technician to check function key error messages and to check for loose cable connections in the IPSS system. I informed the technician if the hardware was okay to pull all the system reports. Then I informed the supervisor that it was okay to do a complete system shutdown and startup. The Electronic Technician got an okay from the supervisor. I proceeded to tell the Electronic Technician to do a cold/warm start on the upper bus to get rid of the software error. I had the technician reconnect the site-to-site and I reconnected the VIP/VAP. The reason for doing the cold/warm complete system startup is to save the images at the P&DC side of operations. Once both the P&DC side was down have to be sent back over to the P&DC for processing.

As a result the Electronic Technician at the Savannah, GA P&DC plant informed the supervisor that the IPSS system was up and running to process the mail without any plant failure. My sixteen (16) years in the U.S. Postal Service, as well as my USPS training has helped me to understand projects and contractors work as a team to identify problem areas in order to have the system up and running with no delay in mail processing or delivery.

KSA #8: Ability to prepare and present technical reports.

In my experience as an Electronic Technician and MPE Mechanic, I have prepared reports and presented them to maintenance supervisors and managers. While attending college as an electronics student, I had to prepare and present technical and lab reports.

I had to prepare and present reports on the IPSS system when it has malfunctions to an SCSI lockup and software error. For example, I was reading a step-by-step procedure to perform an SCSI lockup and to format the image disk drives during the maintenance window, at a certain step in the procedures were to press any key to continue the image disk drive formatting in which one of the image disk drives crashed. I presented my report to the IPSS system coordinator and informed her of the software error. In the report I informed the IPSS system coordinator to inform others about the problem and to skip that part of the image disk drive formatting until that software error was corrected. The other remote encoding centers and processing and distribution centers were also informed.

As a result, I have the knowledge to prepare and present technical reports to maintenance supervisors and managers and IPSS system coordinators. I have prepared and presented technical reports on U.S. Postal Service equipment as an Electronic Technician and MPE Mechanic.

**ELECTRONIC
TECHNICIAN,
ANNOUNCEMENT
#PRP483
KSA #8**

SITUATION, TASK, ACTION, RESULT (STAR)

KAREN SWAIN

SSN: 000-00-0000

ISS/REC SUPERVISOR, ANNOUNCEMENT #XYZ123

ISS/REC SUPERVISOR, Announcement #XYZ123 Management KSA #1

KSA #1: Knowledge of data entry operations, including an understanding of production, quality control methods, and procedures

The three situations described below illustrate my knowledge as well as my ability to expertly apply my knowledge in this area.

STAR: While supervising on the ISS operation at the Boston P & DC, I detected that the Return to Sender mail was being incorrectly keyed. I notified the MDO that the mail was being misdirected because the REC keyers could not see the RTS stamp. I furthermore contacted the MDO at the REC and informed her that all of the images should be keyed as RTS until further notice. I also notified the ET to disconnect the ISS from the REC in order to prevent current mail from being combined with the RTS mail. **Result: This action on my part prevented loop and misdirected mail of the Return to Sender.**

STAR: During my detail as acting supervisor at the BREC, I reviewed the accuracy rates of all employees assigned to my pay location. I began daily edits for players who were below the 98% accuracy requirement. I also talked with each employee, addressing their errors. During these discussions, I discovered that many of the keyers were unclear on the coding rules. I took the time to explain the rules and made sure they understood what they were supposed to do. **Result: At the end of my assignment, there was a major improvement in the quality of those employees' performance, and this action on my part further resulted in providing the BREC with highly valuable keyers who were subsequently considered expert at their jobs.**

STAR: In a position as a Data Collection Technician, I worked independently on a daily basis. I ensured that all trucks were logged accurately and that all documentation for outbound mail was in compliance with appropriate policies and procedures. On one occasion, we experienced an unexpected surge in mail volume. My proficiency in data collection and my high quality control standards led to uninterrupted documentation in spite of the fact that I was handling a workload greatly in excess of the norm.

KSA #2: Ability to quickly and efficiently respond to fluctuations in work load requirements and utilize employees and equipment accordingly

There are two situations which demonstrate my ability to quickly and efficiently respond to fluctuations in work load requirements and utilize human and physical resources appropriately.

STAR: There were occasions when the Cambridge P & DC experienced power outages preventing images from transferring to the Boston REC. On one such occasion, I had approximately 80 keyers under my supervision and a rapidly decreasing mail volume from Cambridge due to the disconnection. Since we support three (3) other plants, I contacted each and advised them of our situation with the Cambridge plant. I requested that they send all the mail they had in their facility to be processed by the ISS. I had all available consoles switched from Cambridge to accommodate the other three (3) plants. **Result: This action allowed early clearance for the three plants. Upon reconnection to Cambridge, I was able to place all keyers on Cambridge consoles and this action on my part prevented a plant failure.**

STAR: While working as the ISS Supervisor at the Boston plant, I was notified that we would be receiving mail from the Cambridge plant to process. I reassigned employees at the other operations to relieve those operating the ISSs during lunch and breaks to ensure a continuous operation. I also contacted the Boston REC and requested maximum number of keyers to contend with the extra mail volume. **Result: This action allowed us to process all the mail and prevented plant failure.**

SITUATION, TASK, ACTION, RESULT (STAR)

KAREN SWAIN

SSN: 000-00-0000

ISS/REC SUPERVISOR, ANNOUNCEMENT #XYZ123

**ISS/REC SUPERVISOR,
Announcement #XYZ123
Management KSA #3**

KSA #3: Ability to forecast mail volume and handle changing work force requirements

The three situations described briefly below illustrate my ability to predict future mail volume and human resources needs.

STAR: While working as the ISS Supervisor at the Cape Cod plant, I was notified that we would be receiving mail from the Westchester plant to process. I reassigned employees at the other operations to relieve those operating the ISSs during lunch and breaks to ensure a continuous operation. I also contacted the Cape Cod REC and requested maximum number of keyers to contend with the extra mail volume.
Result: This action allowed us to process all the mail in our operation and prevented plant failure.

STAR: There were occasions when the Cambridge P & DC experienced power outages preventing images from transferring to the Boston REC. On one such occasion, I had approximately 80 keyers under my supervision and a rapidly decreasing mail volume from Cambridge due to the disconnection. Since we support three (3) other plants, I contacted each and advised them of our situation with the Cambridge plant. I requested that they send all the mail they had in their facility to be processed by the ISS. I had all available consoles switched from Cambridge to accommodate the other three (3) plants.
Result: This action allowed early clearance for the three plants. Upon reconnection to Cambridge, I was able to place all keyers on Cambridge consoles and this action on my part prevented a plant failure.

STAR: While assigned as a 204-B at the Cape Cod REC, I was monitoring the Westchester plant status reports when I noticed that we had a very low volume of images to process. The plant's projections reflected a high volume of mail to be processed and identified the need for the maximum number of keyers to be assigned to our consoles. I informed the plant of the situation and requested that they turn off the RCR, thereby permitting a quicker transfer of images.
Result: This action on my part allowed us to process all the images and meet the plant's clearance time.

KSA #4: Ability to prepare, maintain, and interpret reports related to productivity, work hours, mail volume, operating budget, injuries and accidents, and time and attendance

The two situations described below illustrate my ability pertaining to this requirement.

Situation: As Chief of Operations for the Systems Management Division (1995-97), my main responsibilities involved maintaining records for three flying squadrons consisting of 240 crew members. I ensured that all documents related to crew members' flight hours, physical examinations, qualifications, and numerous other documentation were updated, maintained, and secured. In one situation, our division was tested under live-fire conditions and some damage occurred to buildings and property while three individuals suffered minor burns.

Task: Ensured that investigations were conducted and reports of incident as well as many other records were prepared and distributed in a timely and accurate manner.

Action: Upon learning of the damage to persons and property, I immediately prepared numerous reports and records related to this live-fire incident. I initiated a thorough investigation of the incident so that safety reports could be prepared and so that a complete accounting could be made of the incident.

Result: As a result of the extreme care which I exercised in preparing, updating, and maintaining accurate paperwork, we received a perfect evaluation during a rigorous audit of our record keeping activities, I was the recipient of a prestigious medal recognizing my personal initiative and take-charge attitude in responding with poise and professionalism to this incident. As a further positive outcome of this incident, I utilized the reports which I prepared in authoring a new Standard Operating Procedure which instituted a new standard safety procedure which was used in future live-fire exercises.

Situation/Task/Action/Result: While working as the ISS Supervisor at the Boston plant, I was notified that we would be receiving mail from the Westchester plant to process. I immediately analyzed demand and prepared a report containing the forecasts for labor needs to handle the increased volume. Because of this report, employees were reassigned to cover the volume predicted and my request for a maximum number of keyers from Boston REC was granted in order to deal with the extra mail volume.

Result: This action allowed us to process all the mail in our operation and prevented plant failure.

ISS/REC SUPERVISOR, Announcement #XYZ123 Management KSA #4

Not all your STARs have to come from post office experience. Notice that the first STAR on this page describes a situation from military service which illustrates this ability.

SITUATION, TASK, ACTION, RESULT (STAR)
KAREN SWAIN
SSN: 000-00-0000

ISS/REC SUPERVISOR, ANNOUNCEMENT #XYZ123

ISS/REC SUPERVISOR, Announcement #XYZ123 Management KSA #5

KSA #5: Ability to manage the work of others to meet productivity, safety, and quality goals, including scheduling, coordinating, monitoring, and evaluating the work

The four situations below illustrate my ability pertaining to this requirement/factor.

STAR: During my detail as acting supervisor at the Boston REC, I reviewed the accuracy rates of all employees assigned to my pay location. I began daily edits for players who were below the 98% accuracy requirement. I also talked with each employee, addressing their errors. During these discussions, I discovered that many of the keyers were unclear on the coding rules. I took the time to explain the rules and made sure they understood what they were supposed to do.

Result: At the end of my assignment, there was a major improvement in the quality of those employees' performance, and this action on my part further resulted in providing the BREC with highly valuable keyers who were subsequently considered expert at their jobs.

Sometimes giving one or two examples is sufficient to address the KSA. On the other hand, providing one example and giving lots of detail about the methodology you used to, for example, solve a problem can be just as effective.

STAR: During my tour at the BREC, I became aware of a productivity problem among the keyers. I utilized my oral communication skills to make the keyers aware of the shortfall, and I received authorization from the proper channels to embark upon training programs to upgrade the skills and productivity of keyers.

Result: The increase in productivity at the plant allowed us to process the mail in a timely manner and there was a noticeable improvement in morale as well as a new dedication to the pursuit of quality standards and productivity among keyers. Some of the keyers whom I trained have gone on to become some of most productive keyers in the postal system.

STAR: While in a supervisory position at the BREC, I was responsible for employee performance evaluations in my assigned pay location. For the majority of my tour, there was one other supervisor and myself monitoring the work floor. In order for us to perform our evaluations, we would rotate in order to supervise productivity and meet with our employees.

Result: By working together, this allowed us to complete our job requirements in a timely manner with the added result that morale and productivity increased because of employees' perception that we were listening to them and concerned with establishing and maintaining harmonious work relationships.

STAR: During my employment as the Training Instructor for Boeing Support Systems, I was responsible for the supervision and instruction of prospective Data Conversion Operators. With individuals working at their own pace, I was required to work one-on-one in their training to ensure their understanding of the coding rules.

Result: As a result, the last 190 employees hired by Boeing were under my instruction, and many hold positions now with the U.S. Postal Service at the Boston REC.

KSA #6: Ability to establish and maintain effective team and individual work relationships with employees, other managers, and union representatives

The three situations below illustrate my ability pertaining to this requirement/factor.

STAR: During my detail as acting supervisor at the Boston REC, I reviewed the accuracy rates of all employees assigned to my pay location. I began daily edits for players who were below the 98% accuracy requirement. I also talked with each employee, addressing their errors. During these discussions, I discovered that many of the keyers were unclear on the coding rules. I took the time to explain the rules and made sure they understood what they were supposed to do.
Result: At the end of my assignment, there was a major improvement in the quality of those employees' performance, and this action on my part further resulted in providing the BREC with highly valuable keyers who were subsequently considered expert at their jobs.

STAR: While in a supervisory position at the BREC, I was responsible for employee performance evaluations in my assigned pay location. For the majority of my tour, there was one other supervisor and myself monitoring the work floor. In order for us to perform our evaluations, we would rotate in order to supervise productivity and meet with our employees.
Result: By working together, this allowed us to complete our job requirements in a timely manner with the added result that morale and productivity increased because of employees' perception that we were listening to them and concerned with establishing and maintaining harmonious work relationships.

STAR: While supervising at the Boston REC, I was often responsible for establishing the master edits to be utilized in monitoring employee performance. On one such occasion, employees argued that an image did not appear in its entirety on their monitors. Upon hearing their dissatisfaction with the edit, I requested the "ET" to bring the image up on these monitors and adjust the screen in all directions to give the keyers every possible view.
Result: After seeing that the image was clearly visible, the employees were satisfied with the edit results, and this situation resulted in a more harmonious working environment.

SITUATION, TASK, ACTION, RESULT (STAR)

KAREN SWAIN
SSN: 000-00-0000
ISS/REC SUPERVISOR, ANNOUNCEMENT #XYZ123

**ISS/REC SUPERVISOR,
Announcement #XYZ123
Management KSA #7**

KSA #7: Ability to implement and monitor building, equipment, and systems maintenance activities and programs

The two situations below illustrate my ability pertaining to this requirement/factor.

STAR: While supervising at the Boston REC, I was often responsible for establishing the master edits to be utilized in monitoring employee performance. On one such occasion, employees argued that an image did not appear in its entirety on their monitors. Upon hearing their dissatisfaction with the edit, I requested the "ET" to bring the image up on these monitors and adjust the screen in all directions to give the keyers every possible view. After a thorough analysis of the image problem, we realized that the monitors were not being operated or adjusted properly and were failing to receive recommended maintenance in order to product top-notch results. After some discussion with the vendors of the monitors, a special session was organized so that vendor personnel could demonstrate the proper use, maintenance, and upkeep of the monitors.
Result: The employees were trained to properly maintain and adjust the screens, and this situation resulted in a more harmonious working environment. Thereafter, a routine schedule of maintenance was established for the monitors and a brief training session was developed to teach employees techniques in maintenance and adjustment.

You do not have to use only post office experiences as evidence of your ability, knowledge, or knowledge. Notice that one of these STARs is from military experience.

STAR: During my ten years of military service, I rose to the rank of E-7 while earning as reputation as an expert in the field of building, property, and systems maintenance. On one occasion, I was handpicked for a position which required me to take charge of an organization which had neglected its need for maintenance of property, equipment, and systems. One result of this negligence was that the organization had failed miserably its three prior annual evaluations. After I assumed the position, I established a team of employees to analyze the deficiencies and help me develop a report of findings and recommendations. Employees slowly became enthusiastic about this project, and we identified numerous problems and solutions. The result was that, within three months, we were able to correct all problems and deficiencies in inventory, equipment, and systems and we earned an outstanding evaluation on the next annual evaluation.

KSA #8: Ability to communicate effectively in order to train and give guidance to employees

The three situations below illustrate my ability pertaining to this requirement/factor.

STAR: During my employment as the Training Instructor for Boeing Support Systems, I was responsible for the supervision and instruction of prospective Data Conversion Operators. With individuals working at their own pace, I was required to work one-on-one in their training to ensure their understanding of the coding rules.
Result: As a result, the last 190 employees hired by Boeing were under my instruction, and many hold positions now with the U.S. Postal Service at the Boston REC.

STAR: During my detail as acting supervisor at the BREC, I reviewed the accuracy rates of all employees assigned to my pay location. I began daily edits for players who were below the 98% accuracy requirement. I also talked with each employee, addressing their errors. During these discussions, I discovered that many of the keyers were unclear on the coding rules. I took the time to explain the rules and made sure they understood what they were supposed to do.
Result: At the end of my assignment, there was a major improvement in the quality of those employees' performance, and this action on my part further resulted in providing the BREC with highly valuable keyers who were subsequently considered expert at their jobs.

STAR: While in a supervisory position at the BREC, I was responsible for employee performance evaluations in my assigned pay location. For the majority of my tour, there was one other supervisor and myself monitoring the work floor. In order for us to perform our evaluations, we would rotate in order to supervise productivity and meet with our employees.
Result: By working together, this allowed us to complete our job requirements in a timely manner with the added result that morale and productivity increased because of employees' perception that we were listening to them and concerned with establishing and maintaining harmonious work relationships.

SITUATION, TASK, ACTION, RESULT (STAR)

NESTOR HERNANDEZ

SSN: 000-00-0000

SUPERVISOR, ANNOUNCEMENT #483PRP

SUPERVISOR, Announcement #483PRP KSA #1

KSA #1: ORAL COMMUNICATIONS: Ability to communicate information, instructions, or ideas orally in a clear and concise manner in individual or group situations

Situation #1: In April 1997, in my capacity as Platform Supervisor, I observed that platform clerks were not following the posted work schedule. We were short manpower in the bullpen which delayed the unloading of incoming mail trucks.

Action: I used my oral communication skills to locate a platform clerk who was not following the posted schedule and who was not in his assigned position. I utilized tact, instructional techniques, and motivational skills to inform and persuade this worker about the importance of his precisely following the work schedule.

Result: As a result of my oral communication effectiveness:
- The trucks were able to be unloaded on schedule, and
- The worker gained a new appreciation of how much he was needed in the position for which he was assigned. I was proud that I was able to achieve this result while actually improving worker morale and making the worker aware of his importance to the overall mission.

Situation #2: With the implementation of the RBCS mail flow, it became imperative that we increase the percentage of mail canceled everyday to forty percent. It then became my job to inform and motivate my crew to achieve the desired cancellations rate by 1,800.

Action: To accomplish this mission, I held a service talk and informed my crew of the new goals and explained to them the new methodology that would be used to get the job done. I stressed the importance of gathering all raw mail from behind each star route as it arrives rather than staging the containers. I also identified the mail in a central location. After the talk and the change in the way of identifying staging the raw mail, my crew achieved the 40 percent cancellations rate for two consecutive weeks.

Result: After the initial two weeks of the new cancellation program, there was some fluctuating in the obtainment of the forty percent goal due to experimentation with manpower needs. However, the foundation was set to achieve the goal on a consistent basis which is now the situation.

KSA #2: LEADERSHIP: Ability to direct or coordinate individual or group action in order to accomplish a task or goal

Situation #1: In February 1999, in my capacity as Manual Operation Supervisor, I was responsible for staffing all floor functions, which included the box section, letter case, city bump table, damaged mail, priority, outgoing and secondary letters, and SCF. This involved the assignment of tasks to 20 individuals. On February 15, 1999, a key employee involved in customer service called in sick, thereby causing serious strain on the SCF operation with the potential of causing numerous customer problems.

Action: I realized that there was no one trained to perform the job of the individual on sick leave, but I wanted to make sure that whatever plan I developed met with the approval of union personnel. After extensive consultation with management and union personnel using the proper channels of communication, it was agreed that it was necessary to develop a plan to ensure productivity. Therefore, utilizing my leadership and decision-making abilities, I developed such a plan. I identified a clerk who was, in my opinion, rapidly trainable. I immediately gave this clerk a "crash course" in the handling of large parcels and completing paperwork, and I utilized my leadership ability to provide this individual with the confidence to do this job for which he had no prior training.

Result: All parcels were posted with no diminishing of customer service or customer satisfaction.

Situation #2: While detailed to the Supervisor of Distribution Operations position from June 15, 1998 to September 5, 1998, we were having trouble making timely dispatches from all machines.

Action: I examined possible causes of the problem and devised a new methodology on how to solve the problem. I ensured that prior to each dispatch, the sweeper would pull the dispatch ten minutes before and stage it for the expediter.

Result: Consequently, dispatch discipline improved and overnight ODIS scores for our neighboring MSC improved.

SITUATION, TASK, ACTION, RESULT (STAR)

NESTOR HERNANDEZ

SSN: 000-00-0000

SUPERVISOR, ANNOUNCEMENT #483PRP

SUPERVISOR, Announcement #483PRP KSA #3

KSA #3: HUMAN RELATIONS: Ability to interact tactfully and relate well with others

Situation #1: In January 1999, in my capacity as Manual Operation Supervisor, I experienced a situation which tested my human relations skills. An employee whom I supervise approached me with a complaint that he was not called in to arrive two hours early for overtime, although his fellow workers had been called. This employee emphasized that this had happened several times previously. The employee was highly agitated and distressed.

Action: I immediately decided to assign a Shop Steward to hear his grievance. The Shop Steward and employee had a discussion which lasted approximately 15 minutes, after which I was called into the office to join the Shop Steward and the employee. When I was asked by the Shop Steward to recommend a course of action, I offered to let the employee work an extra two hours of overtime at the end of his tour on that day and come in two hours early the next day.

Result: The employee was satisfied with the solution I recommended, and he also seemed very pleased with the fact that we took prompt action to listen to his complaint. Therefore, this matter was resolved in a manner which maximized human relations effectiveness within the post office.

Situation #2: While detailed to the Supervisor of Distribution Operations position on the platform, I was confronted with a situation when an important task came up and a spontaneous job reassignment had to be made to cover the emergency. I reassigned an employee to solve the problem; however, I failed to notify his group leader that I had reassigned him. As a result, the group leader became upset. I immediately became aware that I had made a mistake by not informing the reassigned employee's group leader of his new status.

Action: I immediately pulled both employees to the side and apologized for not using the chain of command before making the reassignment. As a result of our conversation, it became apparent that this was a common occurrence that had caused problems in the past.

Result: The result of the meeting was that a new awareness was created concerning the importance of using the chain of command in making personnel changes and a better working environment was created. Through this incident, I feel that my own human relations skills were refined, and I gained insight into how to avoid such a problem in the future.

KSA #4: PROBLEM ANALYSIS: Ability to analyze problems, work performance, suggestions, and complaints by listening, observing, gathering, organizing, and interpreting information

Situation #1: In October 1999, in my capacity as Manual Operation Supervisor, I observed a problem which could have caused serious detriment to productivity. Specifically, outgoing and surface mail were being left behind on the SCF cases. I further observed that a lot of mail was Atlanta-postmarked for that day.

Action: I immediately organized personnel to pull down the surface and outgoing mail and take it back to the outgoing operation to be finalized for dispatch. This was accomplished without detriment to any other internal activities.

Result: All Atlanta-postmarked mail was finalized and dispatched on time, thereby assuring outstanding customer service.

Situation #2: On a reoccurring basis, we were finishing our 892 program well after our scheduled cutoff time.

Action: The first thing I did was to analyze the mail flow to see what was causing the problem. My investigation showed that the late allocation of keyers by the Rec Site was creating an avalanche of excessive 892 mail that could not be processed timely before cutoff time on one DBCS. I decided that in order to meet cutoff time, I needed to start another DBCS at 2100. This adjustment allowed us to clear our volume by 2230. It did, however, create more tied-out bundles for the airlift sacks due to the fact that full trays were not created on second DBCS by the end of distribution. It did ensure, however, that all overnight surface mail was finalized by cutoff time.

Result: The final outcome of the decision was to have 892 mail distributed and ready for dispatch in a timely manner and enhanced service standards not only for overnight delivery but also for two-day and three-day delivery.

SITUATION, TASK, ACTION, RESULT (STAR)

NESTOR HERNANDEZ

SSN: 000-00-0000

SUPERVISOR, ANNOUNCEMENT #483PRP

SUPERVISOR, Announcement #483PRP KSA #5

KSA #5: DECISION MAKING: Ability to develop plans, evaluate their anticipated effectiveness, make decisions, and take appropriate action

Situation #1: In July 1998, in my capacity as Manual Operation Supervisor, I observed that a large volume of mail was being sent to the Manual Cases from Automation at the end of each tour. This practice had caused our efficiency rate to plummet to an all-time-low of 83%!

Action: I tracked the mail and found that three-day states mail was weighed to the outgoing operation. The mail was then counted as a Plan Failure and delayed volume and recorded on the DMCR. After determining that these flawed procedures were causing the problem, I made prudent decisions to remedy the inefficiency. Specifically, I decided that immediate and intensive retraining of workers in the proper procedures was in order. I trained several manual runners in operations such as weight scales and opening unit codes. This retraining was accomplished carefully over a two-week period.

Result: The manual runners were trained to recognize their own mail and place mail pieces in the correct operation, thereby reducing Plan Failures and the delayed volume. The result was that efficiency soared to an acceptable 92% and increased gradually thereafter until achieving a 98% efficiency rate.

Situation #2: In my capacity as Manual Operation Supervisor, I observed a problem which could have caused serious detriment to productivity. Specifically, outgoing and surface mail was being left behind on the SCF cases. I further observed that a lot of mail was Boston-postmarked for that day.

Action: I immediately organized personnel to pull down the surface and outgoing mail and take it back to the outgoing operation to be finalized for dispatch. This was accomplished without any detriment to any other internal activities or staffing needs.

Result: All Boston-postmarked mail was finalized and dispatched on time, thereby assuring outstanding customer service.

KSA #6: WRITTEN COMMUNICATIONS: Ability to write letters, simple reports, and employee evaluations clearly and effectively and to complete standardized reporting forms accurately

Situation #1: In my capacity as Supervisor, I am responsible for preparing employee evaluations. This is a tool utilized to ascertain if the employee is compatible with postal standards. On one occasion I prepared a written employee evaluation which identified numerous deficiencies and errors in the employee's work habits, including such things as a lack of focus on key tasks which resulted in unacceptable efficiency.

Action: I prepared an employee evaluation and provided written as well as oral feedback in a counseling session. At first the employee was distressed to see his faults identified specifically and in writing. However, I emphasized that his flaws could be improved and made recommendations for his improved efficiency.

Result: This employee, with my help and leadership, learned the scheme in half the time and became one of our main keyers for local mail. This result occurred because I prepared precise, detailed, and constructive written communication which helped transform this employee from a marginal to an excellent and highly motivated worker.

Situation #2: In my position as Supervisor, I am responsible for preparing numerous reports related to OSHA and safety practices. On one occasion an employee had an accident on the job during which he suffered an injury to his back.

Action: I immediately assured that the employee was provided with proper medical treatment in a hospital environment. After assuring the proper care of the employees, I then proceeded to analyze the incident and determine causal factors. I prepared numerous reports related to medical matters, OSHA regulations, and other federally regulated issues.

Result: The employee was properly cared for medically, all reports were prepared by me in an expeditious manner, and the safety issues surrounding the accident were addressed both in writing and verbally with other employees. A major attempt was made to try to prevent a reoccurrence of the problem, and I was asked to author a written report about the incident to be distributed at supervisory levels.

SITUATION, TASK, ACTION, RESULT (STAR)

NESTOR HERNANDEZ

SSN: 000-00-0000

SUPERVISOR, ANNOUNCEMENT #483PRP

KSA #7: MATHEMATICAL COMPUTATIONS: Ability to perform addition, subtraction, multiplication, and division with whole numbers, fractions, and decimals

Situation #1: A part of my duties when supervising the ISS System is to keep a continuous count of my own time, the image generation rate of mail I am running, the amount of images on hand, and the keying rate of the DCOs at the Rec Center.

Action: In order to do this, I constantly have to calculate percentages and convert my findings into projections that allow me to process the mail by clearance time. To do this I keep a count of my script and meter volume and then multiply these different volumes by the image that will be generated. I then add this estimate to the images already in the system. Once I obtain this figure, I multiply the keying rate of DCOs by the number of Keyers I have allocated. By doing this, I get an idea of how long it will take me to process my on-hand volume and how much volume I will need to divert to downstream operations in order to meet my clearance time. By using this procedure, I have been able to project my processing window accurately on a consistent basis. This has facilitated our ability to clear our mail in a timely fashion. For example: When I took over the buffer on the ISSs from Tour II, I had 38,348 images with 42 DCOs keying at 894 images per hour. In the next hour, if they maintained their keying rate I could process 37,548 images per hour stage. In front of ISS was approximately 500 feet or approximately 125,000 pieces of script mail. Using a 65% image generation rate I calculated that I could generate an additional 81,250 pieces of mail by adding the buffer count to the projected images.

Result: I came up with a total of 119,598 images, and I had three hours and eleven minutes run time. I added another twenty minutes run time to compensate for breaks by the DCOs; that gave me a total of 3 hours and thirty minutes run time. Therefore, I could run to 1830 with on-hand volume without having to divert to MPLSM.

STAR: As a military professional I was handpicked for a job as Chief of Current Operations, which required me to manage an $11 million budget while maintaining accurate flying records for the squadron. I performed accurate calculations of specific budget items as well as flight hours, and I trained others to do the same. On one occasion when calculating specific budget items, I became aware of a variance which puzzled me. I recalculated totals on line items and recomputed critical mathematical computations which had historically been produced in an erroneous fashion. As a result of my identification of a chronic miscalculation in the budget, errors were corrected which actually resulted in funds being freed up for operations. I received a prestigious medal for my identification and resolution of a problem which had eluded my predecessors.

KSA #8: SAFETY: Knowledge of safety procedures needed to ensure that safe working conditions are maintained. Included is knowledge of the procedures and techniques established to avoid injuries. Also included is knowledge of normal accident prevention measures and emergency procedures

Situation #1: In August 1998, accidents were on the increase, primarily with regard to APCs and BMCs. The injuries sustained caused more than seven days absence for one individual as well as numerous lost days for other individuals.

Action: I identified that the safety problems were occurring because employees were not operating the equipment properly. I immediately instituted refresher safety classes for employees. I determined that there was a need for employees to learn proper techniques of safely operating heavy equipment. I and other supervisors took turns teaching those safety classes weekly.

Result: There was an immediate decrease in the number of safety accidents and incidents, and there was a cost savings because of fewer manhours lost due to injuries. Employees became skilled in identifying damaged equipment and quickly removing the dangerous equipment from the floor, thereby anticipating potential safety problems. We intensified STOP procedures and addressed the issue in weekly safety classes.

Situation #2: Within a short period of time, we had a rash of accidents concerning the proper usage of all-purpose containers (APCs). All of the accidents revolved around the proper securing of the top shelf and the proper closing and securing of the top gate.

Action: On my own initiative I held a safety briefing on the proper usage of all-purpose containers. I explained the importance of securing the top shelf in the "up" position by making sure that all restraints were used and properly seated to prevent the shelf from accidentally falling. I also stressed the point that the top gate should be securely seated and checked before moving. I added that if any of the safety devices were defective, that the container would be tagged orange and put out of circulation until it was properly fixed by maintenance.

Result: By monitoring the usage of all-purpose containers and making on-the-spot corrections when they were discovered to be mishandled, I was able to eliminate all-purpose container accidents under my supervision. We intensified our emphasis on STOP procedures and addressed the matter in weekly safety classes.

SITUATION, TASK, ACTION, RESULT (STAR)

NESTOR HERNANDEZ

SSN: 000-00-0000

SUPERVISOR, ANNOUNCEMENT #483PRP

**SUPERVISOR,
Announcement
#483PRP
KSA #9**

KSA #9: JOB KNOWLEDGE: Knowledge of the operating procedures and the goals of the function to be supervised

Situation #1: I began working with the postal service in 1991 as an LSM operator and received two awards for maintaining 100% keystroke accuracy. Since 1993 I have functioned in supervisory capacities, and I have been assigned to Manual Operation, Automation, and Platform, which has given me an opportunity to acquire excellent job knowledge in all areas.

Action: As an LSM Operator and Supervisor, I have aggressively sought out all training opportunities in order to advance my job knowledge. For example, I completed a course in External First Class Measurement System in November, 1998.

Result: In addition to receiving two awards as an LSM Operator, I have acquired the respect of my fellow supervisors and am consulted frequently because of my job knowledge related to Manual Operation, Automation, and Platform.

Situation #2: Having worked for the U.S. Postal Service in excess of five years, I have gained valuable knowledge of many operations from an employee's perspective. I desired in-depth knowledge of every operation in the Atlanta Processing Distribution for my personal fulfillment; therefore, I volunteered for the Supervisory Training Program (204B) and rapidly grasped the intricacies of the 010 and platform operations.

Action: I asked for and received training on the flat sorting machine (which enabled me to see the down flow from the flat's canceler), 010 Flats Operation, and the Bump table to the FSM and manual flats (O60). Next I received training as (LSM) Letter Sorting Machine, Manual operations and Automation Supervisor. Respectfully, after excelling as SDO of all Tour III operations, I requested training as a Manager of Distribution Operations and performed well when needed in this capacity on seven occasions. I have become a vital member of the management trainee program and obtained valuable knowledge of goals and procedures of each area. I achieved a record-setting volume as Automation SDO on October 22, 1996, of 1,442,254, and on September 11, 1997 we set a new record at 1,460,458 and the highest cancellation of 45% as 010 SDO.

Result: These accomplishments, in addition to completion of every available course and classroom training, have given me many of the tools to excel as a full-time supervisor not only for the challenges of the USPS, but also for myself.

As the editor of this book, I would like to give you some tips on how to make the best use of the information you will find here. Because you are considering a career change, you already understand the concept of managing your career for maximum enjoyment and self-fulfillment. The purpose of this book is to provide expert tools and advice so that you *can* manage your career. Inside these pages you will find resumes and cover letters that will help you find not just a job but the type of work you want to do.

Overview of the Book

Every resume and cover letter in this book actually worked. And most of the resumes and cover letters have common features: most are one-page, most are in the chronological format, and most resumes are accompanied by a companion cover letter. In this section you will find helpful advice about job hunting. Step One begins with a discussion of why employers prefer the one-page, chronological resume. In Step Two you are introduced to the direct approach and to the proper format for a cover letter. In Step Three you learn the 14 main reasons why job hunters are not offered the jobs they want, and you learn the six key areas employers focus on when they interview you. Step Four gives nuts-and-bolts advice on how to handle the interview, send a follow-up letter after an interview, and negotiate your salary.

The cover letter plays such a critical role in a career change. You will learn from the experts how to format your cover letters and you will see suggested language to use in particular career-change situations. It has been said that "A picture is worth a thousand words" and, for that reason, you will see numerous examples of effective cover letters used by real individuals to change fields, functions, and industries.

The most important part of the book is the Real-Resumes section. Some of the individuals whose resumes and cover letters you see spent a lengthy career in an industry they loved. Then there are resumes and cover letters of people who wanted a change but who probably wanted to remain in their industry. Many of you will be especially interested by the resumes and cover letters of individuals who knew they definitely wanted a career change but had no idea what they wanted to do next. Other resumes and cover letters show individuals who knew they wanted to change fields and had a pretty good idea of what they wanted to do next.

Whatever your field, and whatever your circumstances, you'll find resumes and cover letters that will "show you the ropes" in terms of successfully changing jobs and switching careers.

Before you proceed further, think about why you picked up this book.
- Are you dissatisfied with the type of work you are now doing?
- Would you like to change careers, change companies, or change industries?
- Are you satisfied with your industry but not with your niche or function within it?
- Do you want to transfer your skills to a new product or service?
- Even if you have excelled in your field, have you "had enough"? Would you like the stimulation of a new challenge?
- Are you aware of the importance of a great cover letter but unsure of how to write one?
- Are you preparing to launch a second career after retirement?
- Have you been downsized, or do you anticipate becoming a victim of downsizing?
- Do you need expert advice on how to plan and implement a job campaign that will open the maximum number of doors?
- Do you want to make sure you handle an interview to your maximum advantage?

- Would you like to master the techniques of negotiating salary and benefits?
- Do you want to learn the secrets and shortcuts of professional resume writers?

Using the Direct Approach

As you consider the possibility of a job hunt or career change, you need to be aware that most people end up having at least three distinctly different careers in their working lifetimes, and often those careers are different from each other. Yet people usually stumble through each job campaign, unsure of what they should be doing. Whether you find yourself voluntarily or unexpectedly in a job hunt, the direct approach is the job hunting strategy most likely to yield a full-time permanent job. The direct approach is an active, take-the-initiative style of job hunting in which you choose your next employer rather than relying on responding to ads, using employment agencies, or depending on other methods of finding jobs. You will learn how to use the direct approach in this book, and you will see that an effective cover letter is a critical ingredient in using the direct approach.

Lack of Industry Experience Not a Major Barrier to Entering New Field

"Lack of experience" is often the last reason people are not offered jobs, according to the companies who do the hiring. If you are changing careers, you will be glad to learn that experienced professionals often are selling "potential" rather than experience in a job hunt. Companies look for personal qualities that they know tend to be present in their most effective professionals, such as communication skills, initiative, persistence, organizational and time management skills, and creativity. Frequently companies are trying to discover "personality type," "talent," "ability," "aptitude," and "potential" rather than seeking actual hands-on experience, so your resume should be designed to aggressively present your accomplishments. Attitude, enthusiasm, personality, and a track record of achievements in any type of work are the primary "indicators of success" which employers are seeking, and you will see numerous examples in this book of resumes written in an all-purpose fashion so that the professional can approach various industries and companies.

The Art of Using References in a Job Hunt

You probably already know that you need to provide references during a job hunt, but you may not be sure of how and when to use references for maximum advantage. You can use references very creatively during a job hunt to call attention to your strengths and make yourself "stand out." Your references will rarely get you a job, no matter how impressive the names, but the way you use references can boost the employer's confidence in you and lead to a job offer in the least time.

You should ask from three to five people, including people who have supervised you, if you can use them as a reference during your job hunt. You may not be able to ask your current boss since your job hunt is probably confidential.

A common question in resume preparation is: "Do I need to put my references on my resume?" No, you don't. Even if you create a references page at the same time you prepare your resume, you don't need to mail, e-mail, or fax your references page with the resume and cover letter. Usually the potential employer is not interested in references until he meets you, so the earliest you need to have references ready is at the first interview. Obviously there are exceptions to this standard rule of thumb; sometimes an ad will ask you to send references with your first response. Wait until the employer requests references before providing them.

The "direct approach" is the style of job hunting most likely to yield the maximum number of job interviews.

Using references in a skillful fashion in your job hunt will inspire confidence in prospective employers and help you "close the sale" after interviews.

An excellent attention-getting technique is to take to the first interview not just a page of references (giving names, addresses, and telephone numbers) but an actual letter of reference written by someone who knows you well and who preferably has supervised or employed you. A professional way to close the first interview is to thank the interviewer, shake his or her hand, and then say you'd like to give him or her a copy of a letter of reference from a previous employer. Hopefully you already made a good impression during the interview, but you'll "close the sale" in a dynamic fashion if you leave a letter praising you and your accomplishments. For that reason, it's a good idea to ask supervisors during your final weeks in a job if they will provide you with a written letter of recommendation which you can use in future job hunts. Most employers will oblige, and you will have a letter that has a useful "shelf life" of many years. Such a letter often gives the prospective employer enough confidence in his opinion of you that he may forego checking out other references and decide to offer you the job on the spot or in the next few days.

Whom should you ask to serve as references? References should be people who have known or supervised you in a professional, academic, or work situation. References with big titles, like school superintendent or congressman, are fine, but remind busy people when you get to the interview stage that they may be contacted soon. Make sure the busy official recognizes your name and has instant positive recall of you! If you're asked to provide references on a formal company application, you can simply transcribe names from your references list. In summary, follow this rule in using references: If you've got them, flaunt them! If you've obtained well-written letters of reference, make sure you find a polite way to push those references under the nose of the interviewer so he or she can hear someone other than you describing your strengths. Your references probably won't ever get you a job, but glowing letters of reference can give you credibility and visibility that can make you stand out among candidates with similar credentials and potential!

The approach taken by this book is to (1) help you master the proven best techniques of conducting a job hunt and (2) show you how to stand out in a job hunt through your resume, cover letter, interviewing skills, as well as the way in which you present your references and follow up on interviews. Now, the best way to "get in the mood" for writing your own resume and cover letter is to select samples from the Table of Contents that interest you and then read them. A great resume is a "photograph," usually on one page, of an individual. If you wish to seek professional advice in preparing your resume, you may contact one of the professional writers at Professional Resume & Employment Publishing (PREP) for a brief free consultation by calling 1-910-483-6611.

Part One: Some Advice About Your Job Hunt

What if you don't know what you want to do?

Your job hunt will be more comfortable if you can figure out what type of work you want to do. But you are not alone if you have no idea what you want to do next! You may have knowledge and skills in certain areas but want to get into another type of work. What *The Wall Street Journal* has discovered in its research on careers is that most of us end up having at least three distinctly different careers in our working lives; it seems that, even if we really like a particular kind of activity, twenty years of doing it is enough for most of us and we want to move on to something else!

That's why we strongly believe that you need to spend some time figuring out *what interests you* rather than taking an inventory of the skills you have. You may have skills that you simply don't want to use, but if you can build your career on the things that interest you, you will be more likely to be happy and satisfied in your job. Realize, too, that interests can change over time; the activities that interest you now may not be the ones that interested you years ago. For example, some professionals may decide that they've had enough of retail sales and want a job selling another product or service, even though they have earned a reputation for being an excellent retail manager. We strongly believe that interests rather than skills should be the determining factor in deciding what types of jobs you want to apply for and what directions you explore in your job hunt. Obviously one cannot be a lawyer without a law degree or a secretary without secretarial skills; but a professional can embark on a next career as a financial consultant, property manager, plant manager, production supervisor, retail manager, or other occupation if he/she has a strong interest in that type of work and can provide a resume that clearly demonstrates past excellent performance in *any* field and *potential* to excel in another field. As you will see later in this book, "lack of exact experience" is the last reason why people are turned down for the jobs they apply for.

> Figure out what interests you and you will hold the key to a successful job hunt and working career. (And be prepared for your interests to change over time!)

> "Lack of exact experience" is the last reason people are turned down for the jobs for which they apply.

How can you have a resume prepared if you don't know what you want to do?

You may be wondering how you can have a resume prepared if you don't know what you want to do next. The approach to resume writing which PREP, the country's oldest resume-preparation company, has used successfully for many years is to develop an "all-purpose" resume that translates your skills, experience, and accomplishments into language employers can understand. What most people need in a job hunt is a versatile resume that will allow them to apply for numerous types of jobs. For example, you may want to apply for a job in pharmaceutical sales but you may also want to have a resume that will be versatile enough for you to apply for jobs in the construction, financial services, or automotive industries.

Based on more than 20 years of serving job hunters, we at PREP have found that your best approach to job hunting is **an all-purpose resume** and **specific cover letters tailored to specific fields** rather than using the approach of trying to create different resumes for every job. If you are remaining in your field, you may not even need more than one "all-purpose" cover letter, although the cover letter rather than the resume is the place to communicate your interest in a narrow or specific field. An all-purpose resume and cover letter that translate your experience and accomplishments into plain English are the tools that will maximize the number of doors which open for you while permitting you to "fish" in the widest range of job areas.

Your resume will provide the script for your job interview.

When you get down to it, your resume has a simple job to do: Its purpose is to blow as many doors open as possible and to make as many people as possible want to meet you. So a well-written resume that really "sells" you is a key that will create opportunities for you in a job hunt.

This statistic explains why: The typical newspaper advertisement for a job opening receives more than 245 replies. And normally only 10 or 12 will be invited to an interview.

But here's another purpose of the resume: it provides the "script" the employer uses when he interviews you. If your resume has been written in such a way that your strengths and achievements are revealed, that's what you'll end up talking about at the job interview. Since the resume will govern what you get asked about at your interviews, you can't overestimate the importance of making sure your resume makes you look and sound as good as you are.

Your resume is the "script" for your job interviews. Make sure you put on your resume what you want to talk about or be asked about at the job interview.

So what is a "good" resume?

Very literally, your resume should motivate the person reading it to dial the phone number or e-mail the screen name you have put on the resume. When you are relocating, you should put a local phone number on your resume if your physical address is several states away; employers are more likely to dial a local telephone number than a long-distance number when they're looking for potential employees.

If you have a resume already, look at it objectively. Is it a limp, colorless "laundry list" of your job titles and duties? Or does it "paint a picture" of your skills, abilities, and accomplishments in a way that would make someone want to meet you? Can people understand what you're saying? If you are attempting to change fields or industries, can potential employers see that your skills and knowledge are transferable to other environments? For example, have you described accomplishments which reveal your problem-solving abilities or communication skills?

The one-page resume in chronological format is the format preferred by most employers.

How long should your resume be?

One page, maybe two. Usually only people in the academic community have a resume (which they usually call a *curriculum vitae*) longer than one or two pages. Remember that your resume is almost always accompanied by a cover letter, and a potential employer does not want to read more than two or three pages about a total stranger in order to decide if he wants to meet that person! Besides, don't forget that the more you tell someone about yourself, the more opportunity you are providing for the employer to screen you out at the "first-cut" stage. A resume should be concise and exciting and designed to make the reader want to meet you in person!

Should resumes be functional or chronological?

Employers almost always prefer a chronological resume; in other words, an employer will find a resume easier to read if it is immediately apparent what your current or most recent job is, what you did before that, and so forth, in reverse chronological order. A resume that goes back in detail for the last ten years of employment will generally satisfy the employer's curiosity about your background. Employment more than ten years old can be shown even more briefly in an "Other Experience" section at the end of your "Experience" section. Remember that your intention is not to tell everything you've done but to "hit the high points" and especially impress the employer with what you learned, contributed, or accomplished in each job you describe.

Once you get your resume, what do you do with it?
You will be using your resume to answer ads, as a tool to use in talking with friends and relatives about your job search, and, most importantly, in using the "direct approach" described in this book.

When you mail your resume, always send a "cover letter."
A "cover letter," sometimes called a "resume letter" or "letter of interest," is a letter that accompanies and introduces your resume. Your cover letter is a way of personalizing the resume by sending it to the specific person you think you might want to work for at each company. Your cover letter should contain a few highlights from your resume—just enough to make someone want to meet you. Cover letters should always be typed or word processed on a computer—never handwritten.

Never mail or fax your resume without a cover letter.

1. Learn the art of answering ads.
There is an "art," part of which can be learned, in using your "bestselling" resume to reply to advertisements.

Sometimes an exciting job lurks behind a boring ad that someone dictated in a hurry, so reply to any ad that interests you. Don't worry that you aren't "25 years old with an MBA" like the ad asks for. Employers will always make compromises in their requirements if they think you're the "best fit" overall.

What about ads that ask for "salary requirements?"
What if the ad you're answering asks for "salary requirements?" The first rule is to avoid committing yourself in writing at that point to a specific salary. You don't want to "lock yourself in."

What if the ad asks for your "salary requirements?"

There are two ways to handle the ad that asks for "salary requirements."
First, you can ignore that part of the ad and accompany your resume with a cover letter that focuses on "selling" you, your abilities, and even some of your philosophy about work or your field. You may include a sentence in your cover letter like this: "I can provide excellent personal and professional references at your request, and I would be delighted to share the private details of my salary history with you in person."

Second, if you feel you must give some kind of number, just state a range in your cover letter that includes your medical, dental, other benefits, and expected bonuses. You might state, for example, "My current compensation, including benefits and bonuses, is in the range of $30,000-$40,000."

Analyze the ad and "tailor" yourself to it.
When you're replying to ads, a finely tailored cover letter is an important tool in getting your resume noticed and read. On the next page is a cover letter which has been "tailored to fit" a specific ad. Notice the "art" used by PREP writers of analyzing the ad's main requirements and then writing the letter so that the person's background, work habits, and interests seem "tailor-made" to the company's needs. Use this cover letter as a model when you prepare your own reply to ads.

Date

Exact Name of Person
Exact Title
Exact Name of Company
Address
City, State, Zip

Dear Exact Name of Person (or Dear Sir or Madam if answering a blind ad):

With the enclosed resume, I would like to express my interest in exploring employment opportunities with your organization.

As you will see from my resume, I have excelled in a track record of promotion with the United States Postal Service. I have earned a reputation as a gifted problem solver while performing as an Engineer. Although I excelled in the USPS and am held in high regard, I am selectively exploring opportunities in other organizations that are involved in engineering "leading-edge" solutions for our complex modern problems.

I believe that my success in the engineering field thus far has been due to my ability to look at each problem I encounter with a creative yet practical problem-solving approach. To use the vernacular, I am able to "think outside the box." I take pride in the numerous contributions I have made to the USPS, and I offer an ability to work effectively with others at all organizational levels.

I hope you will call or write me soon to suggest a time convenient for us to meet and discuss your current and future needs and how I might serve them. Thank you in advance for your time.

Sincerely,

Jared Coolidge

Alternate last paragraph:
I hope you will welcome my call soon to arrange a brief meeting to discuss your current and future needs and how I might serve them. Thank you in advance for your time.

Employers are trying to identify the individual who wants the job they are filling. Don't be afraid to express your enthusiasm in the cover letter!

2. Talk to friends and relatives.

Don't be shy about telling your friends and relatives the kind of job you're looking for. Looking for the job you want involves using your network of contacts, so tell people what you're looking for. They may be able to make introductions and help set up interviews.

About 25% of all interviews are set up through "who you know," so don't ignore this approach.

3. Finally, and most importantly, use the "direct approach."

More than 50% of all job interviews are set up by the "direct approach." That means you actually mail, e-mail, or fax a resume and a cover letter to a company you think might be interesting to work for.

The "direct approach" is a strategy in which you choose your next employer.

To whom do you write?

In general, you should write directly to the *exact name* of the person who would be hiring you: say, the vice-president of marketing or data processing. If you're in doubt about to whom to address the letter, address it to the president by name and he or she will make sure it gets forwarded to the right person within the company who has hiring authority in your area.

How do you find the names of potential employers?

You're not alone if you feel that the biggest problem in your job search is finding the right names at the companies you want to contact. But you can usually figure out the names of companies you want to approach by deciding first if your job hunt is primarily geography-driven or industry-driven.

In a **geography-driven job hunt,** you could select a list of, say, 50 companies you want to contact **by location** from the lists that the U.S. Chambers of Commerce publish yearly of their "major area employers." There are hundreds of local Chambers of Commerce across America, and most of them will have an 800 number which you can find through 1-800-555-1212. If you and your family think Atlanta, Dallas, Ft. Lauderdale, and Virginia Beach might be nice places to live, for example, you could contact the Chamber of Commerce in those cities and ask how you can obtain a copy of their list of major employers. Your nearest library will have the book which lists the addresses of all chambers.

In an **industry-driven job hunt,** and if you are willing to relocate, you will be identifying the companies which you find most attractive in the industry in which you want to work. When you select a list of companies to contact **by industry,** you can find the right person to write and the address of firms by industrial category in *Standard and Poor's, Moody's,* and other excellent books in public libraries. Many Web sites also provide contact information.

Many people feel it's a good investment to actually call the company to either find out or double-check the name of the person to whom they want to send a resume and cover letter. It's important to do as much as you feasibly can to assure that the letter gets to the right person in the company.

On-line research will be the best way for many people to locate organizations to which they wish to send their resume. It is outside the scope of this book to teach Internet research skills, but librarians are often useful in this area.

What's the correct way to follow up on a resume you send?

There is a polite way to be aggressively interested in a company during your job hunt. It is ideal to end the cover letter accompanying your resume by saying, "I hope you'll welcome my call next week when I try to arrange a brief meeting at your convenience to discuss your current and future needs and how I might serve them." Keep it low key, and just ask for a "brief meeting," not an interview. Employers want people who show a determined interest in working with them, so don't be shy about following up on the resume and cover letter you've mailed.

STEP THREE: Preparing for Interviews

It pays to be aware of the 14 most common pitfalls for job hunters.

But a resume and cover letter by themselves can't get you the job you want. You need to "prep" yourself before the interview. Step Three in your job campaign is "Preparing for Interviews." First, let's look at interviewing from the hiring organization's point of view.

What are the biggest "turnoffs" for potential employers?

One of the ways to help yourself perform well at an interview is to look at the main reasons why organizations *don't* hire the people they interview, according to those who do the interviewing.

Notice that "lack of appropriate background" (or lack of experience) is the *last* reason for not being offered the job.

The 14 Most Common Reasons Job Hunters Are Not Offered Jobs *(according to the companies who do the interviewing and hiring):*

1. Low level of accomplishment
2. Poor attitude, lack of self-confidence
3. Lack of goals/objectives
4. Lack of enthusiasm
5. Lack of interest in the company's business
6. Inability to sell or express yourself
7. Unrealistic salary demands
8. Poor appearance
9. Lack of maturity, no leadership potential
10. Lack of extracurricular activities
11. Lack of preparation for the interview, no knowledge about company
12. Objecting to travel
13. Excessive interest in security and benefits
14. Inappropriate background

Department of Labor studies have proven that smart, "prepared" job hunters can increase their beginning salary while getting a job in *half* the time it normally takes. (4½ months is the average national length of a job search.) Here, from PREP, are some questions that can prepare you to find a job faster.

Are you in the "right" frame of mind?

It seems unfair that we have to look for a job just when we're lowest in morale. Don't worry *too* much if you're nervous before interviews. You're supposed to be a little nervous, especially if the job means a lot to you. But the best way to kill unnecessary fears about job hunting is through 1) making sure you have a great resume and 2) preparing yourself for the interview. Here are three main areas you need to think about before each interview.

Do you know what the company does?

Don't walk into an interview giving the impression that, "If this is Tuesday, this must be General Motors."

Research the company before you go to interviews.

Find out before the interview what the company's main product or service is. Where is the company heading? Is it in a "growth" or declining industry? (Answers to these questions may influence whether or not you want to work there!)

Information about what the company does is in annual reports, in newspaper and magazine articles, and on the Internet. If you're not yet skilled at Internet research, just visit your nearest library and ask the reference librarian to guide you to printed materials on the company.

Do you know what you want to do for the company?

Before the interview, try to decide how you see yourself fitting into the company. Remember, "lack of exact background" the company wants is usually the last reason people are not offered jobs.

Understand before you go to each interview that the burden will be on you to "sell" the interviewer on why you're the best person for the job and the company.

How will you answer the critical interview questions?

Anticipate the questions you will be asked at the interview, and prepare your responses in advance.

Put yourself in the interviewer's position and think about the questions you're most likely to be asked. Here are some of the most commonly asked interview questions:

Q: *"What are your greatest strengths?"*

A: Don't say you've never thought about it! Go into an interview knowing the three main impressions you want to leave about yourself, such as "I'm hard-working, loyal, and an imaginative cost-cutter."

Q: *"What are your greatest weaknesses?"*

A: Don't confess that you're lazy or have trouble meeting deadlines! Confessing that you tend to be a "workaholic" or "tend to be a perfectionist and sometimes get frustrated when others don't share my high standards" will make your prospective employer see a "weakness" that he likes. Name a weakness that your interviewer will perceive as a strength.

Q: *"What are your long-range goals?"*

A: If you're interviewing with Microsoft, don't say you want to work for IBM in five years! Say your long-range goal is to be *with* the company, contributing to its goals and success.

Q: *"What motivates you to do your best work?"*

A: Don't get dollar signs in your eyes here! "A challenge" is not a bad answer, but it's a little cliched. Saying something like "troubleshooting" or "solving a tough problem" is more interesting and specific. Give an example if you can.

Q: "What do you know about this organization?"

A: Don't say you never heard of it until they asked you to the interview! Name an interesting, positive thing you learned about the company recently from your research. Remember, company executives can sometimes feel rather "maternal" about the company they serve. Don't get onto a negative area of the company if you can think of positive facts you can bring up. Of course, if you learned in your research that the company's sales seem to be taking a nose-dive, or that the company president is being prosecuted for taking bribes, you might politely ask your interviewer to tell you something that could help you better understand what you've been reading. Those are the kinds of company facts that can help you determine whether or not you want to work there.

Go to an interview prepared to tell the company why it should hire you.

Q: "Why should I hire you?"

A: "I'm unemployed and available" is the wrong answer here! Get back to your strengths and say that you believe the organization could benefit by a loyal, hard-working cost-cutter like yourself.

In conclusion, you should decide in advance, before you go to the interview, how you will answer each of these commonly asked questions. Have some practice interviews with a friend to role-play and build your confidence.

STEP FOUR: Handling the Interview and Negotiating Salary

Now you're ready for Step Four: actually handling the interview successfully and effectively. Remember, the purpose of an interview is to get a job offer.

A smile at an interview makes the employer perceive of you as intelligent!

Eight "do's" for the interview

According to leading U.S. companies, there are eight key areas in interviewing success. You can fail at an interview if you mishandle just one area.

1. **Do wear appropriate clothes.**

You can never go wrong by wearing a suit to an interview.

2. **Do be well groomed.**

Don't overlook the obvious things like having clean hair, clothes, and fingernails for the interview.

3. **Do give a firm handshake.**

You'll have to shake hands twice in most interviews: first, before you sit down, and second, when you leave the interview. Limp handshakes turn most people off.

4. **Do smile and show a sense of humor.**

Interviewers are looking for people who would be nice to work with, so don't be so somber that you don't smile. In fact, research shows that people who smile at interviews are perceived as more intelligent. So, smile!

5. **Do be enthusiastic.**

Employers say they are "turned off" by lifeless, unenthusiastic job hunters who show no special interest in that company. The best way to show some enthusiasm for the employer's operation is to find out about the business beforehand.

6. Do show you are flexible and adaptable.

An employer is looking for someone who can contribute to his organization in a flexible, adaptable way. No matter what skills and training you have, employers know every new employee must go through initiation and training on the company's turf. Certainly show pride in your past accomplishments in a specific, factual way ("I saved my last employer $50.00 a week by a new cost-cutting measure I developed"). But don't come across as though there's nothing about the job you couldn't easily handle.

7. Do ask intelligent questions about the employer's business.

An employer is hiring someone because of certain business needs. Show interest in those needs. Asking questions to get a better idea of the employer's needs will help you "stand out" from other candidates interviewing for the job.

8. Do "take charge" when the interviewer "falls down" on the job.

Employers are seeking people with good attitudes whom they can train and coach to do things their way.

Go into every interview knowing the three or four points about yourself you want the interviewer to remember. And be prepared to take an active part in leading the discussion if the interviewer's "canned approach" does not permit you to display your "strong suit." You can't always depend on the interviewer's asking you the "right" questions so you can stress your strengths and accomplishments.

An important "don't": Don't ask questions about salary or benefits at the first interview. Employers don't take warmly to people who look at their organization as just a place to satisfy salary and benefit needs. Don't risk making a negative impression by appearing greedy or self-serving. The place to discuss salary and benefits is normally at the second interview, and the employer will bring it up. Then you can ask questions without appearing excessively interested in what the organization can do for you.

Now...negotiating your salary

Even if an ad requests that you communicate your "salary requirement" or "salary history," you should avoid providing those numbers in your initial cover letter. You can usually say something like this: "I would be delighted to discuss the private details of my salary history with you in person."

Once you're at the interview, you must avoid even appearing *interested* in salary before you are offered the job. Make sure you've "sold" yourself before talking salary. First show you're the "best fit" for the employer and then you'll be in a stronger position from which to negotiate salary. **Never** bring up the subject of salary yourself. Employers say there's no way you can avoid looking greedy if you bring up the issue of salary and benefits before the company has identified you as its "best fit."

Don't appear excessively interested in salary and benefits at the interview.

Interviewers sometimes throw out a salary figure at the first interview to see if you'll accept it. You may not want to commit yourself if you think you will be able to negotiate a better deal later on. Get back to finding out more about the job. This lets the interviewer know you're interested primarily in the job and not the salary.

When the organization brings up salary, it may say something like this: "Well, Mary, we think you'd make a good candidate for this job. What kind of salary are we talking about?" You may not want to name a number here, either. Give the ball back to the interviewer. Act as though you hadn't given the subject of salary much thought and respond something like this: "Ah, Mr. Jones, I wonder if you'd be kind enough to tell me what salary you had in mind when you advertised the job?" Or ... "What is the range you have in mind?"

Don't worry, if the interviewer names a figure that you think is too low, you can say so without turning down the job or locking yourself into a rigid position. The point here is to negotiate for yourself as well as you can. You might reply to a number named by the interviewer that you think is low by saying something like this: "Well, Mr. Lee, the job interests me very much, and I think I'd certainly enjoy working with you. But, frankly, I was thinking of something a little higher than that." That leaves the ball in your interviewer's court again, and you haven't turned down the job either, in case it turns out that the interviewer can't increase the offer and you still want the job.

Salary negotiation can be tricky.

Last, send a follow-up letter.

Mail, e-mail, or fax a letter right after the interview telling your interviewer you enjoyed the meeting and are certain (if you are) that you are the "best fit" for the job. The people interviewing you will probably have an attitude described as either "professionally loyal" to their companies, or "maternal and proprietary" if the interviewer also owns the company. In either case, they are looking for people who want to work for *that* company in particular. The follow-up letter you send might be just the deciding factor in your favor if the employer is trying to choose between you and someone else.

A follow-up letter can help the employer choose between you and another qualified candidate.

A cover letter is an essential part of a job hunt or career change.

Many people are aware of the importance of having a great resume, but most people in a job hunt don't realize just how important a cover letter can be. The purpose of the cover letter, sometimes called a **"letter of interest,"** is to introduce your resume to prospective employers. The cover letter is often the critical ingredient in a job hunt because the cover letter allows you to say a lot of things that just don't "fit" on the resume. For example, you can emphasize your commitment to a new field and stress your related talents. The cover letter also gives you a chance to stress outstanding character and personal values. On the next two pages you will see examples of very effective cover letters.

A cover letter is an essential part of a career change.

Please do not attempt to implement a career change without a cover letter. A cover letter is the first impression of you, and you can influence the way an employer views you by the language and style of your letter.

Special help for those in career change

We want to emphasize again that, especially in a career change, the cover letter is very important and can help you "build a bridge" to a new career. A creative and appealing cover letter can begin the process of encouraging the potential employer to imagine you in an industry other than the one in which you have worked.

As a special help to those in career change, there are resumes and cover letters included in this book which show valuable techniques and tips you should use when changing fields or industries. The resumes and cover letters of career changers are identified in the table of contents as "Career Change" and you will see the "Career Change" label on cover letters in Part Two where the individuals are changing careers.

PART FIVE:
Resumes and Cover Letters for Job Hunting Outside the USPS

In this section, you will find resumes and cover letters of professionals seeking employment outside the USPS. In some cases, these individuals have spent some time in USPS employment, or in the postal function outside the USPS, and now seek career change. Some of these individuals have worked as Data Conversion Operator, Flat Sorter Operator, Fleet Maintenance Supervisor, Mail Carrier, Mail Distribution and Window Clerk, Maintenance Manager, Personnel Administration Manager, Postal Clerk, Postal Detachment Clerk, Postal Supervisor, Postal Worker, Supervisory Supply Specialist, Traffic Specialist, and Wheeled Vehicle Mechanic.

Changing fields: Newcomers to an industry *sometimes* have advantages over more experienced professionals. In a job hunt, junior professionals can have an advantage over their more experienced counterparts. Prospective employers often view the less experienced workers as "more trainable" and "more coachable" than their seniors. This means that the mature professional who has already excelled in a first career can, with credibility, "change careers" and transfer skills to other industries.

Newcomers to the field may have disadvantages compared to their seniors. Almost by definition, the inexperienced professional—the young person who has recently entered the job market, or the individual who has recently received respected certifications—is less tested and less experienced than senior managers, so the resume and cover letter of the inexperienced professional may often have to "sell" his or her potential to do something he or she has never done before. Lack of experience in the field she wants to enter can be a stumbling block to the junior employee, but remember that many employers believe that someone who has excelled in anything—academics, for example—can excel in many other fields.

Some advice to inexperienced professionals...
If senior professionals could give junior professionals a piece of advice about careers, here's what they would say: Manage your career and don't stumble from job to job in an incoherent pattern. Try to find work that interests you, and then identify prosperous industries which need work performed of the type you want to do. Learn early in your working life that a great resume and cover letter can blow doors open for you and help you maximize your salary.

Date

Exact Name of Person
Title or Position
Exact Name of Company
Address
City, State, Zip

DATA CONVERSION OPERATOR

Dear Exact Name of Person: (or Dear or Madam if answering a blind ad.)

I would appreciate an opportunity to talk with you soon about how I could contribute to your organization through my experience and personal qualities.

As you will see from my resume, I have excelled as a Data Conversion Operator with the USPS in Minneapolis, and I have proven my ability to produce quality results under tight deadlines. I am interested in making a career within an organization which can utilize my strong management and communication skills.

I hope you will call or write me soon to suggest a time convenient for us to meet and discuss your current and future needs and how I might serve them. Thank you in advance for your time.

Sincerely,

Suzanne Koller

Alternate last paragraph:

I hope you will welcome my call soon to suggest a time convenient for us to meet and discuss your current and future needs and how I might serve them. Thank you in advance for your time.

SUZANNE KOLLER

1110½ Hay Street, Fayetteville, NC 28305 • preppub@aol.com • (910) 483-6611

OBJECTIVE

To apply my background in data entry, personnel administration, and customer service coupled with my excellent clerical and public relations skills to an organization that can use a dedicated and conscientious employee who can provide excellent references.

EXPERIENCE

DATA CONVERSION OPERATOR. U.S. Postal Service, Minneapolis, MN (2004-present). Am involved in processing up to 1 million pieces of outgoing mail per day by inputting zip codes, addresses, and often business names.
- Maintain an average keying speed greater than 7,150 keystrokes per minute.

DATA ENTRY OPERATOR. XYZ Systems, Inc., Minneapolis, MN (2002-04). Keyed and processed mail images on the computer, maintaining a minimum keying speed in order to ensure that production goals were met.

NIGHT AUDITOR and **RESERVATIONS CLERK.** Various hotels, Minneapolis/St. Paul, MN (1998-02). Provided a number of customer relations and administrative tasks while ensuring customer service to guests during their stay at several local hotels.
- Checked guests into and out of the hotel; scheduled and canceled guest reservations.
- Answered multi-line telephone and operated a switchboard, directing guests' calls to the correct extension and taking messages when guests were not available.
- Provided assistance to guests, addressing and resolving questions and complaints when possible.
- Operated a cash register, credit card imprinter, and ten-key calculator.

PRODUCTION WORKER. Swingline, Inc., St. Paul, MN (1996-98). Performed assembly tasks on various power tools for a local facility of this large national manufacturer.

ASSISTANT PERSONNEL ADMINISTRATION SUPERVISOR. U.S. Army, Fort Snelling, MN (1989-96). Provided supervisory, personnel administration, clerical, and training support to an organization with as many as 450 employees.
- Supervised, trained, and assisted six employees in the Personnel Administration Center, ensuring that all tasks were performed accurately and in a timely manner.
- Performed a wide variety of word processing, data entry, and clerical tasks, including the processing of evaluation reports, unit fund reports, and feeder reports.
- Assumed all duties and responsibilities of the Personnel Administration Center Supervisor in his absence.
- Developed and implemented new control systems for meal card logs, leaves, and passes.
- During a three-month absence by the Supervisor, took on the additional responsibilities of that position, preparing the organization for a major inspection. Due to my efforts, the organization received a satisfactory rating with no major areas of deficiency.
- On an official evaluation, received the highest possible marks in all measured proficiencies, and was cited for my "excellent leadership potential."

EDUCATION

Completed numerous personnel administration and leadership courses as part of my military training, including the personnel senior supervisor course, training management systems course, and primary leadership development course.

PERSONAL

Outstanding personal and professional references are available upon request.

Date

Exact Name of Person
Title or Position
Exact Name of Company
Address
City, State, Zip

FLAT SORTER OPERATOR

Dear Exact Name of Person: (or Dear or Madam if answering a blind ad.)

I would appreciate an opportunity to talk with you soon about how I could contribute to your organization through my experience and personal qualities.

As you will see from my resume, I served my country with distinction prior to joining the U.S.P.S. as a Flat Sorter Operator. During my military career, I was promoted ahead of my peers because of my outstanding problem-solving abilities, and I received numerous medals and other awards in recognition of my bottom-line management results.

I hope you will call or write me soon to suggest a time convenient for us to meet and discuss your current and future needs and how I might serve them. Thank you in advance for your time.

Sincerely,

Ulric Mason

Alternate last paragraph:
I hope you will welcome my call soon to suggest a time convenient for us to meet and discuss your current and future needs and how I might serve them. Thank you in advance for your time.

ULRIC MASON

1110½ Hay Street, Fayetteville, NC 28305 • preppub@aol.com • (910) 483-6611

OBJECTIVE To offer my multiple technical skills along with my education, experience, and accomplishments to an organization that can benefit from my skill in operating and supervising highly sophisticated communications and information gathering systems.

EDUCATION Attend University of Kentucky-Hopkinsville Community College, Hopkinsville, KY.
B.S., Computer Information Systems, Hopkinsville Community College, 2004.
Completed the **Computer Repair Technician** course, Central Texas College, 2002.

EXPERIENCE **FLAT SORTER OPERATOR.** U.S. Postal Service, Hopkinsville, KY (2003-present). Operate a keypad at 45 wpm.

During a 10-year career in the U.S. Army, served as a voice interpreter, transcriber, and training manager while coordinating training for active and reserve personnel as well as U.S. Marines. Taught courses in the following languages: Spanish, Russian, French, Korean, and German.
SUPERVISOR. Fort Campbell, KY (2002-03). Supervised and provided technical guidance to intelligence electronic warfare surveillance team with an 18-hour no-notice deployment capability.
* Intercepted, identified, and recorded foreign voice transmissions; established voice and data links; controlled network communications in support of the 101st Airborne Division.

PROGRAM MANAGER. Fort Lewis, WA (2000-01). Developed and maintained a classified program of instruction based on a variety of job descriptions while providing lesson plans and training.
* Managed and coordinated training with national-level agencies and all military services in order to provide subcourses in Spanish, Russian, Persian Farsi, Arabic, and German.

TEAM SUPERVISOR. Fort Lawton, WA (1998-00). Supervised a team of highly skilled voice interception technicians with additional responsibilities for training personnel and overseeing the maintenance of high-tech equipment.

SUPPLY MANAGER. Italy and Korea (1993-98). Earned an Army Achievement Medal for my accomplishments in moving property to a new location during a relocation project as the supply specialist in charge of accountability, turn in, and issue of supplies.
* Became thoroughly knowledgeable of unit, organizational, and installation property management.

TRAINING Received extensive military training which included professional leadership development and supervisory skills as well as technical schools emphasizing electronic warfare, voice interception, supply operations, and airborne training.

SPECIAL SKILLS Through experience, education, and training have developed skills in the following areas:
computer operating systems: Microsoft Windows
word processing software: Microsoft Software: Word, Excel, and PowerPoint
typing: type 50 wpm and keypad at 50 wpm

PERSONAL Speak Spanish fluently. Earned numerous awards and medals.

Date

Exact Name of Person
Title or Position
Name of Company
Address (no., street)
Address (city, state, zip)

FLEET MAINTENANCE SUPERVISOR

Dear Exact Name of Person (or Dear Sir or Madam if answering a blind ad):

I would appreciate an opportunity to talk with you soon about how I could contribute to your organization through my expertise in large fleet maintenance management along with my experience in managing assets and personnel.

In my present position as Fleet Maintenance Supervisor for the U.S. Postal Service, Sacramento, CA, I oversee a general support maintenance shop maintaining a fleet of more than 600 vehicles. I advise a senior official on potential problem areas and recommend solutions. Previously while serving in the U.S. Army, I oversaw activities including automotive, fuel, and electric component repair and rebuild operations.

My technical abilities, insistence on high-quality performance from my employees, and enthusiastic and energetic personality have enabled me to succeed while serving in every position held. As you will see from my resume, I have a B.S. degree in Interdisciplinary Studies from Darton College, Albany, GA.

I feel certain that you would find me to be an articulate and persuasive leader with a "track record" of success in building teams, increasing productivity and efficiency, and managing multimillion-dollar assets.

I hope you will welcome my call soon to arrange a brief meeting at your convenience to discuss your current and future needs and how I might serve them. Thank you in advance for your time.

Sincerely yours,

Jason L. Reaves

Alternate last paragraph:
I hope you will call or write soon to suggest a time convenient for us to meet and discuss your current and future needs and how I might serve them. Thank you in advance for your time.

JASON LEE REAVES

1110½ Hay Street, Fayetteville, NC 28305   •   preppub@aol.com   •   (910) 483-6611

OBJECTIVE

To benefit an organization that can use an astute manager who offers a proven ability to manage transportation services and vehicle maintenance for maximum safety and profitability.

EDUCATION

B.S., Interdisciplinary Studies, GPA 3.66, Darton College, Albany, GA, 1997.

TRAINING

Completed training programs which included logistics management and leadership schools as well as training as a military police officer.

EXPERIENCE

FLEET MAINTENANCE SUPERVISOR. U.S. Postal Service, Sacramento, CA (2004-present). Oversee maintenance support activities for a fleet of more than 600 vehicles. Collect data and prepare status reports on numbers of vehicles available for immediate use and on hold for repair parts.
- Distribute information on safety and equipment maintenance issues.
- Advise a senior official on potential problem areas and recommend solutions.
- Am known as an assertive manager who leads the way in producing quality results on a timely basis.

Refined my skills while serving my counter in the U.S. Army:
MECHANIZED INFANTRY PLATOON LEADER. U.S. Army, Germany (1998-03). In my first assignment as an officer, supervised and trained 30 people, controlled a $10 million equipment inventory, and oversaw equipment maintenance activities.
- Quickly earned a reputation as a young professional who could be counted on to react rapidly and use sound judgment when making decisions.
- Became effective in solving problems and operating under pressure and was selected to lead a support team to Bosnia which completed its mission with no incidents.
- Executed all missions without incident or loss to personnel or property.

FULL-TIME STUDENT. Darton College, Albany, GA (1995-97). Selected for a special program sponsored by the U.S. Army, attended college full time and upon graduation was commissioned into active duty service.
- Displayed a high level of leadership skills, personal drive, and dedication which resulted in my selection for this educational opportunity.

MILITARY POLICE TEAM LEADER. U.S. Army, Fort Meade, MD (1993-95). Advanced quickly to the leadership role of my three-person team of military police officers providing law enforcement, traffic management, traffic investigation, and crime prevention support to a military community.
- Became highly effective as a leader and motivator; learned to welcome responsibility while ensuring that all tasks and duties were carried out successfully.
- Was singled out for my maturity and leadership qualities as a member of an advance task force providing relief following the devastation of a hurricane in Florida.
- Earned the honor of "Post Soldier of the Quarter" after winning at the company and battalion level against many more experienced candidates.

COMPUTERS

Proficient with numerous software programs including the Microsoft Office Suite.

PERSONAL

Married, one son. Enjoy the outdoors, cars, family, biking, sailing, and sports.

Date

Exact Name of Person
Exact Title
Exact Name of Company
Address
City, State, Zip

MAIL CARRIER   Dear Exact Name of Person: (or Dear Sir or Madam if answering a blind ad):

With the enclosed resume, I would like to make you aware of my background as a versatile professional with exceptional communication skills, a strong customer service orientation, and experience in a variety of challenging service-intensive environments.

As you will see from my resume, I offer experience as a Purchasing Agent, and I have become skilled at processing a high volume of orders while solving a variety of problems and maintaining zero customer complaints. I was cited in an official evaluation for my strong problem-solving and customer service skills as well as for my cheerful disposition and personal initiative.

In a previous position as a Medical Clerk for a busy clinic in Italy, I was praised for diplomacy and compassion that resulted in many patient complaints being avoided during a time when the clinic was heavily understaffed. In addition to being a key player in the integration of a new scheduling system after the clinic scaled up to a round-the-clock operation, I handled a multi-line switchboard and answered numerous customer inquiries in a courteous and professional manner.

In prior experience I proudly served my country as a Military Policeman and Customs Inspector.

Although I was highly regarded by my the U.S. Postal Service in my most recent position and can provide excellent personal and professional references at the appropriate time, I resigned in order to seek full-time permanent employment in an organization that can make use of my strong customer service, administrative, and problem-solving abilities. I feel there is a good "fit" between my skills and your company's needs, and I would appreciate the opportunity to speak with you soon about how I can contribute to your operation.

If you can use an outgoing, articulate individual whose exceptional interpersonal skills and customer focus have been proven in a variety of challenging environments, then I hope you will welcome my call soon when I try to arrange a brief meeting to discuss your goals and how my background might serve your needs.

Sincerely,

Shannon Smith

SHANNON SMITH

1110½ Hay Street, Fayetteville, NC 28305   •   preppub@aol.com   •   (910) 483-6611

OBJECTIVE   To benefit an organization that can use an experienced professional with exceptional communication and interpersonal skills who offers a versatile background in customer service and administrative environments as well as the ability to work with little supervision.

COMPUTERS   Skilled with the Windows operating system, Microsoft Word, Excel, and PowerPoint.

EXPERIENCE   **MAIL CARRIER.** U.S. Postal Service, Pierre, SC (2004). Provided exceptional service to residential U.S. mail customers while ensuring the timely and accurate delivery of correspondence, packages, and parcels; organized mail for each day's deliveries to ensure that the route was completed in the most efficient manner.

PURCHASING AGENT. U.S. Army, Fort Jackson, SC (2001-03). Performed purchasing, rental, and leasing of supplies, services, and equipment to support the operations of this military installation; trained two new employees with no previous purchasing experience to assume the duties of my position.
- Became known for my strong problem-solving skills; retained vendor/customer satisfaction while achieving stringent quality control and bottom-line goals.
- Processed a high volume of customer purchase orders requiring administrative action, solving all problems and disputes while **maintaining zero customer complaints.**
- Was cited in an official evaluation for my **"gracious manner in helping both vendors and customers with any of their contracting problems."**
- Continuously exceeded production requirements despite personally handling most purchases over the competition threshold and the majority of difficult ADP purchases.
- Ensured compliance with all applicable rules and regulations regarding the open market and formal competitive bid processes, as well as with adequate pricing in competition, price reasonable, and small business determinations and sole source justifications.

MEDICAL CLERK. Italy Army Regional Medical Center, Italy (1999-01). Provided customer service, administrative, and receptionist support, exercising tact and diplomacy in dealing with patients who were often tense and fearful.
- Demonstrated exceptional attention to detail while maintaining the appointment calendar; scheduled, rescheduled, and cancelled patient appointments.
- Answered a high volume of inquiries in a courteous and professional manner, both over the phone and in person; utilized a multi-line phone system.
- In an official performance appraisal, my supervisor stated that **"due to her diplomacy and compassion, many patient complaints were avoided."**

Highlights of earlier experience:
CUSTOMS INSPECTOR. U.S. Customs Service, Spain. Supervised and coordinated all movements of household and cargo items being exported out of the area, ensuring that no contraband entered the U.S. from items transported from Spain.
- Served as **Senior Inspector** and was the civilian liaison for military and civilian personnel processing through the facility; maintained outstanding relationships.

Proudly served my country as a **MILITARY POLICE OFFICER** and **CUSTOMS INSPECTOR** in the U.S. Army, supervising and training up to 20 personnel responding to emergency and non-emergency situations requiring law enforcement assistance.

PERSONAL   Excellent personal/professional references available on request. Skilled problem solver.

Date

Exact Name of Person
Title or Position
Exact Name of Company
Address
City, State, Zip

**MAIL DISTRIBUTION
& WINDOW CLERK**

Dear Exact Name of Person: (or Dear Sir or Madam if answering a blind ad.)

I would appreciate an opportunity to talk with you soon about how I could contribute to your organization through my versatile experience, positive attitude, and dedication to high quality customer service and quality control.

With a keen eye for detail and ability to quickly learn and apply new ideas and concepts, I offer a reputation as a professional who can be depended on for personal integrity, resourcefulness, and dedication to excellence in everything I attempt.

You will see from my enclosed resume that the bulk of my experience has been with the U.S. Postal Service and the U.S. Army where I was successful in jobs where my attention to detail, research and analytical skills, and clerical and office operations skills were of prime importance. With a typing speed of 60 wpm and experience in using most standard office machines, I offer familiarity with numerous popular software programs and operating systems.

I hope you will call or write me soon to suggest a time convenient for us to meet and discuss your current and future needs and how I might serve them. Thank you in advance for your time.

Sincerely,

Mary Tanner

MARY TANNER

1110½ Hay Street, Fayetteville, NC 28305 • preppub@aol.com • (910) 483-6611

OBJECTIVE	To offer a versatile background and skills to an organization that can benefit from my ability to utilize computers and all standard office equipment, my research and analytical skills, and my ability to motivate and manage personnel for outstanding results.
SPECIAL SKILLS	Through training and experience, offer skills and knowledge in the following areas: *computers:* familiar with various software; utilized customized government contracting programs *equipment:* type 60 wpm, ten-key adding machines, data entry equipment, mail automation equipment, copiers, and cash registers *other:* working knowledge of Department of Defense contracting, procurement, and budget process
EDUCATION & TRAINING	Have completed approximately 30 credit hours of college course work as well as extensive training in the areas of accounting, budgeting, and personnel supervision.
EXPERIENCE	**MAIL DISTRIBUTION AND WINDOW CLERK.** U.S. Postal Service, Anchorage, AK (2004-present). Maintain a high level of production while involved in sorting, identifying, and processing mail and ensuring it is distributed according to strict guidelines.

ACTING CUSTOMER SERVICE SUPERVISOR. U.S. Postal Service, Bethel, AK (2002-04). Began as a Letter Sorting Machine Operator in 2002, and earned promotion to Acting Customer Service Supervisor; supervised and motivated 25 employees with an emphasis on safety, proper handling and delivery of mail to postal patrons, and the preparation of reports.
- Provided leadership which kept production high and labor costs within budget restraints.
- Contributed to team unity while investigating grievances and listening to both sides.

U.S. Army experience:
SUPPLY TECHNICIAN. Fort Bragg, NC (2000-01). Developed quality control guidelines for a medical material branch including maintaining files and records; received an Exceptional Performance Award for implementing a program in which expired medical supplies were returned rather than destroyed and which saved the government more than $30,000 in a six-month period.

BUDGET ASSISTANT. Korea (1999-00). Processed complex travel claims and vouchers for and researched government regulations to ensure compliance; managed supply accounts.

PROCUREMENT CLERK. Italy (1998-99). Provided support for supply activities by inputting data into an automated system, reviewing and coordinating corrections, assembling and distributing correspondence, and preparing a wide range of reports; was cited for my sound judgment and ability to work independently.

WINDOW CLERK/DISTRIBUTION CLERK. U.S. Postal Service, Eagle River, AK (1994-98). Sorted and processed mail as well as answering customers' questions and controlling funds received for mail services.
- Selected as Acting Operations Supervisor, frequently filled in by overseeing services for a community of more than 10,000 people including maintaining detailed statistical and accounting records and preparing finance reports for the district finance office.

PERSONAL	Honest individual; positive attitude. Extensive quality control/customer service experience.

Date

Exact Name of Person
Title or Position
Name of Company
Address
City, State, Zip

**MAINTENANCE
MANAGER**

Dear Exact Name of Person (or Dear Sir or Madam if answering a blind ad):

I would appreciate an opportunity to talk with you soon about how I could contribute to your organization through my excellent performance record which includes both technical and mechanical skills as well as the ability to provide training, supervision, and managerial abilities.

As you will see from my resume, I offer more than ten years of experience as a light and heavy wheeled vehicle mechanic and power generation equipment technician. In my current position as Shop Supervisor at Allied Auto Electric, Annapolis, MD, I have been credited with turning around a failing maintenance operation. I direct two clerks and five mechanics in all aspects of maintenance support.

In a previous job with the U.S. Postal Service, Baltimore, MD, I supervised five persons and was awarded three awards in recognition of my efforts. Throughout my employment, I have earned a reputation as a creative leader who could be counted on to see that the details were taken care of which ensured that operations ran smoothly. I have consistently been singled out for advancement and described as a professional who meets challenges head on and achieves outstanding results through leadership by example.

My versatile background has included providing direct supervision for up to 27 employees, overseeing all aspects of running maintenance operations, developing and conducting effective training programs, and managing logistics support activities. I have received numerous commendation and achievement awards for my exceptional duty performance, leadership and concern for my employees, and contributions which directly resulted in success for my department and for the organization as a whole.

I believe you would find me to be an enthusiastic and ambitious individual who works well under stress and time constraints.

I hope you will welcome my call soon to arrange a brief meeting at your convenience to discuss your current and future needs and how I might serve them. Thank you in advance for your time.

Sincerely yours,

Jerry C. O'Reilly

JERRY CHAD O'REILLY

1110½ Hay Street, Fayetteville, NC 28305   •   preppub@aol.com   •   (910) 483-6611

OBJECTIVE

To offer a combination of excellent electrical and mechanical skills along with outstanding managerial and supervisory abilities to an organization that can use a mature, detail-oriented professional who is also recognized as a hard-charging and creative trainer and motivator.

TECHNICAL KNOWLEDGE

Experienced in reading schematics and wiring diagrams, am highly skilled in the repair, service, and inspection of a wide range of equipment including, but not limited to:

generators up to 100KW	trucks up to 10 tons	trailers up to 40 feet
air compressors up to 250CFM	floodlights	gas and diesel heaters
4,000 and 6,000-lb. forklifts	4,000-lb. cranes	hoists
water and fuel pumps up to 350GPM		

gas engines: up to 20HP Hercules engines
diesel engines: Cummins, Detroit, and White V-6, V-8, and V-10 straight 6, 4, and 2-cylinders
Use diagnostic equipment including calibrators, potentiometers, and multimeters

EXPERIENCE

MAINTENANCE MANAGER. Allied Auto Electric, Annapolis, MD (2004-present). Credited with turning around a failing maintenance operation, directed two clerks and five mechanics in all aspects of support for a $1 million inventory of 80 generators.
- Displayed my knowledge and versatility overseeing activities ranging from dispatching, to training, to using computers for report preparation and record keeping.
- Molded employees into a team which went from failing to "no faults found" ratings.

MAINTENANCE SUPERVISOR. U.S. Postal Service, Baltimore, MD (2000-03). Developed a maintenance program which led to commendable 95% availability rates as the manager of a five-person department with 33 line items of equipment valued in excess of $2 million.
- Was singled out to conduct the organization's maintenance training program.
- Exceeded standards by averaging 6% zero balance for a 180-line-item inventory.
- Was awarded *three* awards in recognition of my efforts and long hours which directly resulted in the shop's superior rating in a major inspection which found no faults in the areas of automated records and inventory.
- Supervised five employees and ensured error-free operation of the automated logistics system including all aspects of ordering parts and maintaining records.

POWER GENERATION SHOP FOREMAN. Hood Construction Company, Baltimore, MD (1996-99). Earned advancement to a supervisory role and several awards for my performance in supervising up to 27 people maintaining and operating as many as 50 vehicles, 17 power units, and 234 items of material-handling equipment.
- Was consistently evaluated as displaying technical competence, sound judgment, and a true concern for ensuring high standards of training for and performance by employees.
- Motivated and led employees to outstanding accomplishments under tight deadlines.

POWER GENERATION EQUIPMENT INSPECTOR. U.S. Army, Germany (1993-95). After contributing skills and knowledge which led to a low maintenance backlog, was chosen to oversee quality control and provide technical guidance for eight separate companies.

TRAINING

Excelled in training including power generation mechanics, wheeled vehicle mechanics, fuel handling, leadership development, and maintenance management.

PERSONAL

Have a Secret security clearance. Excel in motivating others through my strong work ethic, insistence on results, and positive approach. Am available for relocation worldwide.

Date

Exact Name of Person
Exact Title
Exact Name of Company
Address
City, State, Zip

PERSONNEL
ADMINISTRATION
MANAGER

Dear Exact Name of Person: (or Dear Sir or Madam if answering a blind ad):

With the enclosed resume, I would like to make you aware of my interest in exploring employment opportunities with your organization and to acquaint you with my distinguished track record of achievements as a manager.

As you will see from my resume, I have excelled in positions requiring top-notch management, communication, and organizational skills while serving my country in the U.S. Army. While gaining experience with numerous popular software programs including Microsoft Word, Excel, and others, I refined my knowledge of human resources and personnel administration. In my most recent position, I directed a personnel services organization of 54 employees involved in handling personnel administration for hundreds of people. Praised for my leadership ability and strong personal initiative, I organized a new Personnel Administration Center "from scratch' and led my team to receive nine commendable ratings on quality control inspections.

In previous jobs in locations all over the world, I trained and supervised employees in all aspects of personnel administration. On numerous occasions I was selected for hotseat jobs which required a proven leader with strong problem-solving abilities. For example, I served as a Postal Supervisor in Iraq, and I was credited with transforming inefficient facilities and services into quality operations which met or exceeded customer expectations.

If you can use a hard worker with a proven ability to manage multiple priorities and produce outstanding bottom-line results under tight deadlines, I hope you will contact me to suggest a time when we might meet to discuss your needs. Thank you in advance for your time.

Sincerely,

Michelle Dennis

MICHELLE DENNIS

1110½ Hay Street, Fayetteville, NC 28305   •   preppub@aol.com   •   (910) 483-6611

OBJECTIVE

To benefit an organization that can use a skilled administrative manager with exceptional communication and organizational skills who offers a background in personnel supervision, training, and administration, operations management, and office administration.

COMPUTERS

Familiar with many of the most popular computer operating systems and software, including: Windows XP, Microsoft Word, Excel, and PowerPoint, and others.

EXPERIENCE

Promoted ahead of my peers and advanced to positions of increasing responsibility while serving my country in the U.S. Army and Army Reserves (1998-present):
2004-present: **PERSONNEL ADMINISTRATION MANAGER.** U.S. Army and Army Reserves, Oversee administrative support activities, directing a personnel service organization of 54 employees in the timely and accurate preparation of personnel actions.
- Manage the processing of all administrative actions, such as in and out-processing of personnel, submission of evaluations and awards, and preparation of recurring reports.
- Established a Personnel Administration Center (PAC) "from scratch," coordinating with the operations office to ensure that the center effectively met the organization's needs.

2003-04: **POSTAL SUPERVISOR.** U.S. Army, Iraq. Supervised four postal clerks while overseeing service delivery of postal financial services to approximately 1,000 personnel in support of War on Terror; held final responsibility for equipment and an inventory of stamps, money orders, and other postal stock with a combined value of more than $50,000.
- Initiated an in-depth training program and oversaw quality assurance of all mail sacks and letter trays; reduced operational and finance errors by 40%.
- Conducted in-depth regular inspections of six separate mail rooms; praised for bringing about a 100% improvement of the postal facility and services for the organization.
- Received nine commendable ratings on organizational-level inspections.
- Was cited in an official evaluation for possessing "unparalleled leadership abilities" and for using my vast expertise to overcome obstacles that would stop others.

2001-03: **PERSONNEL SUPERVISOR.** U.S. Army, Iraq. Managed personnel functions for an organization of more than 2,000 personnel in support of Operation Iraqi Freedom; oversaw preparation of officer and enlisted evaluations and accountability of personnel records, as well as personnel actions such as promotions, reassignments, and transfers.
- Supervised and trained nine employees in all aspects of personnel administration; conducted training classes on my own time to increase the unit's proficiency.
- Reorganized the Personnel Accountability System, improving accountability.

1999-01: **PROCESSING SUPERVISOR.** U.S. Army, Fort Drum, NY. Started as a Processing Clerk and advanced to this position, supervising as many as ten military and civilian personnel processing 40-80 applicants for military service daily; prepared enlistment documents and orders, travel arrangements, and submission of security investigation data.

1998-99: **CUSTODIAN OF POSTAL EFFECTS.** U.S. Army, Korea. Managed three postal clerks and more than $50,000 worth of equipment and postal stocks; conducted weekly audits on postal clerks and consolidated, prepared, and submitted monthly reports.

EDUCATION

Completed 98 college hours towards Bachelor's degree, City Colleges of Chicago, Chicago IL.

PERSONAL

Excellent personal and professional references are available upon request.

Exact Name of Person
Title or Position
Exact Name of Company
Address
City, State, Zip

POSTAL CLERK   Dear Exact Name of Person: (or Dear or Madam if answering a blind ad.)

I would appreciate an opportunity to talk with you soon about how I could contribute to your organization through my experience and personal qualities.

As you will see from my resume, I excelled in a track record of promotion in retail and customer service environments prior to my current job as a Postal Clerk. I have discovered that the U.S.P.S. is a dynamic organization with an aggressive customer service orientation, and I have gained experience in using computer systems and programs that improve processing time and productivity.

I hope you will call or write me soon to suggest a time convenient for us to meet and discuss your current and future needs and how I might serve them. Thank you in advance for your time.

Sincerely,

Paul Moser

Alternate last paragraph:
I hope you will welcome my call soon to suggest a time convenient for us to meet and discuss your current and future needs and how I might serve them. Thank you in advance for your time.

PAUL MOSER

1110½ Hay Street, Fayetteville, NC 28305   •   preppub@aol.com   •   (910) 483-6611

OBJECTIVE   To contribute to an organization that can use an intelligent young professional with a reputation as an innovative thinker who can motivate others to work toward common goals by applying natural leadership abilities.

EDUCATION   Earned a **Bachelor of Arts (B.A.) in Political Science** with a minor in **Psychology,** Lincoln University, Jefferson City, MO, 2001.
•   Named to Dean's List in recognition of scholastic accomplishments and high GPA.
Completed college transfer degree program, Lincoln University, Jefferson City, MO, 1998.

EXPERIENCE   **POSTAL CLERK.** U.S. Postal Service, St. Louis, MO (2004-present). Gained experience using computer programs specific to the postal service while processing mail for commercial flights and for truck dispatches while working out of a busy airport.

Refined communication skills and the ability to deal with people while learning to manage my time for highest productivity during a period when I was simultaneously attending college and financing my education in part-time and seasonal jobs:
RETAIL SALES ASSOCIATE. Oxy Clean Products, Jefferson City, MO (2001-04). Achieved outstanding results while polishing sales and customer service skills in the jewelry department of this major retail outlet. **Ranked #1 in sales** per hour while excelling in creating attractive, eye-catching displays and operating an automated inventory control system.
•   Was recognized as the most productive associate in the area of selling customers on the advantages of extended service plans on merchandise. Placed third in overall sales despite having less experience in sales of luxury items than most other associates.

STOCK ASSISTANT. Rack Room Shoes, Jefferson City, MO (1998-00). Learned to set up and coordinate pleasing merchandise displays; helped in all aspects of stock control from receiving and processing incoming stock to keeping stock on the floor.

TEAM LEADER. Pizza Hut, Jefferson City, MO (1996-97). Developed and refined personnel management abilities as well as customer service and organizational skills.

SALESMAN. Jenny Craig & Jefferson Fitness Center, Jefferson City, MO (1995). Learned to talk with customers and provide them with quality programs that would fit their needs.

ACADEMIC &   As a student at Union Senior High School, Jefferson City, MO, participated in scholastic and
COMMUNITY   extracurricular as well as community service activities including the following:
INVOLVEMENT   •   Was named in Who's Who Among American High School Students and received recognition from the U.S. Achievement Academy for my accomplishments and scholastic excellence in the field of mathematics.
•   Held membership in the Alpha Club and SAIL — a program for gifted students — as well as attending advanced placement courses.
•   Member, Vocational Club with concentration in Technical Drafting and Law Enforcement.
•   Helped organize a chapter of SADD (Students Against Drunk Driving) which grew to 150 students and met at least once a month: created flyers which were widely distributed and encouraged young people to avoid the dangers of driving or riding with anyone under the influence of alcohol or drugs.

PERSONAL   Helped with roadside cleaning, lawn maintenance, and other services as a volunteer with a local fire department. Am able to easily handle deadlines and pressure.

Date

Exact Name of Person
Title or Position
Exact Name of Company
Address
City, State, Zip

POSTAL CLERK   Dear Exact Name of Person: (or Dear or Madam if answering a blind ad.)

I would appreciate an opportunity to talk with you soon about how I could contribute to your organization through my experience and personal qualities.

As you will see from my resume, I have skills and abilities that could make me a valuable part of your team. In addition, I feel certain that you would find me to be hard-working and reliable professional who prides myself on doing any job to the best of my ability. I can provide excellent personal and professional references if you request them.

I hope you will call or write me soon to suggest a time convenient for us to meet and discuss your current and future needs and how I might serve them. Thank you in advance for your time.

Sincerely,

Alicia Charles

Alternate last paragraph:
I hope you will welcome my call soon to suggest a time convenient for us to meet and discuss your current and future needs and how I might serve them. Thank you in advance for your time.

ALICIA CHARLES

1110½ Hay Street, Fayetteville, NC 28305   •   preppub@aol.com   •   (910) 483-6611

OBJECTIVE

To benefit an organization that can use a dedicated hard worker who offers excellent organizational and communication skills.

EXPERIENCE

POSTAL CLERK. U.S. Postal Service, U.S. Army, Italy (2004-present). While serving customers and processing mail in a busy post office, learned all aspects of the postal system and earned recognition for my dedication and technical skills.

- Sell stamps and money orders; requisition supplies.
- Weigh packages for mailings; sell express mail services.
- Process and routed mail; resolved problems and inquiries.
- Learned post office regulations and how to read zone and rate charts.
- Post changes of address; manage accountable mail deliveries.
- Became knowledgeable of Department of Defense and Department of the Army special mail policies.
- Prepare error-free financial reports.

CUSTODIAL WORKER. Italy Health Clinic, Italy (2003). Cleaned offices, storerooms, clinical rooms and other areas; used my "eye for detail" to maintain strict sanitary requirements.

KITCHEN WORKER. Army Dining Center, Italy (2002). During a major Army training project, worked in a dining facility serving up to 1,500 people a day.

SALES CLERK. AAFES Post Exchange, Fort Bragg, NC (2001-02). In the lady's wear section of this busy department store, assisted customers, stocked merchandise, and operated a cash register.

CLERK/TYPIST. U.S. Army, Germany (2000-01). Earned a reputation for dependability while performing typing, filing, and office supply management duties for a nine-person office.

MILITARY POLICEWOMAN/MAIL CLERK. U.S. Army, Fort Rucker, AL (1997-00). Served as a law enforcement officer for one year; as a mail clerk, sorted and delivered mail and change box combinations when needed.

Other U.S. Army experience (1994-97): Performed general office duties, made military ID cards, and sorted mail.

TRAINING

Completed U.S. Army and civil service courses related to management, mail handling, law enforcement, and child care.

SPECIAL SKILLS

Am a certified family child care provider.
Operate a U.S. Postal Service equipment, computers, and vehicles.

PERSONAL

Held a **SECRET security clearance**. Have always maintained perfect accountability of mail. With an excellent knowledge of postal operations, have improved efficiency in post offices and have been sought out to train others. Am an excellent motivator.

Date

Exact Name of Person
Exact Title
Exact Name of Company
Address
City, State, Zip

Dear Exact Name of Person: (or Dear Sir or Madam if answering a blind ad.)

With the enclosed resume, I would like to introduce my exceptional skills in maximizing human and fiscal resources, building teams of productive employees, and increasing customer service along with my specialized experience in the management of mail handling and processing operations.

As you will see from my resume, I am presently serving in the U.S. Air Force as a Postal Detachment Chief in Germany. Assigned to facilities at Germany International Airport, I oversee all aspects of mail processing and transportation while supervising a nine-person work force which supports more than 28,000 postal patrons. Until my retirement from the U.S. Air Force, I will be involved in a wide range of actions including acting as liaison for customs issues with the America Embassy, German officials, and U.S. government agencies and organizations.

In earlier assignments I have supervised military post office and processing operations in Iraq, Afghanistan, Germany, and Korea where I have learned to deal with, supervise, and coordinate with people from these and other countries. I am excelled in large part due to my communication skills and ability to establish mutual respect with representatives and employees from other countries in international settings.

I have been cited in official performance reports for my depth of technical knowledge of regulations and procedures and for my ability to pass that knowledge on to others. Known for my honesty and personal integrity, I have been entrusted with a Top Secret security clearance.

If you can use a confident and mature professional with an eye for the bottom line as well as the fine details which lead to customer satisfaction, profitability, and productivity, I hope you will welcome my call soon when I try to arrange a brief meeting to discuss your goals and how my background might serve your needs. I can provide outstanding references at the appropriate time.

Sincerely,

Simeon Anderson

Alternate Last Paragraph:
I hope you will write or call me soon to suggest a time when we might meet to discuss your needs and goals and how my background might serve them. I can provide outstanding references at the appropriate time.

SIMEON ANDERSON

1110½ Hay Street, Fayetteville, NC 28305 • preppub@aol.com • (910) 483-6611

OBJECTIVE

To contribute to the management of mail handling operations in an organization that can benefit from my expertise in maximizing resources.

EXPERIENCE

Was known as a talented problem solver who could be counted on to find ways to make operations run smoothly while emphasizing customer service, U.S. Air Force:
POSTAL DETACHMENT CHIEF. Germany (2004-present). Supervise nine people; oversee all aspects of training, production, mail movement, and transportation as well as providing technical guidance in support of 28,000 customers.
- Manage a $41K annual operating budget and $350K supply/equipment account.
- Provide support for military mail customs issues and movement with the German officials and numerous U.S. agencies and organizations.

AIR POST OFFICE (APO) CHIEF. Iraq (2003-04). Simultaneously managed a post office with five employees and an aerial mail terminal operation (AMT) with four employees while directing acceptance, receipt, delivery, and dispatch of mail.

POSTMASTER. Afghanistan (2002-03). Was the driving force behind a massive renovation project which resulted in a more convenient and workable facility as manager of postal operations in support of 650 military and civilian contracting personnel at a remote site.

POSTMASTER. Germany (2000-02). Managed the complexities of preparing for a base closure while operating a facility which supported eight units with 2,300 customers.
- Supervised and evaluated four employees and a large volunteer force.
- Negotiated a unique agreement guaranteeing forwarding of first class mail for one year when the normal period had been only two months during other base closures.
- Provided expert mail service for the largest force deployment: processed 136K pounds of outgoing mail for 3,500 people and more than 181K pounds (8,100 pieces) of mail delivered to personnel in Afghanistan and Iraq.

MAIL PROCESSING SUPERVISOR. Korea (1998-00). Supervised nine employees and was credited with initiating coordination with international air carriers which resulted in prompt, accurate, and safe movement of more than 2.5 million pounds of mail monthly.

POSTAL SERVICE CENTER SUPERVISOR. Germany (1996-98). Provided timely service to more than 10,000 customers of the largest facility of its kind in Germany.

NCOIC, ADMINISTRATIVE COMMUNICATIONS. Hill AFB, UT (1991-96). Provided direct support to the Chief of Administration: supervised six employees.
- Developed and implemented procedures for document control, security, administrative orders, and operation of the Base Information Transfer System (BITS).
- Conducted customer education programs to improve administrative correspondence and surveys to determine the effectiveness of operations. Maintained a 95% rating while overcoming a 75% turnover in personnel and a workforce at half its allotted strength.

EDUCATION & TRAINING

Am currently attending a course in **Computer Information Systems,** Central Michigan University, Mt. Pleasant, MI, 2004-present.
Received extensive training in quality control and personnel/resource management at the NCO Academy and in numerous Air Force courses such as Quality Air Force Awareness and the U.S. Air Force Administration Management Specialist Course.

Date

Exact Name of Person
Title or Position
Exact Name of Company
Address
City, State, Zip

POSTAL SUPERVISOR   Dear Exact Name of Person: (or Dear or Madam if answering a blind ad.)

I would appreciate an opportunity to talk with you soon about how I could contribute to your organization through my experience and personal qualities.

As you will see from my resume, I served with distinction as a Postal Supervisor in my most recent position, and part of my responsibility involved serving a tour in Iraq, where I established postal operations from scratch in a combat environment. I am the recipient of numerous medals and awards, and I am known for my strong problem-solving abilities and management skills.

I hope you will call or write me soon to suggest a time convenient for us to meet and discuss your current and future needs and how I might serve them. Thank you in advance for your time.

Sincerely,

Lloyd Crow

Alternate last paragraph:
I hope you will welcome my call soon to suggest a time convenient for us to meet and discuss your current and future needs and how I might serve them. Thank you in advance for your time.

LLOYD CROW

1110½ Hay Street, Fayetteville, NC 28305 • preppub@aol.com • (910) 483-6611

SUMMARY OF QUALIFICATIONS

Over ten years experience as a personnel management clerk, processing clients records and status reports. Performed general clerical duties as an administrative office assistant. Ten years experience as a supervisor and trainer of personnel. Received regional recognition for outstanding performance of duties.

PERSONNEL CLERK

Compiled and processed status reports and client records quickly and efficiently for over 10,000 personnel. Created and implemented an office procedure that ensured delivery of information in a timely manner. Used a computer system to update personnel information. Prepared and maintained personnel reports and statistics for upper-level management.

SUPERVISOR TRAINER

Supervised personnel performing typing, general clerical, and administrative duties. Cross trained personnel in job duties which resulted in reduced supervision requirements and a saving in overtime hours. Trained personnel in the maintenance of records and preparation of work orders.

EXPERIENCE

POSTAL SUPERVISOR. U.S. Army, Fort Campbell, KY (2002-present). Served a five-month tour in Iraq, January-May 2003. Supervised four postal clerks while overseeing service delivery of postal financial services to approximately 1,000 personnel in support of War on Terror; held final responsibility for equipment and an inventory of stamps, money orders, and other postal stock with a combined value of more than $50,000.
- Initiated an in-depth training program and oversaw quality assurance of all mail sacks and letter trays; reduced operational and finance errors by 40%.
- Conducted in-depth regular inspections of six separate mail rooms; praised for bringing about a 100% improvement of the postal facility and services for the organization.
- Received nine commendable ratings on organizational-level inspections.
- Was cited in an official evaluation for possessing "unparalleled leadership abilities" and for using my vast expertise to overcome obstacles that would stop others.

ADMINISTRATIVE SUPERVISOR. U.S. Army, Fort Campbell, KY (2000-01). Was awarded *three* awards in recognition of my efforts and long hours which directly resulted in the shop's superior rating in a major inspection which found no faults in the areas of automated records and inventory.
- Supervised five employees and ensured error-free operation of the automated logistics system including all aspects of ordering parts and maintaining records.

Highlights of other experience:
OPERATION TRAINING SUPERVISOR. U.S. Army, Fort Campbell, KY (1999-00).
TRAINING SUPERVISOR. U.S. Army, Fort Leonard Wood, MO (1995-99).
EDUCATION COORDINATOR. U.S. Army, Germany (1992-95).
LEGAL ADMINISTRATIVE SUPERVISOR. U.S. Army, Fort Drum, NY (1987-92).

EDUCATION

A.A.S. degree, Business Administration, Virginia State University, Petersburg, VA, 1982.
Senior Command & Staff Course, U.S. Army, Fort Leonard Wood, MO, 1996.
Upper Level Management Course, U.S. Army, Fort Jackson, SC, 1993.
Administrative Management Course, U.S. Army, Fort Drum, NY, 1991.

PERSONAL

Outstanding personal and professional references available on request.

Date

Exact Name of Person
Title or Position
Name of Company
Address
City, State, Zip

POSTAL SUPERVISOR   Dear Exact Name of Person: (or Sir or Madam if answering a blind ad.)

With the enclosed resume, I would like to formally enquire about the possibility of joining your organization in some capacity which could utilize my experience as a junior military officer as well as my prior sales experience in Fortune 500 company environments.

As you will see from my enclosed resume, I hold a Master's degree, Bachelor of Science degree, and Associate of Science degree, and I have also excelled in extensive training as a military officer. In particular, I have excelled in formal training related to postal operations management as well as human resources and personnel administration.

In my current job as a General Manager, I am functioning as the equivalent of a Postal Supervisor at one of the U.S. military bases, where I am in charge of 15 people in the largest active-duty postal company in the continental U.S. On my own initiative, I have developed a comprehensive safety program, a plan for emergency operations, as well as training procedures which have boosted employee productivity.

In my previous job as a Human Resources Manager, I was handpicked for a job normally held by a Major, and I was praised for reinvigorating dormant programs and evaluated in writing as performing "brilliantly and tactfully" while supervising 51 employees.

I am proud that I have had the opportunity to serve my country in the active duty Army as well as in the National Guard and the ROTC. In fact, while earning my Master's degree, I was selected as Cadet Battalion Commander over eight ROTC schools and also received the Distinguished Military Graduate award upon graduation.

Prior to military service, I excelled as an Account Manager and Assistant Territory Manager in Fortune 500 companies, and I became skilled at managing my time for maximum efficiency. I have also worked as an Outside Tax Collector and learned a great deal from the experience of meeting delinquent tax payers face-to-face and negotiating with them to pay back taxes.

I have excelled in every job I have held and can provide outstanding references from all previous employers. If you can use a highly motivated and dynamic individual who would take pride in rapidly becoming a valuable member of your team, I hope you will call or write me to suggest a time when we might meet in person to discuss your needs.

Yours sincerely,

Eric Landon

ERIC LANDON

1110½ Hay Street, Fayetteville, NC 28305　•　preppub@aol.com　•　(910) 483-6611

OBJECTIVE　　To benefit an organization that can use a highly motivated professional who offers a track record of accomplishments in the academic arena and in the public and private sectors.

EDUCATION　　**Master of Liberal Arts,** Western Kentucky University, Bowling Green, KY, 2002.
Bachelor of Science in Music and Business, Sullivan College, Louisville, KY, 1997.
Associate of Science in General Education, Sullivan College, Louisville, KY, 1995.
Completed 21 credit hours in **Criminal Justice** studies, University of Kentucky, 1998.
Completed **Constitutional Law** and **Property Law** Courses, Western Kentucky University, 1996.
As a military officer, completed training including the following:
- **Postal Operations** and **Postal Supervisors Course**
- **Adjutant General (Personnel Administration)** Course

Other military training related to areas such as:

Karate Hand-to-Hand	Operation of 9mm and M-16	Airborne School
Range Control Operations	Rappelling	Hand Grenades

Operation and maintenance of vehicles including HMMV, 2 ½ ton and 5 ton trucks

EXPERIENCE　　**GENERAL MANAGER (POSTAL SUPERVISOR).** U.S. Army, Fort Hood, TX (2004-present). As a First Lieutenant, am serving as a Platoon Leader in charge of 15 people in the largest active-duty postal company within the continental U.S.; am excelling as a Postal Supervisor.
- Developed a comprehensive safety program which improved safety awareness and which was adopted as the model safety program by the parent organization.
- Implemented a postal training program which led the two mail operations I supervise to pass rigorous inspections and to achieve 100% accountability of all mail items.
- Control use and maintenance of eight wheeled vehicles and equipment worth $400,000.
- Developed a plan for emergency deployment of the company within 18 hours.

HUMAN RESOURCES MANAGER. U.S. Army, Fort Hood, TX (2000-04). As a Second Lieutenant, was handpicked for a job normally held by a Major; supervised 51 individuals providing personnel administration services for 1,800 employees.
- On my own initiative, developed systems that resulted in a 40% increase in efficiency in 18 key areas; dramatically decreased late evaluation reports, awards, and promotions.
- Reinvigorated dormant programs including the safety and sponsorship programs.
- Improved team work and communication with unit leaders.
- Improved organizational efficiency through prudent reassignment of personnel.
- Planned and orchestrated a Corps Summer Formal which exceeded all expectations.
- Was praised in writing for performing "brilliantly and tactfully."

STUDENT, ADJUTANT GENERAL OFFICER BASIC COURSE. U.S. Army, Fort Campbell, KY (1998-00). Was selected as First Class Leader, and was evaluated as setting "a sterling example" and for possessing "a rare combination of vision and attention to detail."

Other experience (Fortune 500 company environments): Became skilled in opening new accounts and new territories:
ACCOUNT EXECUTIVE. Wal-Mart, Lexington, KY (1997-98). Received Fortune 500 sales training and then opened new territory in SC by establishing distributor accounts.

PERSONAL　　Proficient with Word and PowerPoint. Known for my motivated nature and integrity.

Date

Exact Name of Person
Exact Title
Exact Name of Company
Address
City, State, Zip

POSTAL WORKER & MAIL HANDLER

A versatile job hunt is what Ms. Pratt has in mind. She is primarily oriented toward social services environments, nonprofit organizations, and teaching.

Dear Exact Name of Person (or Dear Sir or Madam if answering a blind ad):

With the enclosed resume, I would like to offer my services to a company that can make use of a confident and highly motivated professional with strong organizational and communication skills and a firm commitment to making a difference in the lives of others.

As you will see, I have recently completed my Bachelor of Arts in Sociology. While pursuing my degree, I worked as a student teacher and attended extracurricular seminars in order to further prepare myself to work in this field. Being a mother of two and a military spouse, I feel that my personal experience as well as my education and background make me uniquely qualified to serve the needs of our community.

In previous positions, I have shown myself to be a versatile and results-oriented team player who also works well with little or no supervision. For example, I quickly learned the spreadsheet program used by First Union to access and modify account information and I also compiled and published the bank's monthly newsletter.

If you can use an enthusiastic and knowledgeable counselor or teacher, I hope you will contact me to suggest a time when we might meet to discuss your present and future needs, and how I might meet them. I can assure you in advance that I could rapidly become an asset to your organization.

Sincerely,

Edith Pratt

EDITH PRATT

1110½ Hay Street, Fayetteville, NC 28305   •   preppub@aol.com   •   (910) 483-6611

OBJECTIVE   To benefit an organization that can use a confident and highly motivated individual with strong organizational and communication skills along with a firm commitment to making a difference in the lives of others.

EDUCATION   **Bachelor of Arts in Sociology,** Albion College, Albion, MI, 2004.
Attended numerous seminars to supplement my degree program, including modules on good parenting, the difficult child, homework skills, and abuse issues.

COMPUTERS   Proficient with numerous popular software programs including Word.

EXPERIENCE   **POSTAL WORKER/MAIL HANDLER.** U.S. Postal Service, Jacksonville, FL (2004-present). Excelled in this physically strenuous and mentally stressful environment, performing a variety of different tasks; as an Equipment Operator, operated mail processing machines, binding machines, automated labeling equipment, embossing and addressing machines, bundle belt, return-to-sender machines, as well as machines for casing, stacking, lifting, and loading.

KINDERGARTEN STUDENT TEACHER. Roosevelt Elementary School, Albion, MI (2004). Was a Student Teacher Assistant while completing my Bachelor's degree.
- Planned and executed various activities, such as reading to the students, arts and crafts, and music.
- Supported the regular classroom teacher in the implementation of lesson plans.
- Developed excellent rapport with the children under my care; assisted those having difficulty with reading, spelling, and math.

COLLEGE STUDENT. Albion College, Albion, MI (2001-04). Completed my Bachelor of Arts degree in Sociology.

ADMINISTRATIVE ASSISTANT, LOAN DEPARTMENT. First Union Bank, Albion, MI (2001-03). In a part-time job, prepared consumer loan paperwork and entered it into a database; compiled and published the bank's monthly newsletter.
- Entered consumer loan information into a computer; utilized the software to retrieve and modify existing files.
- Utilized computers to check account balances and payment status of existing loans.
- Prepared financial documents and maintained the filing system.

MICROFILMING TECHNICIAN. State Board of Health, Jacksonville, FL (1999-2000). Transferred official documents from hard copy to microfilm; prepared/sealed documents to be microfilmed; produced microfilm of birth certificates, marriage certificates, and adoption papers; once the documents were transferred to microfilm, packed original paper copies for long-term storage.

Other experience: **TUTOR** and **SUPERVISOR.** Albion Urban League, Albion, MT. Excelled in summer jobs for two summers. In the first summer, worked as a Tutor for young children; in the second summer, supervised 25 young tutors aged 16-20 in tutoring children aged K-5 in reading and writing.

PERSONAL   Excellent personal and professional references on request.

Date

Exact Name of Person
Title or Position
Exact Name of Company
Address
City, State, Zip

SUPERVISORY
SUPPLY SPECIALIST
with prior
experience as a
Postal Clerk

Dear Exact Name of Person: (or Dear or Madam if answering a blind ad.)

I would appreciate an opportunity to talk with you soon about how I could contribute to your organization through my experience and personal qualities.

As you will see from my resume, in my current position I supervise six specialists involved in keeping automated records of supply transactions while ensuring adequate quantities of all vital supplies and equipment. I was awarded an achievement medal in recognition of my contributions toward reestablishing control of supply operations upon the company's return from the Middle East.

I hope you will call or write me soon to suggest a time convenient for us to meet and discuss your current and future needs and how I might serve them. Thank you in advance for your time.

Sincerely,

Robert Jackson

Alternate last paragraph:
I hope you will welcome my call soon to suggest a time convenient for us to meet and discuss your current and future needs and how I might serve them. Thank you in advance for your time.

ROBERT JACKSON

1110½ Hay Street, Fayetteville, NC 28305   •   preppub@aol.com   •   (910) 483-6611

OBJECTIVE

To offer my experience in the acquisition, storage, and distribution of equipment and supplies to an organization that can use a detail-oriented professional with skills related to employee supervision, material handling equipment operations, and postal procedures.

EXPERIENCE

SUPERVISORY SUPPLY SPECIALIST. U.S. Army, Fort Devens, MA (2004-present). Advanced in the supply management field to this role overseeing all details of controlling more than $7 million worth of equipment used to provide for the needs of the 140-person headquarters department of an engineering company.

- Supervise six specialists involved in keeping automated records of all supply transactions and ensuring adequate quantities of all vital supplies and equipment.
- Was awarded an achievement medal in recognition of my contributions toward reestablishing control of supply operations upon the company's return from the Middle East. Play a valuable role in identifying excess equipment, establishing up-to-date records of shortages, and accounting for all equipment.
- Earned the respect of superiors for successfully training a supply specialist and a weapons specialist to my own high standards.

SUPPLY OPERATIONS SPECIALIST/VEHICLE OPERATOR. U.S. Army, Iraq (2003-04). Received an achievement medal and other certificates of appreciation for my accomplishments while supervising three subordinates and handling arrangements for moving large amounts of equipment and supplies to various sites during preparations for combat and throughout the War on Terror.

- Cited for my "unparalleled enthusiasm" and ability to work long hard hours, earned a reputation as a self starter who could be counted on to see that the work is done.
- Handled the stress of frequently moving entire support operations — including vehicles and large items of engineering equipment — from site to site.
- Gained experience in operating the 300-foot sky crane while unloading at the port.

SUPPLY SPECIALIST. U.S. Army, Fort Devens, MA (2001-03). Performed a variety of activities related to the receipt, issue, replenishment, and interim storage of authorized supply items for an engineering organization.

- Became skilled in operating heavy equipment including forklifts and sky cranes to load and unload trucks and move materials to and from their proper storage areas.
- Was recognized by my superiors as being dedicated to training and self improvement while always being willing to share my knowledge with others.

POSTAL CLERK. U.S. Army, Fort Devens, MA (1999-01). Completed special training resulting in qualification as a Postal Clerk: provided services related to the sorting, handling, and dispensing of mail to individuals and companies.

SPECIAL KNOWLEDGE

Through training and experience, am qualified to operate vehicles and equipment including:

up to 5-ton dump trucks	up to 10k forklifts
up to 2 1/2-ton cargo trucks	tractor trailers

TRAINING

Completed military training programs in the areas of supply operations, leadership development, and postal operations as well as airborne training and emergency lifesaving.

PERSONAL

Have been entrusted with a Secret security clearance. Have some knowledge of Spanish. Am a team player who motivates others through my own enthusiasm and hard work.

Date

Exact Name of Person
Title or Position
Name of Company
Address
City, State, Zip

TRAFFIC SPECIALIST

with experience as a Data
Conversion Operator

Dear Exact Name of Person: (or Dear Sir or Madam if answering a blind ad.)

With the enclosed resume, I would like to make you aware of my interest in exploring employment opportunities with your organization.

As you will see from my resume, I most recently have worked in manufacturing environments. In my current job the company depends on me as its Traffic Specialist, which makes me responsible for organizing shipments of manufactured telecommunications products to customers all over the east coast. In my previous position, I worked for a company which manufactured bottles used by major soft drink companies, and I was in charge of assuring that major customers received on-time delivery of their orders.

In both the positions above I made significant contributions to profitability and efficiency through my ability to solve problems resourcefully. I am well known for my intense dedication to the highest standards of safety, quality, and cost control.

Prior to entering the manufacturing industry, I excelled as General Manager of a country club, where I was responsible for supervising up to 40 employees. I offer highly refined supervisory and communication skills.

If you can use a dedicated professional with a sincere desire to make enduring contributions to the bottom line, I hope you will contact me to suggest a time when we might discuss your current and future needs and how I might serve them.

Sincerely,

Liana Rasco

LIANA RASCO

1110½ Hay Street, Fayetteville, NC 28305 • preppub@aol.com • (910) 483-6611

OBJECTIVE

To benefit an organization that can use a motivated professional with experience in the management of human and physical resources, interviewing and hiring, training and staff development who also offers exceptional data entry skills.

EXPERIENCE

TRAFFIC SPECIALIST & MANUFACTURING LIAISON. Westfall Manufacturing Center, Atlanta, GA (2004-present). Started with Westfall working part-time in Data Entry and then quickly advanced, first to a full-time position, and then to the Traffic Department, where I am currently excelling in handling all aspects of load scheduling for this busy regional manufacturer of telecommunications devices.

- Schedule all loads to be dropped and assist the gate by locating and providing load numbers when the driver doesn't have a load number.
- Sign all freight bills, and update receivers by keying additional information from the freight bills into the computer.
- Enter all Void To Return (VTR) items into the system, removing merchandise that has been slotted in the wrong physical location so that it can be reentered into the computer and slotted correctly.
- Generate and reconcile the 4631 & 4632 reports; check the physical warehouse to verify whether or not stock has been slotted, then ensure that receivers for merchandise that is already slotted are keyed as complete.

PACKAGING COORDINATOR. Morgan Bottling Company, Morgan, GA (1999-04). For a company which manufactured bottles used by major soft drink makers, coordinated all aspects of the packaging, loading, shipping, and delivery of products to customers all over the east coast.

- Accepted customer orders for delivery on the next business day from bulk accounts drivers, then keyed these orders into the system to generate loading cards.
- Sorted printed loading cards, organizing them according to the order in which the deliveries were to be made. Contacted customers in order to schedule delivery times; provided exceptional customer service to all vendors.

DATA CONVERSION OPERATOR. U.S. Postal Service, Atlanta, GA (1994-99). Provided data entry services at this large regional distribution center, encoding mail for Atlanta, Macon, and Savannah plants through the use of computer-generated images.

- Maintained a 98% accuracy rate while keying more than 1,000 pieces of mail per hour; facility goal is 750 pieces per hour.

GENERAL MANAGER. Payne Country Club, Payne, GA (1992-94). Oversaw all operational aspects, including human resources, purchasing, events coordination, and bookkeeping for this local country club.

- Supervised 40 employees, including the kitchen staff, bartenders, and wait staff.
- Performed all bookkeeping functions, including accounts payable, accounts receivable, payroll, W-2s, income tax reports, and ABC reports.
- Conducted periodic employee appraisals and wrote weekly employee schedules.
- Interviewed, hired, and trained all new employees.
- Booked parties and scheduled special events; was responsible for purchasing.

EDUCATION

Associate's degree in Accounting, Los Angeles City College, Los Angeles, CA, 1992.

PERSONAL

Excellent personal and professional references are available upon request.

Date

Exact Name of Person
Title or Position
Name of Company
Address
City, State, Zip

**WHEELED VEHICLE
MECHANIC**

Dear Exact Name of Person (or Dear Sir or Madam if answering a blind ad):

I would appreciate an opportunity to talk with you soon about how I could contribute to your organization through my skills in troubleshooting, repairing, and maintaining heavy- and light-wheeled vehicles and power generation equipment.

As you will see from my resume, I am serving with the U.S. Postal Service with distinction while becoming known as a highly skilled troubleshooter who excels in repairing the stubborn mechanical problems that have baffled others. I am skilled in using diagnostic equipment, hand and power tools, and special tools for disassembly, repair, reassembly, and testing of components and major end items, and I am experienced in repairing/maintaining brake systems, hydraulic systems, pneumatic systems, electrical systems, as well as the clutch and transmission.

A self-motivated individual, I received more than 11 separate medals and awards while serving my country, and I am proud of my reputation as an extremely "quality-conscious, safety-first" individual. I can provide excellent personal and professional references, and I would be willing to relocate worldwide to suit your needs.

I hope you will write or call me soon to suggest a time when we might meet to discuss your needs and how I might serve them. Thank you in advance for your time.

Sincerely yours,

David C. Dante

Alternate last paragraph:
I hope you will welcome my call soon to arrange a brief meeting at your convenience to discuss your current and future needs and how I might serve them. Thank you in advance for your time.

DAVID CHRISTOPHER DANTE

1110½ Hay Street, Fayetteville, NC 28305 • preppub@aol.com • (910) 483-6611

OBJECTIVE	To offer my mechanical skills and management potential to an organization that can use a seasoned troubleshooter who has earned a reputation for being able to solve difficult problems, often with limited resources.
TECHNICAL SKILLS	• Experienced in the repair and maintenance of heavy- and light-wheeled vehicles and generators. • Skilled in diagnostic and repair procedures for drive train, hydraulic, electrical, and brake systems. Familiar with repair parts ordering procedures. • Knowledgeable of the use of service and technical manuals, am experienced in reading electrical and hydraulic schemes as well as blueprints and diagrams. • Troubleshoot and repair Detroit and Detroit Allison products, Cummins products, Caterpillar products, and Mercedes-Benz diesel products. • Operate and repair forklifts; skilled in using diagnostic equipment, hand and power tools, and special tools including oxyacetylene welding for disassembly, repair, reassembly, and testing of components and major end items. • Experienced in repairing/maintaining brake systems, hydraulic systems, pneumatic systems, electrical systems, as well as the clutch and transmissions.
EXPERIENCE	**WHEELED VEHICLE MECHANIC** and **ACTING SUPERVISOR.** U.S. Postal Service, San Diego, CA (2004-present). Because of my reputation as a highly skilled mechanic with a knack for troubleshooting the most difficult diesel and mechanical problems, am sometimes put in charge of between six to 20 mechanics in the absence of the manager. • Perform wheeled vehicle maintenance and repair on a multimillion-dollar fleet of vehicles; assured the highest standards of quality control and supervised road testing before equipment was returned to customers. • Frequently train junior mechanics in mechanical techniques, use of tools, and analytical processes needed to diagnose and repair problems; assist and advise mechanics in the servicing and overhaul of drivetrains and hydraulic and electrical systems. • Maintain a perfect safety record. Perform troubleshooting, repair, preventative maintenance, and modification of heavy-wheeled vehicles. **WHEELED VEHICLE MECHANIC.** Carter Construction Company, Germany (2001-04). Serviced numerous makes and models of both light- and heavy-wheeled equipment as well as generators for an organization which had a fleet of 241 heavy-wheeled vehicles along with hundreds of other pieces of equipment, generators, and light-wheeled vehicles. • Became experienced in all phases of gasoline, diesel, and electrically powered equipment ranging from preventative maintenance checks and services through complete service. • Learned to make skillful repairs under tight deadlines, and assured conformity of all repairs, with schedules, time tables, as well as federal and local OSHA regulations. **Other experience:** Learned mechanical skills as an adolescent and have been repairing mechanical components for several years; worked in construction prior to the U.S.P.S.
EDUCATION	At the St. Louis Vehicle School, excelled in the Heavy-Wheeled Vehicle Mechanic Course; graduated 2000. Also completed Wheeled Vehicle Recovery Specialist Course, 1999. Completed the ICS Automotive Course, 1997.
PERSONAL	Am a self-motivated individual who prides myself on performing quality work at all times. Am extremely safety conscious. Enjoy teaching and training less experienced workers.

Date

Exact Name of Person
Title or Position
Name of Company
Address
City, State, Zip

VOLLEYBALL COACH
with experience as a
Postal Supervisor
is writing to high school
principals seeking
teaching and coaching
opportunities.

Dear Principal:

With the enclosed resume, I would like to make you aware of my interest in exploring employment opportunities with your school.

As you will see from my resume, I am currently a Volleyball Coach and played an important part in the development of successful high school and middle school girls' volleyball teams. I have assumed the responsibility for holding tryouts, making decisions on the potential of each candidate, and teaching sports skills when no faculty member was familiar enough with the sport to take charge. I selected the 16 members of the high school team which came in fourth place in state finals competition—a major accomplishment for a first-year team in a school which had gone seven years with no team!

I offer enthusiasm, energy, and drive to an organization that can use a dedicated professional who can provide proven managerial and administrative skills. Prior to teaching, I excelled in business environments as an Administrative Assistant and Legal Clerk.

I am confident that I could become a valuable teaching and coaching resource for your school.

I hope you will call or write me soon to suggest a time convenient for us to meet to discuss your current and future needs. Thank you in advance for you time.

Sincerely yours,

Shelia Gold

Alternate last paragraph:
I hope you will welcome my call soon to suggest a time convenient for us to meet and discuss your current and future needs and how I might serve them. Thank you in advance for your time.

SHELIA GOLD

1110½ Hay Street, Fayetteville, NC 28305   •   preppub@aol.com   •   (910) 483-6611

OBJECTIVE To offer my enthusiasm, energy, and drive to an organization that can use a dedicated professional who can provide managerial and administrative skills along with a very strong commitment to helping young adults and contributing to their growth.

EDUCATION Earned **Bachelor of Science in Physical Education**, University of Cheyenne, WY, 2002.

EXPERIENCE **VOLLEYBALL COACH & PHYSICAL EDUCATION TEACHER.** Cheyenne, WY (2002-present). Play an important part in the development of successful high school and middle school girls' volleyball teams.
- Was chosen to take on the responsibility for holding tryouts, making decisions on the potential of each candidate, and teaching basic skills when no faculty member was familiar enough with the sport to take charge.
- Work with students at Wagner Middle School and Easton High School from seventh grade through seniors in high school.
- Select the 16 members of the high school team which came in fourth place in state finals competition—a major accomplishment for a first-year team in a school which had gone seven years with no team!
- Was successful in teaching the middle school team members the skills which would enable them to advance to the high school team and help it continue to grow.
- Learned the importance of treating young adults with respect in order to earn respect.

ADMINISTRATIVE ASSISTANT. Blend Heating, Inc., Cheyenne, WY (2002). Originally hired as a Clerk/Typist, became known for my attention to detail while tracking the progress of new projects and keeping work flowing smoothly.

POSTAL SUPERVISOR. U.S. Postal Service, Rock Springs, WY (2001-02). Trained and directed seven mail clerks involved in the metering section of the main post office where all mail was processed and then turned over to the U.S. Postal Service for final processing.
- Gained experience in quality control operations as an inspector.

ADMINISTRATIVE SPECIALIST. Hannah & Associates, Rock Springs, WY (2001). Was selected to provide clerical support for a highly confidential project to obtain bids and oversee development of a software product.

PERSONNEL RECORDS CLERK. J&B Enterprises, Inc., Rock Springs, WY (1995-00). Processed and maintained the personnel records for people attending training programs; serviced approximately 175 people attending each of several 90-day training programs.

LEGAL CLERK. Law Offices of Redwood, Rock Springs, WY (1993-95). Provided a supply services organization with clerical and office administration support.

TRAINING Completed training programs including courses for postal operators, administrative specialists, and a leadership development course.

SPECIAL SKILLS Offer experience with IBM, Microsoft Word and processing programs.

PERSONAL Received several awards and medals for professionalism and dedication. Completed one semester of general studies at the college level. Excellent references.

ABOUT THE EDITOR

Anne McKinney holds an MBA from the Harvard Business School and a BA in English from the University of North Carolina at Chapel Hill. A noted public speaker, writer, and teacher, she is the senior editor for PREP's business and career imprint, which bears her name. Early titles in the Anne McKinney Career Series (now called the Real-Resumes Series) published by PREP include: *Resumes and Cover Letters That Have Worked, Resumes and Cover Letters That Have Worked for Military Professionals, Government Job Applications and Federal Resumes, Cover Letters That Blow Doors Open,* and *Letters for Special Situations.* Her career titles and how-to resume-and-cover-letter books are based on the expertise she has acquired in 25 years of working with job hunters. Her valuable career insights have appeared in publications of the "Wall Street Journal" and other prominent newspapers and magazines.

PREP Publishing Order Form You may purchase our titles from your favorite bookseller! Or send a check, money order or your credit card number for the total amount, plus $4.00 for postage and handling, to PREP, 1110 1/2 Hay Street, Suite C, Fayetteville, NC 28305. You may also order our titles on our website at www.prep-pub.com and feel free to e-mail us at preppub@aol.com or call 910-483-6611 with your questions or concerns.

Name: _____

Address: _____

E-mail address: _____

Payment Type: ☐ Check/Money Order   ☐ Visa   ☐ MasterCard

Credit Card Number: _____ Expiration Date: _____

Put a check beside the items you are ordering:

☐ $16.95—REAL-RESUMES FOR RESTAURANT, FOOD SERVICE & HOTEL JOBS. Anne McKinney, Editor

☐ $16.95—REAL-RESUMES FOR MEDIA, NEWSPAPER, BROADCASTING & PUBLIC AFFAIRS JOBS. Anne McKinney, Editor

☐ $16.95—REAL-RESUMES FOR RETAILING, MODELING, FASHION & BEAUTY JOBS. Anne McKinney, Editor

☐ $16.95—REAL-RESUMES FOR HUMAN RESOURCES & PERSONNEL JOBS. Anne McKinney, Editor

☐ $16.95—REAL-RESUMES FOR MANUFACTURING JOBS. Anne McKinney, Editor

☐ $16.95—REAL-RESUMES FOR AVIATION & TRAVEL JOBS. Anne McKinney, Editor

☐ $16.95—REAL-RESUMES FOR POLICE, LAW ENFORCEMENT & SECURITY JOBS. Anne McKinney, Editor

☐ $16.95—REAL-RESUMES FOR SOCIAL WORK & COUNSELING JOBS. Anne McKinney, Editor

☐ $16.95—REAL-RESUMES FOR CONSTRUCTION JOBS. Anne McKinney, Editor

☐ $16.95—REAL-RESUMES FOR FINANCIAL JOBS. Anne McKinney, Editor

☐ $16.95—REAL-RESUMES FOR COMPUTER JOBS. Anne McKinney, Editor

☐ $16.95—REAL-RESUMES FOR MEDICAL JOBS. Anne McKinney, Editor

☐ $16.95—REAL-RESUMES FOR TEACHERS. Anne McKinney, Editor

☐ $16.95—REAL-RESUMES FOR CAREER CHANGERS. Anne McKinney, Editor

☐ $16.95—REAL-RESUMES FOR STUDENTS. Anne McKinney, Editor

☐ $16.95—REAL-RESUMES FOR SALES. Anne McKinney, Editor

☐ $16.95—REAL ESSAYS FOR COLLEGE AND GRAD SCHOOL. Anne McKinney, Editor

☐ $25.00—RESUMES AND COVER LETTERS THAT HAVE WORKED. McKinney, Editor

☐ $25.00—RESUMES AND COVER LETTERS THAT HAVE WORKED FOR MILITARY PROFESSIONALS. McKinney, Ed.

☐ $25.00—RESUMES AND COVER LETTERS FOR MANAGERS. McKinney, Editor

☐ $25.00—GOVERNMENT JOB APPLICATIONS AND FEDERAL RESUMES: Federal Resumes, KSAs, Forms 171 and 612, and Postal Applications. McKinney, Editor

☐ $25.00—COVER LETTERS THAT BLOW DOORS OPEN. McKinney, Editor

☐ $25.00—LETTERS FOR SPECIAL SITUATIONS. McKinney, Editor

☐ $16.95—REAL-RESUMES FOR NURSING JOBS. McKinney, Editor

☐ $16.95—REAL-RESUMES FOR AUTO INDUSTRY JOBS. McKinney, Editor.

☐ $24.95—REAL KSAs--KNOWLEDGE, SKILLS & ABILITIES--FOR GOVERNMENT JOBS. McKinney, Editor

☐ $24.95—REAL RESUMIX AND OTHER RESUMES FOR FEDERAL GOVERNMENT JOBS. McKinney, Editor

☐ $24.95—REAL BUSINESS PLANS AND MARKETING TOOLS ... Samples to use in your business. McKinney, Ed.

☐ $16.95—REAL-RESUMES FOR ADMINISTRATIVE SUPPORT, OFFICE & SECRETARIAL JOBS. Anne McKinney, Editor

☐ $16.95—REAL-RESUMES FOR FIREFIGHTING JOBS. Anne McKinney, Editor

☐ $16.95—REAL-RESUMES FOR JOBS IN NONPROFIT ORGANIZATIONS. Anne McKinney, Editor

☐ $16.95—REAL-RESUMES FOR SPORTS INDUSTRY JOBS. Anne McKinney, Editor

☐ $16.95—REAL-RESUMES FOR LEGAL & PARALEGAL JOBS. Anne McKinney, Editor

☐ $16.95—REAL-RESUMES FOR ENGINEERING JOBS. Anne McKinney, Editor

☐ $22.95—REAL-RESUMES FOR U.S. POSTAL SERVICE JOBS. Anne McKinney, Editor

_____ **TOTAL ORDERED**

_____ **(add $4.00 for shipping and handling)**

_____ **TOTAL INCLUDING SHIPPING**

Would you like to explore the possibility of having PREP's writing
team create a resume for you similar to the ones in this book?

For a brief free consultation, call 910-483-6611
or send $4.00 to receive our Job Change Packet to
PREP, 1110 1/2 Hay Street, Fayetteville, NC 28305. Visit our
website to find valuable career resources: www.prep-pub.com!

QUESTIONS OR COMMENTS? E-MAIL US AT PREPPUB@AOL.COM